From the Knowledge Argu

MW00855955

This book presents a strong case for substance dualism and offers a comprehensive defence of the knowledge argument, showing that materialism cannot accommodate or explain the 'hard problem' of consciousness. Bringing together the discussion of reductionism and semantic vagueness in an original and illuminating way, Howard Robinson argues that non-fundamental levels of ontology are best treated by a conceptualist account, rather than a realist one. In addition to discussing the standard versions of physicalism, he examines physicalist theories such as those of McDowell and Price, and accounts of neutral monism and panpsychism from Strawson, McGinn and Stoljar. He also explores previously unnoticed historical parallels between Frege and Aristotle and between Hume and Plotinus. His book will be a valuable resource for scholars and advanced students of philosophy of mind, in particular those looking at consciousness, dualism and the mind–body problem.

Howard Robinson is University Professor in the Department of Philosophy at Central European University, Budapest; Senior Fellow at Rutgers Center for Philosophy of Religion, New Brunswick; and a Visiting Scholar at Fordham University, New York. He is the author of *Matter and Sense: A Critique of Contemporary Materialism* (Cambridge, 1982) and *Perception* (1994).

From the Knowledge Argument to Mental Substance

Resurrecting the Mind

Howard Robinson

CAMBRIDGE
UNIVERSITY PRESS

CAMBRIDGE
UNIVERSITY PRESS

University Printing House, Cambridge CB2 8BS, United Kingdom

One Liberty Plaza, 20th Floor, New York, NY 10006, USA

477 Williamstown Road, Port Melbourne, VIC 3207, Australia

4843/24, 2nd Floor, Ansari Road, Daryaganj, Delhi - 110002, India

79 Anson Road, #06-04/06, Singapore 079906

Cambridge University Press is part of the University of Cambridge.

It furthers the University's mission by disseminating knowledge in the pursuit of education, learning and research at the highest international levels of excellence.

www.cambridge.org
Information on this title: www.cambridge.org/9781107455481

First published 2016
First paperback edition 2017

A catalogue record for this publication is available from the British Library

Library of Congress Cataloging in Publication data
Robinson, Howard.
From the knowledge argument to mental substance : resurrecting the mind / Howard Robinson.
New York : Cambridge University Press, 2016. | Includes bibliographical references and index.
LCCN 2015036048 | ISBN 9781107087262
LCSH: Philosophy of mind. | Knowledge, Theory of. | Materialism.
LCC BD418.3 .R754 2016 | DDC 128/.2–dc23
LC record available at http://lccn.loc.gov/2015036048

ISBN 978-1-107-08726-2 Hardback
ISBN 978-1-107-45548-1 Paperback

For

Jocelyn

Contents

Preface

This book is largely, but not wholly, based on work in the philosophy of mind that I have published in the last twenty-five years. Much has happened since Cambridge University Press published my *Matter and Sense* in 1982, and many sophisticated physicalist and semi-physicalist theories have been developed. It is one of the arguments of this book that this sophistication only disguises the fact that no serious progress has been made: the lucid but inadequate theories of J. J. C. Smart and D. M. Armstrong still remain the best that standard physicalism can achieve.

This book divides into three parts. In Part I, I argue against all the main attacks that have been made on the knowledge argument, but, beyond that, I argue that the knowledge argument does not merely resist all attempts to refute it, but that it has much more powerful consequences than is usually allowed for by either side in the discussion. What it shows is that the qualitative dimension of reality, without which the world can be nothing more than a bare formal system, is something that standard physicalism cannot accommodate. If the knowledge argument were not correct, there could be no manifest image of the world at all, and without the manifest image, there could be no scientific image either. I also try to prove the inadequacy of various non-reductive naturalist strategies, such as neutral monism and those that derive from the work of Wittgenstein and Donald Davidson.

In Part II, I challenge one of the main motivations of physicalism. The physicalist believes in the closure of the physical world. It is a consequence of this that if the mental is not physical, it must be epiphenomenal. I try to show that if the world is closed under *physics* – that is the physical world's most fundamental and microscopic level – then all higher levels, which must include the brain/mind if physicalism is true, will be epiphenomenal: I defend, that is, a version of what Kim calls the *exclusion principle*, and I do this via an investigation of reductionism and semantic vagueness. I carry the conclusion further and argue that there are no strict physical individuals at all: at most there are quality placings in space-time, presumably as the features of events.

In Part III, I try to prove that we must be simple immaterial selves, and as such, minds are the only true individuals in the natural world. In the final chapter I tie this thought up to themes in the history of philosophy. I argue that a doctrine universally ignored by analytical philosophers, namely Plotinus's doctrine of the One, can be used to throw welcome light on the notion of an individual and on modern debates concerning the unity of substances. In fact, the notion of individuality that we project on the world has its source in our own identity as individuals. In this way, Plotinus's metaphysics and Humean conventionalism are both true. In the process, I draw attention to a striking – and, as far as I know, unnoticed – parallel between Frege's treatment of concepts and Aristotle's criticism of Plato's theory of forms, and how this supports a form of neo-Platonism.

If some of my conclusions run against current fashion in a way that provokes resistance, I believe that my arguments on particular issues follow all the normal canons of analytic carefulness and fall well within the framework of contemporary debates. I therefore ask the reader who finds parts of the final outcome rebarbative to try to take seriously the contributions to individual discussions that happen on the way.

Acknowledgements

My plan in writing this book was to bring together the work that I had done on the mind–body problem since *Matter and Sense* was published in 1982. This work therefore draws on much previously published material, which is listed in the Bibliography. Some chapters are only slightly modified from their previously published versions. This includes, for example, Chapters 4, 8, 9 and 10. Others, such as Chapters 5, 6, 7, 13 and 15, draw heavily on published papers. But there is much new material and redesigning throughout, and everything has, I hope, been re-considered in the light of its place in this monograph.

I would like to thank Oxford University Press for permission to print from 'Dennett and the knowledge argument', *Analysis*, 53, 1993, 174–7.

'Substance dualism and its rationale', in *Free Will and Modern Science*, ed. Richard Swinburne, the British Academy and OUP, 2012, 158–77.

'Phenomenal qualities: what they must be and what they cannot be', in *Phenomenal Qualities: Sense, Perception and Consciousness*, eds Paul Coates and Sam. Coleman, OUP, 2015, 103–120.

Routledge for permission to use 'Naturalism and the unavoidability of the Cartesian perspective', in *Contemporary Dualism*, eds Lavazza and Robinson, Routledge, 2014, 154–170.

'Reductionism', in *The Routledge Companion to Metaphysics*, eds P. Simons and P. Lepoidevin, Routledge, 2009, 527–36.

Cambridge University Press for 'Quality, thought and consciousness', in *The Metaphysics of Consciousness*, Royal Institute of Philosophy Supplement 67, eds P. Basile, J. Kiverstein, P. Phemester, Cambridge University Press, Cambridge, 203–16.

MIT Press for 'Why Frank should not have jilted Mary', in *The Case for Qualia*, ed. Edmond Wright, MIT Press, 2008, 223–45.

Notre Dame Press for permission to use 'Qualia, qualities and our conception of the physical world', in *The Case for Dualism* ed. Benedikt Goecke, Notre Dame Press, 2012, 231–263.

The Aristotelian Society for use of 'Vagueness, Realism, Language and Thought', in *Proceedings of the Aristotelian Society*, vol.CIX, 2008-9, 83-101.

When a book is based on material that has been generated over such a long period, it is hard to list the people who have contributed to its final form. I have been a member of a discussion group meeting in the summers in Oxford since well before the appearance of *Matter and Sense* in 1982 and almost everything I have written has passed through that forum. Ralph Walker, Lesley Brown and Julie Jack have been members of that group through the whole period. The late John Foster and the late Michael Woods were regulars for many years. Stephen Blamey, Adrian Moore, Anita Avromides, Penelope Mackie, Bob Frazier and Alex Orenstein are also long-standing members. I owe a great debt of gratitude to my former colleagues in Liverpool and to my present colleagues at Central European University (CEU), particularly Barry Dainton and Kati Farkas. Much of the material in the following pages was presented in Philosophy of Mind courses at CEU and I am grateful to the many students who helped me sharpen my arguments. My time at CEU since 2000 has been a pure delight. My wife, Jocelyn Wogan-Browne, to whom this book is dedicated, is a professor of English at Fordham University and this has led me to be recurrently a visiting scholar at Fordham in the Bronx. The Walsh Library there is a most congenial place in which to sit and work: much of the final writing of this book was done there. Material was also presented – and thoroughly criticised – in a course I taught at Rutgers. I am grateful, too, to Barry Loewer and Kati Balog of Rutgers for many discussions on issues that recur in this book. Also to Ned Block and David Chalmers for inviting me to their NYU mind discussions, and to David Rosenthal for his CUNY cognitive science sessions.

I dedicated *Matter and Sense* to Manchester Grammar School (MGS). The Berkeley Society at the school, between 1961 and 1964, was where it became clear to me that I had to become a philosopher, and the discussions there chaired by John Armstrong continue to be an inspiration. The year 2015 is the five-hundredth anniversary of MGS and though I do not dedicate the book again to the school, neither can I fail to repeat mention, in its quincentennial year, of the debt that I owe it. This is more so as the school's founder, Hugh Oldham, was also a partner in the founding of my college, Corpus, in Oxford, also due for a quincentennial in 2017. My principal tutor there was Christopher Taylor. A better philosophical education than that provided by these institutions is hardly imaginable.

Part I

The power of the knowledge argument

1 Introducing the knowledge argument

1.1 Setting the context

In a book, *Matter and Sense*, which was published in 1982, I attempted to evaluate the various modern materialist accounts of consciousness that had been discussed in the literature up to that time. In this volume I shall be concentrating on the various forms of materialism that have become current since then, and then develop the arguments for mental substance. Much of the discussion in the later period has focused on the so-called knowledge argument (KA), which was brought centre stage by Frank Jackson's 'Epiphenomenal qualia' (1982): hence the title of this book. One important objective of this book is to see whether the versions of materialism that have been developed in the wake of Jackson's knowledge argument manage to avoid what, in 1982, I argued were the fundamental weaknesses of the earlier theories.

A version of KA was not absent from *Matter and Sense*. Indeed a form of it was present on page 4. I set the argument out in the following way.

Imagine that a deaf scientist should become the world's leading expert on the neurology of hearing. Thus, if we suppose neurology more advanced than at present, we can imagine that he knows everything that there is to know about the physical processes involved in hearing, from the ear-drum in. It remains intuitively obvious that there is something which this scientist will not know, namely *what it is like to hear*. The same problem can be setup by imagining investigations carried out on a Martian who possesses a sixth sense that we lack. No matter how much we discover about his nervous system, we will not discover what the experiences he had by that sense were like (unless, perchance, the machinery suggested that it resembled one of our five senses). No amount of new information about the physical process will amount to information about *what it is like* to possess the sense in question. 'What it is like' is the sense viewed from the standpoint of the subject. It is the subjective element which presents a serious challenge to the materialist. (1982: 4–5)

I did not then treat this as a refutation of physicalism, but rather as a way of setting up the problem that faced the physicalist. The passage continues,

3

The mentalist thinks of these subjective states as instances of peculiarly mental properties, such as *feeling a pain* or *sensing redly*. It would seem that the materialist cannot do this and must find some other treatment for subjectivity. (1982: 5)

I thought that the problem I illustrated by the case of the deaf scientist would be generally recognisable – including by physicalists – as a statement of the issue that physicalism faced, and I treated the various forms of physicalism that I discussed as attempts to answer this problem. As we shall see soon, I now think that, once we see the full force of KA, it becomes clear that most of the theories I discussed are hardly responses to it at all.

1.2   Smart, Armstrong and topic neutrality

Although I discussed Donald Davidson, Richard Rorty, Paul Feyerabend and other philosophers, the ones I had mainly in mind were J. J. C. Smart and D. M. Armstrong. The common fundamental feature of their accounts of consciousness is that we are only what they call *topic neutrally* aware of the contents of our own consciousness. In 1982 I thought that if the topic neutral account could be made to work, then it would solve the problem that my deaf scientist raised for the physicalist. I now think that it does not touch that problem. On the other hand, I believe that physicalism keeps being forced back towards the topic neutral approach, and, in some fundamental way, needs it.

Before expounding KA itself, I want to look again at Smart and Armstrong's claim that our knowledge of our experiences is topic neutral, to see why this seems to be difficult for a physicalist to avoid, and to explain why this approach has been largely neglected. Then I'll look at why the topic neutral approach does not work.

Smart illustrates his theory as follows:

The man who reports a yellowish orange after-image does so in effect as follows: *what is going on in me is like what is going on in me when* my eyes are open, the light is normal etc. etc. and there really is a yellowish-orange patch on the wall. In this sentence the word 'like' is meant to be used in such a way that something can be like itself ... with this sense of 'like' the above formula will do for a report that one is having a veridical sense datum too. Notice that the words '*what is going on in me is like what is going on in me when* ... ' are topic neutral. (1963: 94–5)

Armstrong says the following:

The concept of a mental state is primarily the concept of *a state of a person apt for bringing about a certain sort of behaviour* ... In the case of some mental states only they are also *states of the person apt for being brought about by a certain sort of stimulus* . . . (1968: 82)

He adds, slightly later, that his ambition is to

give a satisfactory and complete account of situations covered by the mental concepts in purely physical and topic-neutral terms. (84)

It is important to note that Smart and Armstrong are concerned with identifying conscious states with occurrent physical events, not with higher-order abstract states. It was essentially the abstractness of behavioural dispositions which, in their view, made them unsuitable to be 'raw feels'. It is, therefore, essential to what the identity theorist wants to achieve that the mental state be literally identical to some brain state or process. In Armstrong's case this means that the causal, functional or dispositional state be so identical. We shall see soon that this leads to one of the main problems with the theory, but it is difficult to deny the drive that lies behind Smart and Armstrong's approach: sensations are concrete, occurrent events, not abstract or higher-order states, and it would seem that a physicalist must, therefore, identify them with some physical events, because he holds that physical events are the only events that there are. It is reasonable to presume that they are events in the brain.

So topic neutrality seems to be vital to the physicalism of Smart and Armstrong, and to any form of physicalism that involves mind–brain identity, whether type or token, because of three essential features of such theories.

(i) Conscious states are identical to neural states.
(ii) Neural states possess only those properties recognised by physical science. There are no 'emergent properties'.
(iii) We are not explicitly aware of those physical neural properties in being aware of our own conscious states.

Put these together with the uncontroversial claim that

(iv) we are aware of the contents of our conscious states in some way or other;

it would seem to follow that we must be aware of our brain states in some manner that does not positively reveal any of their actual and physical properties. As the physical properties are the only ones that they possess, we must be aware of those neural states in some way that does not reveal their intrinsic nature, which is the force of saying that our knowledge of our conscious states must be *topic neutral*.

Nevertheless, as far as I can see, few if any physicalists subsequent to Smart and Armstrong explicitly avow the doctrine of topic neutrality, by which I mean that they do not use that term or own up to that pedigree.

Prima facie, it is difficult to see how they can avoid such a commitment. As they are, in general, anti-emergentist, they are committed to (ii) above. They certainly accept (iii), that, in conscious awareness, we are not aware of our brain states as such. Whether they accept (i), the identity theory, is more variable. In general they reject the type–type identity theory of Smart and Armstrong, but in fact token identity theories and any account allowing for the occurrent nature of sensations seem to be caught in the same trap. The fact is that if one wishes to identify conscious states with specific occurrent physical events – and what else is a physicalist to do, given that he regards them as occurrent events? – the forces that pressed for topic neutrality are still there.

It might seem that talk of the *supervenience* of mental states or of their *realisation* in physical states or of their functional role could give mental content more autonomy from the physical than talk of identity allows. But these expressions seem to fit much better with propositional attitude states than with brute sensation. Of course, there is much more to say on these questions, and it will emerge in the course of this book. Nevertheless, I think it is worth bearing in mind how difficult it might prove to be for physicalists to entirely avoid the strategy associated with Smart and Armstrong, if they admit that something that is merely a disposition or a functional role lacks the occurrent specificity of a raw feel.

The idea that the classic identity theorists thought that dispositions (and, by extension, functional states) were too abstract to constitute sensory content, and that they thought that central state identity theory remedied this problem, played a major part in the argument of *Matter and Sense* and will be important at several points in this book, including the present chapter. It is, therefore, important to get a little clearer on what the claim that dispositional and functional states are 'abstract' means. A contemporary functionalist might seek to reject the accusation by pointing out that Smart and Armstrong were responding to Ryle, who thought of dispositions as not being physical states at all, but rather conditional *statements* about which stimuli tend to be correlated with which responses. Modern functionalists reject Ryle's non-realist (what Armstrong (1968: 86) calls his *phenomenalist*) account of dispositions. For them dispositions and functional states are physical and causal processes, and so are quite 'non-abstract' and 'concrete'.

But treating functional states as realised in physical processes does not avoid the accusation that they are too abstract to constitute occurrent conscious states, and this for two reasons. First, functional states are higher-order states and not specific neural states. (See the next section and footnote 3 for further explanation of this.) This means that they are not appropriate objects for the 'internal perception' that Armstrong wants. This is important because identity theorists want sensations to be not just non-abstract states, but specific *objects of awareness*. A complex functional mechanism is not suitable to be that. Second, and perhaps more important in this context, is the fact that 'functional' means rather different things in physical and psychological settings. Physically, a functional state is defined by what physical changes it brings about, but a psychological state is characterised by behaviours that will often have nothing in common. In Ryle's words they 'signify ... not things of one unique kind, but lots of different kinds' (1949: 118). In more modern jargon, they are multi-track dispositions. This is true of even sensory states: there is no unified physical response to seeing something red, for example. Even if one tries to limit the response to 'discriminating similar objects', the physical movements involved in this could be of an indefinite variety. This means that the functional unity of a psychological state is more a matter of interpretation within a certain framework than of brute physical similarity: it is more a product of what Dennett calls *the intentional stance* than a brute physical unity. This is not the non-abstract physical identity for which Smart and Armstrong – and later Lewis – were searching.

There is, I think, a historical explanation for why the 'Australian' approach to 'raw feels' was not more generally adopted. It is because the centre of discussion moved to the United States, and the historical background to the problem there was rather different. The simplest way to see this is to consider the difference between Armstrong's theory and Putnam's.

While it is, on the one hand, natural to regard Putnam's functionalism as very closely related to Armstrong's causal theory of mind, the problem on which it was mainly focused was different. Smart and Armstrong were dissatisfied with the way that the informal behaviourism of Ryle and Wittgenstein coped with raw feels. By contrast, Putnam, like other philosophers who followed Chomsky, was dissatisfied with the crudity of the stimulus-response scientific behaviourism of Skinner and Quine. Whereas the Australians were focused specifically on finding a more adequate account of occurrent conscious states, Putnam was searching for a more sophisticated account of mental processes in general, and this latter required a more complex modelling of the dispositional or functional role of our mental states than a crudely stimulus-response account seemed naturally fitted to give. Topic neutrality figures in the former quest. It is not a wholly unjust generalisation to say that it was not until Nagel's (1974) that modern American philosophers of mind were forced to think seriously about the problem of raw feels as something insufficiently abstract to be treated as a mere functional state, and it came as something of a shock for them to realise that there was an urgent issue of that kind.[1] Jackson's promulgation of the knowledge argument can be seen as a follow-up to Nagel. In a sense, it was only with the reception of Nagel and Jackson that American analytic philosophy was forced to take seriously the problem that Smart and Armstrong's theory had been devised to solve. If Nagel and Jackson are right, neither the approach of Australian identity theorists nor of the American functionalists shows signs of success.

1.3   Problems with the topic neutral analysis

Quite apart from KA, which, as we shall see, itself constitutes a response to the topic neutral analysis, that theory faces objections which are interesting in their own right.

The view that consciousness presents us with states of our central nervous system in a topic neutral fashion has at least five serious faults. The first might be dismissed on the grounds that it is 'merely intuitive'. It is that when we are in an experiential state – for example, having a yellow-orange after-image – it is plainly false that we are unaware of what the mental state in question is like: its being of, or as of, a yellow-orange patch gives it a positive quality.[2] The second and third could be regarded as more systematic versions of the counterintuitiveness accusation. The second is that our conception of the world depends on how it – the world – appears to us. This is the 'manifest image'. But if 'how it seems' is phenomenologically neutral, how can we give content to our manifest image? The third point in a way drives home the first two. It is that Smart's theory reverses an essential order of priority in a way that undermines our perception of the world. Smart characterises the experiential states in terms of what they are naturally brought about by, but how do we know what is out there causing our experiences, except on the basis of what the experiences they cause are like? This is not to deny that we characterise the experiences in terms of what in the external world they seem to be of, but this very fact means that we can, de facto, distinguish the experiences themselves by what they are like. The topic neutral analysis proceeds as if we identify our experiences by correlating them

---

[1] It is true that Herbert Feigl's long essay 'The "Mental" and the "Physical"' (1957) is concerned with 'raw feels', but it is difficult to see that it had a very direct influence on the development of the discussion within the American tradition. Neither Putnam nor Davidson took much notice of raw feels, and the emphasis on the computer analogy, which goes along with functionalism, puts the emphasis on propositional attitudes.

[2] We will find ourselves discussing later, in Chapter 4, the suggestion that we are aware of a (non-existent) intentional object but this account tells us nothing about what it is to be aware of such objects.

with what happens to cause them, but this is not a position any subject could adopt.

It might be argued that this last objection, though it works against Smart, does not apply to Armstrong, because Armstrong emphasises the role of mental states in producing behaviour, rather than their receptivity to certain stimuli. This, put together with his account of perception as the acquiring of a readiness to behave in a certain way, might seem to distinguish him from Smart. Nevertheless, this cannot apply to raw feels, even of a perceptual sort. The phenomenology of 'seeming to see red' is not reportable as 'something is going on in me that makes me feel inclined to red-behave': that is, the phenomenology seemingly presents its object, not our disposition to respond. Armstrong himself says,

> it is part of our notion of seeing or seeming to see something yellow that it is the sort of inner event characteristically produced in us by the action of a yellow physical object. But a full account must do more than this. To show us that he can perceive, a man must show us that ... he can systematically discriminate in his behaviour between certain classes of things. (1968: 81)

In other words, what we topic neutrally know in conscious perception must be a state which is both apt to be brought about by a certain stimulus and apt to cause us to respond appropriately to a stimulus of that kind. But as far as the experience is concerned, it must be its intentional object, rather than some usually deferred, invariably multiform potential response that characterises it, even if the same state plays both roles.

The fourth problem concerns not so much the topic neutrality as the identification of the mental state with the brain state, and it has the causal theory of Armstrong as its target. (So if you think that he avoids the previous objection, you can fall back on this one.) Armstrong's identity theory, which is often labelled the *causal* theory of the mind, shares with functionalism the identification of mental states with their functional or causal role. Armstrong's theory differs from functionalism, however, in identifying the mental states with specific brain states. This is not fundamentally a matter of the functionalist denial of the type identity theory: the problem I am about to describe would arise for a token identity theory.

As I have emphasised, Smart and Armstrong are concerned with identifying conscious states with occurrent physical events, not with higher-order abstract states. It is, therefore, essential for them that the mental state be literally identical to some brain state or process. In Armstrong's case this means that the causal, functional or dispositional state be so identical. The analogy used for mental states by functionalists, that they are like states of a programme, will not do to establish the kind of non-abstract status that sensations require. But the unfortunate fact is that the causal significance of a particular brain process depends entirely on its context: the immediate electronic output of a cluster of neurons has the behavioural/functional significance that it does, only given the rest of the apparatus. Alter the rest of the system and one might reverse the significance of a central process. Behavioural dispositions are, so to speak, long-term dispositions, and not immediate ones, and cannot be identified with a specific central state or its causal output. Thus the conflation of causal role and neural identity that the identity theorist was seeking cannot be brought off.

The failure of the central state identity theorists to identify causal role with localised hardware undermined their attempt to improve on classical behavioural theories. I drew attention to this point in *Matter and Sense*, but, though the fact that functional states are abstract has often been made, I'm not sure that the full nature of the problem of identifying mental content with a brain state or its local causal output, whether that content be phenomenal or propositional, has been fully absorbed.[3]

I said earlier that this objection works against the token, as well as the type, identity theory. This is true, but it does not follow that the type theory is not needed to preserve the role of the identity theory in preserving occurrence. If it is the occurrent state that constitutes the nature of the experience, and if all occurrences of a particular kind of mental state feel similar to a given subject – red is consistent in what it looks like to him – then it better be constituted by the same neural state. But the functional/causal analysis seemed to undermine this appeal to type identity by arguing that the same functional or causal role could be filled by different mechanisms. This is the functionalist doctrine of *multiple realisability*. David Lewis's article 'Mad Pain and Martian Pain' (1983b) was meant to be a response to this problem. He claimed that type identity was species restricted, so that if, in a certain species S, the normal pain state was P, and if in a particular member of S, namely M, P played a different role – say that of how claret tasted – then the member, M, of P had a mad pain: claret tasted painful to him, though he reacted as any other claret drinker would. The idea was that it would still feel to this member of S the way that pain feels to others, both its stimulus – claret taken through the mouth – and the response – saying what a good year that was – would remain the same as for someone who had had what we would call the taste of good claret. But if another creature, N, who was physically indistinguishable from M, had this same state in the claret role in the context of a community where this was the normal claret-taste state, then it would not be mad, but would be a genuine claret taste. The suggestion is not that

---

[3] For a longer version of this argument, see *Matter and Sense*, 53–60 and 67–8.

claret tasted for them like pain felt for us, but they liked it, but that, following multiple realisability in different species, that was the real claret taste for them.

I don't think Lewis's view on this has gained many followers, but this fact has consequences. On the one hand, to preserve the occurrent nature of sensations, the physicalist must identify them with occurrent physical events, and so sensations that feel the same should be identical to physical states that are of the same or similar kinds. On the other hand, any causal analysis seems to indicate that realiser is irrelevant, so long as the functional role is the same. But if the functional role is a long-term disposition, and not the immediate causal property of a neural state, it differs little from an abstract, programme-like state. Lewis's failure to make sense of mad and Martian pains is not the failure of an eccentric theory but the failure of the attempt to combine a genuinely 'occurrentist' account of sensation with a causal one.

The fifth objection is specific to the concerns of this book. It is the fact that topic neutrality is no response to KA.

When, in 1982, I used a version of KA to set up the problem for the physicalist and then discussed Smart's and Armstrong's attempts to solve it, I failed to notice that the appeal to topic neutrality does not even *seem* to be an answer to KA. If Mary or the deaf scientist already knew all the physical facts, then surely coming to acquire the topic neutral information that something or other of a general sort was going on could not add anything. If I know exactly what is going on, the further information that something or other is going on will surely not even seem to me to be further or new information, for it is entailed by what I already know. So topic neutrality might be apt to explain the kind of knowledge possessed by someone who is lacking some information – I might know that *someone* is coming through the garden, without knowing *who*. But once I know that Fred is coming through the garden it adds nothing to be told that *someone* is coming through it. Full and explicit physical knowledge should, therefore, if physicalism is true, cancel out anything new for Mary to learn when she actually sees chromatic colours or for the deaf scientist to learn when he gains his hearing.[4]

I spoke above of (i), (ii) and (iii) as essential to the central state identity theory and as entailing topic neutrality. But we have seen that the neutral account of experience will not work. Which of the three is least harmful

---

[4] One possible response is that our topic neutral knowledge presents itself as new knowledge when it is not. If one were to run together topic neutrality and the phenomenal concept strategy, then one might give rise to such a theory, which is what Janet Levine has recently done. That this cannot escape the problems for topic neutrality I have outlined above, I claim in Section 5.8.

for the physicalist to drop? (ii) is essential to standard physicalism and (iii) is a plain fact of introspection, so it is (i), the identity theory, that must go. But then what of the need to accommodate the occurrent and physical, rather than abstract, nature of raw feels? For any orthodox physicalist, all occurrent events are physical events, so, if the having of a sensation is an occurrent event, it must be a physical event. For something as specific and 'internal' as a sensation, it seems natural, if not inevitable, to think of it, from a physicalist perspective, as an event in the central nervous system. Whether one categorises it as identical to, or as constituted by, neural events, it remains the case that no physical properties of the brain seem to be explicitly presented, and these seem to be the only properties that a strict physicalist will allow. So it looks as if the doctrine of topic neutrality is going to be required for any standard form of physicalism that allows for sensations to be occurrent events.

The story that I have told leading to the failure of topic neutral theories to find a resolution of the raw feels problem is only one of the paths that have led to the current qualia problem.

The physicalist, therefore, seems to be in a serious difficulty. The argument I presented to show that he is committed to accepting topic neutrality runs straight up against KA, which appears to show that topic neutrality will do nothing to explain the apparent knowledge that is gained when a new kind of experience is undergone. I shall try, in the discussions of KA that follow, to relate the various physicalist responses to the topic neutralist strategy, and the argument that seems to make it compulsory for the physicalist.

The physicalist has the following difficult tasks. He must (i) avoid making sensations 'abstract', as propositional attitudes and, in general, functional states might be held to be, and (ii) avoid appealing to topic neutrality in a way that falls foul of KA. We will see that this is a dilemma that the physicalist never manages to resolve. We will also see (in Chapter 8) that KA has a power that even its proponents have barely noticed.

But having set the ground, it is necessary now to consider KA itself.

1.4   The knowledge argument, informally stated

The knowledge argument (KA) is almost certainly the most popular of the contemporary arguments which have been used to show that physicalism faces serious problems. In general outline, the argument has a longish history, Ludlow, Nagasawa and Stoljar (2004) find earlier versions of the argument in Russell, Dunne, Broad, Farrell, Feigl, Meehl and Nagel, as well as the one coincident in time with Jackson by the present author. Jackson's version of the argument is the one that has attracted the discussion and has become canonical. He states it as follows:

> Mary is confined to a black-and-white room, is educated through black-and-white books and through lectures relayed on black-and-white television. In this way she learns everything there is to know about the physical nature of the world. She knows all the physical facts about us and our environment, in a wide sense of 'physical' that includes everything in *completed* physics, chemistry, and neurophysiology, and all there is to know about the causal and relational facts consequent upon all this, including, of course, functional roles. If physicalism is true, she knows all there is to know. For to suppose otherwise is to suppose there is more to know than every physical fact, and that is just what physicalism denies . . . It seems, however, that Mary does not know all there is to know. For when she is let out of the black-and-white room or given a colour television, she will learn what it is like to see something red, say. This is rightly described as *learning* – she will not say 'ho, hum'. Hence, physicalism is false. (Jackson 1986: 291)

Before looking at the argument more closely, I want to make two preliminary points. First, although Jackson characterises what Mary will learn as *what it is like to see* something – for example, red – the knowledge Mary initially lacks and which she later gains concerns what might variously be characterised as *what it is like to see chromatic colours* (henceforth, just 'colour') or *what coloured things normally look like*, or *the phenomenal nature of colour* or *the qualitative nature of colour*. The point, that is, can be made in a way that draws attention to the 'feel' for the subject, or to the qualitative nature of the phenomenon. For our purposes, this is a distinction without a serious difference, for the character of sensory experience is given by its internal phenomenal object: hence *what it is like* for a given subject to experience a given colour is a direct function of the phenomenal nature of colour in his experience – that is, of the way colours look to him. Saying this does not involve denying that there is a distinction between the act and the object of experience, for such a distinction is compatible with the introspectable character of the former being dependent on the latter. This fact, which is surely an innocuous version of the so-called transparency of phenomenal consciousness, will become important in later chapters. The conclusion of the argument is that, since she knows all there is to know about the physical process of seeing, that about which she does not know must not be a physical state of affairs: so that which can be variously referred to as *what it is like to see colours, what coloured things look like* and *the phenomenal and qualitative natures of colour* must be a non-physical feature of vision.

The second preliminary point concerns how one focuses on the intuition that KA is seeking to express as an argument. As Jackson expresses it, the ground for the belief that Mary did not know everything while in her room is that she would learn something upon leaving it, namely what it is like to see a colour such as red. One could instead have said that she obviously lacked something when in her room because there she did not know what it was like to see red, and other chromatic colours, as do people who have not been confined as she has. One might, that is, put weight primarily on the intuition that she will learn something on leaving the room, or on the intuition that she lacks something, compared to the rest of us, while still confined. Our conviction (if we share it) that Mary will feel she has discovered something on leaving the room rests on the same intuition as the conviction that she lacked something when confined. This is a thought experiment, not an actual experiment, so we do not actually learn anything by putting Mary in the room and then letting her out. The supposition of the discovery that she makes on leaving the room is simply a dramatic way of re-expressing the conviction that she lacked something when still confined. In setting the argument out slightly more formally, I shall concentrate on the idea that she initially lacked something, rather than on the idea that she later gained something. This is a distinction without a difference. This is not, I think, a trivial point. Some of the responses to the argument focus on *what it is that Mary later learns*, rather than *what it is she was originally missing*. These ought to be the same, but we will find that the distinction allows wiggle room to the opponent of the argument. How this is so will emerge when we discuss both Dennett's response to KA in Chapter 2 and the *Abilities Hypothesis* in Chapter 3.[5]

1.5   KA and its close relatives

David Chalmers in *The Conscious Mind* (1996) gave a tremendous boost to the discussion of the problem that conscious experience constituted for the physicalist. He coined the happy expression 'the hard problem' to characterise the issue on which KA focused (1996: xii).

Chalmers also grouped KA with several other arguments, which tend to support property dualism, but two in particular have become intertwined with the discussion of KA. One is *the logical possibility of zombies*, generally known as *the conceivability of zombies* (CZ). The other consists in pointing out (following Joseph Levine (1983)) that there is an *explanatory gap* (EG) between the physical and phenomenal realms. Chalmers states this as follows:

---

[5] Nagasawa and Stoljar point out that Jackson adds the point about learning, and cite it as an improvement over the version in Robinson (1982), which omits it; but in their own formal statement of the argument, Mary's ignorance plays a role, but not her subsequent illumination.

The most obvious way (although not the only way) to investigate the logical supervenience of consciousness [on the body/brain] is to consider the logical possibility of a *zombie*: someone or something physically identical to me (or to any other conscious being), but lacking conscious experiences altogether ... So let us consider my zombie twin. This creature is molecule for molecule identical to me, and identical in all the low-level properties postulated be a completed physics, but lacks conscious experience entirely ... What is going on in my zombie twin? He is physically identical to me, and we may well suppose that he is embedded in an identical environment. He will certainly be identical to me *functionally*: ... It is just that none of this functioning will be accompanied by any conscious experience. There will be no phenomenal feel. There is nothing it is like to be a zombie. (1996: 94–5)

Chalmers argues that such creatures are logically possible (and not just imaginable) and so consciousness does not logically supervene on the physical.

The *explanatory gap* argument (EG) is based on CZ:

The very fact that it is logically possible that the physical facts could be the same while the facts about consciousness are different shows us that as Levine (1983) has put it, there is an *explanatory gap* between the physical level and conscious experience.

If this is right, the fact that consciousness accompanies a given physical process is a *further fact*, not explicable simply by telling the story about the physical facts. In a sense, the accompaniment must be brute ... Perhaps we might get some kind of explanation by combining the underlying physical facts with certain further *bridging* principles that link the physical facts with consciousness, but this explanation will not be a reductive one. The very need for explicit bridging principles shows us that consciousness is not being explained reductively, but is being explained in its own terms. (1996: 107)

These arguments clearly make points closely associated with that made by KA, but are also, strictly speaking, different arguments. It is my view that, simply as arguments for property dualism, they add nothing to KA – though the zombie argument raises important issues concerning modality. I shall argue in Chapter 5 that, through no fault of Chalmers's, these other strategies have functioned as distractions from the core claims of the 'hard problem' and KA. At this point I merely want to note some of the differences.

First, the zombie argument, in its straightforward form, presupposes epiphenomenalism and KA does not. This is because a zombie is defined as a creature exactly like a human in construction and behaviour, but without consciousness. This assumes that consciousness has no effect on behaviour. Jackson titled his paper 'Epiphenomenal Qualia', but the epiphenomenalism does not enter into the argument, it is a consequence of the additional assumption that the world is closed under physics, which does not enter into the argument itself.

Second, the zombie argument rests on certain views about modality which are irrelevant to KA for property dualism. P. F. Strawson in *Individuals* (1959), for example, defends a form of property dualism in association with the claim that it is conceptually necessary that the subject of those properties is also the subject of physical properties. KA does not seek to refute Strawson: the modal features of the link between the properties, once their distinction *qua* properties has been established, is another matter.[6]

The important point is that the fact that there is an explanatory gap between our physical account of the world and the features of consciousness is open to either a *de re* or a *de dicto* interpretation. That is, one might either take it to be the case that it is a mystery how conscious properties emerge from physical properties, or of how psychological explanations relate to physical explanations. One might even think that the phrase '*explanatory* gap' suggests the latter. We will see in Chapter 5 that opponents of KA use both the explanatory gap and the zombie argument to suggest that the arguments show only a conceptual dualism, not a property dualism, and that the sliding between the KA, EG and CZ helps them to do this. The KA and the hard problem are much less easily open to this interpretation.

1.6   KA formally stated

For purposes of close discussion, the argument needs to be put in a more formal manner.

(1) Mary knows all those facts about the perception of chromatic colour which can in principle be expressed in the vocabulary of physical science.
(2) Unlike those who have normal visual experiences, Mary does not know the phenomenal nature of chromatic colour (what it is like to perceive chromatic colour).

Therefore

(3) The phenomenal nature of chromatic colour in principle cannot be characterised using the vocabulary of physical science.
(4) The nature of any physical thing, state or property can be expressed in the vocabulary of physical science.

Therefore

---

[6] We shall see in Chapter 14 that E. J. Lowe likens his own dualist theory to Strawson's, so even in more contemporary debate, the modal and dualist issues operate separately.

(5) The phenomenal nature of chromatic colour is not a physical thing, state or property.

One objection that has been made against this argument is that it is not valid. (Churchland 1989c, but also Prinz 2012). Propositional attitude verbs such as 'know' create opaque contexts and perhaps the above argument ignores this fact and moves from two things not being known to be the same to the conclusion that they are not the same. The following argument is not valid because of such opacity.

(6) S knows that Cicero was an orator.
(7) S does not know that Tully was an orator.

Therefore

(8) Cicero is not Tully.

The opacity of 'knows' does not, however, affect our argument, though not for the reason sometimes suggested. It has been suggested that the argument is invulnerable to this objection because 'knows about' or 'knows, concerning' is transparent, not opaque. If we were to argue,

(9) Concerning Cicero, S knows that he was an orator.
(10) Concerning Tully, S does not know that he was an orator.

therefore

(11) Cicero is not Tully,

then the argument would not be valid. The error would lie in (10) because, given that Cicero is identical with Tully then S does know *about* or *concerning* Tully anything he knows about or concerning Cicero, because knowledge about *a* does not imply one knows that what one knows is in fact about *a:* the 'that' which introduces the propositional content of S's knowledge follows the name and hence does not include it within its scope. The relevance of this to our original argument would be brought out by rewriting (1) and (2) as

(1′) Concerning experiencing colour, Mary knows everything which could in principle be expressed in the vocabulary of physical science.
(2′) Concerning seeing, Mary does not know the phenomenal nature of its object, colour.

The knowledge referred to in both (1′) and (2′) concerns seeing and that which is said to be unknown in (2′) must fall outside the class of things said to be known in (1′). As the latter includes everything encompassed by physical science, the former must fall outside that class. Hence (3) follows. This explanation, however, shows that it is not the transparency of 'knows about' which saves the argument but the proviso that Mary knows *everything* that physical science could tell her about seeing.

This is in fact the crucial point. Opacity is created by the fact that things can be objects of mental states under many different aspects or descriptions. What (1) asserts is that Mary knows every physical aspect of the system and hence any aspect under which she does not know it cannot be a physical one. We can see how this would modify the other argument.

(12) S knows everything about Cicero, including that Cicero was an orator.

(13) S does not know that Tully was an orator.

Therefore

(14) Cicero is not Tully.

The argument is valid, because if S knew everything about Cicero he would know that he was Tully, if he were Tully. On the other hand, the transparency of 'knows about' would not alone save the argument, for if we replace (12) by

(15) S knows most things about Cicero, including that he was an orator

the argument to (14) by (15) and (13) would not be valid, for that Cicero was Tully might be one of the things S did not know. Similarly it would be invalid to argue these:

(16) Concerning seeing, Mary knows *most* of the facts which could in principle be expressed in the vocabulary of physical science.

(2') Concerning seeing chromatic colour, Mary does not know the phenomenal nature of its object, chromatic colour.

Therefore

(3) The phenomenal nature of chromatic colour cannot be expressed in the vocabulary of physical science.

This is not valid because *the phenomenal nature of colour* may be one of the physical features Mary does not know about. Hence it is the completeness of Mary's knowledge in the relevant area which makes the argument a good one.

This very fact may open the way to a new objection to the argument, namely that no one ever could know everything that could *in principle* be expressed in the vocabulary of physical science, and perhaps that the very notion of knowing all such facts is a bogus one, because there are indefinitely many. As we shall see, an objection similar to this plays a role in Dennett's objections to KA. For present purposes, it is easily circumvented. This objection, stated bluntly, merely forces one to make the argument more indirect, for the notion of *knowing everything* is merely an aid to easy exposition of the argument. It can be expressed without it. The crucial idea behind the argument is that no possible knowledge of a physical sort would constitute or entail knowledge of the subjective dimension. This can be expressed as follows:

(17) Take any set of facts of the sort in principle expressible in the vocabulary of physical science such that the facts in that set could be known, at one time, by a given subject, and suppose Mary to possess knowledge of that set.

(18) Whichever such set Mary knows, she, unlike those who have normal visual experiences, does not know the phenomenal nature of colour.

Therefore

(19) Knowledge of the phenomenal nature of colour cannot be strictly derived from the knowledge of any set of physical facts, as above.

Therefore

(20) Either (a) knowledge of the phenomenal nature of colour can only be derived from knowledge of some set of physical facts which no individual could ever know at one time or (b) the phenomenal nature of colour cannot in principle be expressed in the vocabulary of physical science (i.e. (3)).

(21) (20)(a) lacks any plausible rationale.

Therefore

(3) The phenomenal nature of colour cannot in principle be expressed in the vocabulary of physical science.

I shall discuss the argument in its original formulation.

(18) parallels (2) and the issues that arise for (2) arise in the same way for (18).

1.7   Possible objections

Given that the argument is valid, is it sound, or are some of the premises defective? I have already dealt with objections to (1), and the principal problems concern (2); but some remarks may be required in defence of (4). It may be objected to (4) that there are a lot of facts about physical objects that are not expressible in scientific jargon – for example, that pen-knives are useful for getting stones out of horses' hooves. Many of such cases will bring in human purposes and perspectives at least indirectly, and may, therefore, be judged dubious as instances of uncontroversially physical properties. Notwithstanding this, such examples are irrelevant to the present issue. Physical science concerns itself with bedrock description and explanation, and those facts which fall outside of it concern larger and looser and more informal perspectives on things. Sensory consciousness will only be thought to come into this latter category if one accepts a reductive social-cum-behavioural analysis of it. Such theories are not, at the moment, in play, and we can accept that sense experience is involved at a more fundamental level in the operation of the human organism. I shall assume, therefore, that (4) applies at the relevant level of description and that any reasonable controversy concerning this will resurface when I discuss the physicalist strategies relevant to (2).[7]

A physicalist who accepts the validity of the argument must challenge the truth of one of the premises, presumably (2). If Mary knows everything physical which is relevant to colour perception, then, from a physicalist perspective, there cannot be anything that she does not know: hence (2) must be rejected.

We can ask either 'what was it Mary lacked before leaving the room?' or 'what was it Mary acquired on leaving the room and experiencing colour?' Everyone agrees that she lacked experience of colour before leaving the room and acquired such experiences after, but the core issue is what way, if any, coming to experience colour can be characterised as gaining knowledge she had previously lacked. There are four responses available to this, as follows.

(1) The boldest – adopted by Dennett – is that Mary lacked nothing cognitive before leaving the room and so gained nothing cognitive on getting outside. Mary was all along in a position to work out what it is like to see colours, if she should choose to do so.

Everyone agrees that Mary lacks something and that what she lacks could be called the *experience of colour*. But whether that involves a lack of *knowledge* is another matter. Dennett is one of the few philosophers who think that she really could work out *what it is like* to see colour, such that she could successfully anticipate the experience before it came. We will consider this outright rejection of the argument in the next chapter.

(2) Mary lacked, and then acquired, some ability or capacity. She gained the knowledge of *how*, not knowledge of any fact.

This is the view associated primarily with Lewis and Nemirow. It is also the approach that one might expect to be associated with behaviourism and functionalism, though we shall see in Chapter 3 that Lewis and Nemirow are strangely compromised on this.

(3) Mary lacked and then gained some particular way or mode (generally labelled 'phenomenal') of knowing something which she had known in a more theoretical way all along.

The major way of developing this line of thought has been the so-called *phenomenal concept strategy*, which originates in the work of Brian Loar and which is the topic of Chapter 5.

The differences between (2) and (3) can disappear in some strategies, especially if one says that the ability acquired is a *capacity to represent* a

---

[7] Part II, especially Chapter 9 on reduction is relevant to this point. I argue there that all non-basic physical levels, which includes the special sciences as well as more ordinary language contexts, presuppose the human perspective.

neural state in a special experiential way. This is the view to which Jackson himself moved when he abandoned KA, as we shall see in Chapter 4.

(4) Mary lacked and later acquired some factual knowledge concerning the nature of phenomenal colour. She gained what Lewis (who rejects it) calls *phenomenal information.*

This is the interpretation required by someone who thinks that the argument successfully refutes physicalism by proving property dualism. The information in question will not be propositional, but be a form of knowledge by acquaintance, but it will still be factual information concerning the nature of colour and colour experience.

By the end of Part I we shall have found that (4) is the only plausible response to the argument.

2   Dennett's denial of Mary's ignorance

2.1   Mary and the blue banana: an argument or a challenge?

Daniel Dennett first discussed the knowledge argument (KA) in *Consciousness Explained* (1991) and replied to critics and developed his argument in his (2007). Dennett's general method in his (1991), as in much of his other work, is what might be called 'the Jericho method': he believes that if he marches around a philosophical problem often enough, proclaiming what are, plausibly, relevant scientific truths, the problem will dissolve before our eyes. Insofar as he is inviting us to adopt new ways of looking at things, abandoning our primitive 'intuition pumps', this method can be quite appropriate. It is, however, also rather indirect, and so moments of direct philosophical argument are to be relished when found. The KA is one strategy that condenses the issue of physicalism and consciousness sufficiently precisely to force Dennett to face his opponent directly.

Dennett is probably the most prominent amongst the philosophers who affirm that Mary, whilst still in her room, is able to work out what it would be like to experience chromatic colours. He claims that we have no good reason to think that, on the basis of her complete scientific knowledge, she could not work it out precisely. We, of course, cannot see how she would do it, but that is another matter. The fact that we cannot imagine how she might do it merely reflects the fact that we cannot imagine what it might be like to have her complete knowledge of the physical processes. He defends this view by using a series of his own thought experiments. The first of these concerns 'Mary and the blue banana' (MBB). When this was challenged, he presented in the later articles the story of 'Swamp Mary' (SM): finding that this fantasy offends his sensibility, he gives it a scientistic reconstruction, in the form of 'RoboMary' (RM). I shall follow this developing line of argument and attempt to show that Dennett is forced to fall back on a version of the abilities hypothesis, which will be discussed in the next chapter. I shall also argue that Dennett's approach suffers from a serious tension; namely one between his behaviourism and his claim that it is our inability to imagine the full extent of Mary's knowledge that makes KA intuitively plausible. He needs both these but, I shall argue, the behaviourism ought to render the detailed physical knowledge irrelevant.

Dennett explains MBB as follows.

And so, one day, Mary's captors decide that it was time for her to see colors. As a trick, they prepared a bright blue banana to present to her as her first color experience ever. Mary took one look at it and said ' Hey! You tried to trick me! Bananas are yellow, but this one is blue!' Her captors were dumbfounded. How did she do it? 'Simple,' she replied. 'You have to remember that I know *everything* – absolutely everything – that could ever be known about the physical causes and effects of color vision. So of course before you brought the banana in, I had written down, in exquisite detail, exactly what physical impression a yellow object or a blue object (or a green object, etc.) would make on my nervous system. So I already knew what *thoughts* I would have (because, after all, the "mere disposition" to think about this or that is not one of your famous qualia, is it?). I was not in the slightest surprised by my experience of blue ... I realize it is *hard for you to imagine* that I could come to know so much about my reactive dispositions that the way blue affected me came as no surprise. Of course it is hard for you to imagine. It is hard for anyone to imagine the consequences of someone knowing absolutely everything physical about anything!' (1991: 399–400)

At first sight one might think that there was here some attempt to explain how Mary performed her trick. She seems to say that, because she knew everything, she was able to write down in detail what physical impression would be made by different colours, and what thoughts would follow therefrom, and so be able to identify the experience. In Robinson (1993c) I was puzzled about how this was meant to work. How does Mary know that what she is seeing is *blue*? She says she had 'written down, in exquisite detail, exactly what physical impression a yellow object or a blue object (or a green object etc.) would make on my nervous system'. I argued that this would enable her to work out that the banana before her was *blue* only if she could know what state her brain was put in by the banana. But, I claimed, she would have no way of knowing that. Her 'scientific omniscience' did not include an automatic knowledge of what particular physical states obtained, only what was contained in or followed from science. No amount of knowledge of the science of neurology would, of itself, tell her what state her brain was in at a given time. So I claimed that Dennett's narrative assumes that Mary knows what her own neurological state is at the moment of seeing the blue banana for otherwise how does she know that she is undergoing what she had written down under 'blue' not 'yellow'. She has not seen chromatic colour before, so she does not recognise that it is blue in the normal way, namely identifying it from the many samples of colour that she has previously experienced. She has no experiential way of telling that *that* is what *blue* looks like. The only way she might do it is if she knows that the states that she is in are of the kind that is associated with blue-seeing (and not yellow-seeing, as she would have expected from a banana). But Mary's perfect scientific knowledge tells her nothing about what is currently going on in her nervous system – such particular information is not part of her scientific omniscience – so there is no way she could tell that she is being affected in a *blue* way.

Dennett (2007, 16, fn 1) rejects this objection in the following words:

Howard Robinson (1993) supposes that I am illicitly helping myself to the premise that Mary knows 'every particular physical thing that is going on' but my claim does not at all depend on such a strong claim, as will be clear from the variations that I develop here.

The 'variations' developed later in the article are SM and RM.

Again it might seem unclear just how the response is meant to work. If it is just that he does not wish to claim that she knows *every* physical fact, then that does not touch my criticism, which required only that he was helping her to certain pieces of knowledge about her current state to which she would have no access: the 'every' came into it only in my attempt to explain why Dennett might have thought that she would know this, namely that her scientific omniscience included such particular information. How might she have seen that she was seeing blue without having such access to her optical states? Perhaps this is revealed in the sentence following the one most recently quoted: 'So I already knew what *thoughts* I would have (because, after all, the mere disposition to think about this or that is not one of your famous qualia, is it?)'.

This is an entirely different line of argument from the one that seemed to involve Mary knowing what state her neural pathways were currently in. The idea may be this. Mary could work out, on the basis of scientific information alone, what thoughts a given physical stimulus would cause, and she would know what thoughts she was actually having just by being conscious of them. So she could work out what the stimulus must be on the basis of the thoughts that she was having. This, I think, is confused. The conscious thought that would result from an unfamiliar stimulus would be something along the lines of 'I wonder what that colour is called'. This thought might be caused by any unfamiliar colour and would not allow one to work out what the stimulus must be. Dennett seems to be assuming that the stimulus would automatically cause a recognitional thought, but it would not, on anyone's theory, if the stimulus was not familiar. This is the contrast between the *thought* stimulated by the experience and the effect on the visual pathways. A blue object will, presumably, make (more or less) the same effect on the optic nerve whether or not one has seen blue before, but it would not prompt the same kind of recognitional thought, which does depend on past experience and memory.

In these criticisms of Dennett, I was trying to construct from his account of MBB some kind of explanation of how, in outline, she might have performed her trick. I still think that Dennett set the story out as if he were giving strong hints about this. Whether or not he originally meant to give these leads, he now denies that they figure in the point of his story. He now claims that it is a mistake to suppose that MBB suggests any sort of explanation of how Mary might have performed the feat. The story, as Dennett now construes it, is a much more direct act of defiance. He was not assuming that knowledge of Mary's current neural state was part of her comprehensive knowledge of the physical facts, nor that knowledge of her own thoughts would reveal it. He was simply telling a counter-Jackson story where Mary *could* tell – because she had worked it out – what it was like to see various colours. I had mistakenly attributed to Dennett a rationale for how she had worked it out, but that was not his intention. MBB is simply a denial of the normal story – but why not? One man's intuition is another man's prejudice: Jackson tells it how it strikes him and Dennett tells it *his* way. Where is the *argument* – or so Dennett wants to say? He shows this by presenting a short dialogue.

TRAD: What on earth do you mean? *How* could Mary do that?

DCD: It wasn't easy. She deduced it, actually, in a 4,765 step proof (for red – once she'd deduced what red would look like to her, green fell into line with a 300-step lemma, and the other colours and all the hues thereof, were relatively trivial extensions of these proofs).

TRAD: You're just making it all up! There are no such proofs!

DCD: This is a thought experiment; I get to make up all sorts of things. Can you prove that there are no such proofs? What established fact or principle am I contradicting when I help myself to a scenario in which she deduces what colors would look like to her from everything she knows about color?

TRAD: Look. It's just obvious! You can't deduce what a color is like if you've never seen one!

DCD: That's an interesting folk theorem, I must say. Here's another: If you burp, sneeze and fart at the same time, you die. Both sound sort of plausible to me, but is there any scientific backing for either of them? (2007: 16–17)

So my mistake in 1993c was to think that MBB gave at least a hint about how Mary might perform the feat. It still seems to me that my original way of reading the story is the natural one. But we must now take Dennett as simply making a contrary assertion to the KA, and claiming that this is as reasonable (or unreasonable) as was the original KA.

2.2   Swamp Mary and RoboMary: how Mary could have pulled it off

From the flow of the narrative in Dennett (2007), he seems to be promising to improve on this situation and that the coming stories of SM and RM will explain how Mary might have worked out her solution to the blue banana. The first is science-fictional (or science fantasy) and leaves a bad taste in Dennett's mouth. The second is a scientist version of the first. Because the first establishes the principle at issue more straightforwardly, my discussion will be mainly in its terms, but it is applicable to both.

The first version is Swamp Mary.

Swamp Mary: Just as standard Mary is about to be released from prison, still virginal regarding colors and aching to experience 'the additional and extreme surprise, the unanticipated delight, or the utter amazement that lie in store for her' (Graham and Horgan 2000: 82), a bolt of lightning rearranges her brain, putting it by Cosmic Coincidence in exactly the brain state she was about to go into *after* first seeing a red rose … So when, a few seconds later, she is released, and sees for the first time a colored thing (that red rose), she says just what she would say on seeing her *second* or *nth* red rose. 'Oh yeah, right, a red rose. Been there, done that.' (2007: 24)

He follows up by pointing out that the lightning did not give her a hallucination of red, but the 'competence state' that normally followed such an experience. In the second version, RoboMary is a non-chromatic-experiencing robot that manages to engineer herself into the same sort of state as the lightning creates in Swamp Mary. So the cases are essentially similar, but RoboMary is more 'technological' and hence less 'miraculous' than the lightning story. So I think we are to understand that Mary-of-the-blue-banana might, as a result of her 4,675 steps, put herself into a state rather of this sort.

Swamp Mary and RoboMary raise interesting questions, but not ones directly relevant to the KA. They challenge the claim that actually having an experience of red in a normal or more or less normal (e.g. hallucinatory) way is the only way that one might come by the knowledge of what seeing red is like. And it is true that this form of experience is the normal way and that this is necessary is the intuition that Dennett puts into Trad's mouth in the dialogue I quoted above. But the fundamental claim of the KA is that knowledge of *what it is like* can only be captured from the first-person perspective, it is not about how that perspective *must* come about. Swamp Mary and RoboMary have not gained their knowledge simply by understanding the relevant processes from a third-person perspective; they need to become the subjects of those states themselves, even if not by having a standard phenomenal experience.

Dennett faces an objection very close to this one, which he states and responds to as follows.

Objection (thanks to the editors of this volume): For RoboMary to self-program herself into [the state she would have been put in by having the experience] is cheating as much as for her to self-program herself into the 'experiencing red' state. What matters is whether Mary (or RoboMary) can *deduce* what it is like to see red from her complete physical knowledge, not whether one can use one's physical knowledge in some way or other to acquire knowledge of what it is like to see in color.

   I just don't see that this is what matters. So far as I can see, this objection presupposes an improbable and extravagant distinction between (pure?) deduction and other varieties of self-enlightenment. I didn't describe RoboMary as 'programming' herself. I said she ... makes all the necessary adjustments and *puts herself into [the state that constitutes seeing colours in others].* If I use my knowledge to imagine myself in your epistemic shoes in some regard, is this 'self-programming'? (2007: 29)

Talk of 'programming' is irrelevant, and so, perhaps, is 'deduction'. The question is whether there is something essential about *getting yourself into the state* rather than knowing it in an intellectual, third-personal manner, as one generally knows scientific facts about things in the world.

   The interesting question to which these cases give rise is how one is to conceive of the knowledge of colours that these two latest Marys possess: how should one characterise their state after they have become like those who have had an experience although they themselves have not had it. This is the same question as 'what are the properties of this normally-post-experiential state?' Dennett describes it as 'a dispositional state':

now she can know just what it is like for her to see a red tomato, because she has managed to put herself into just such a dispositional state ... (2007: 28)

He does not seem, however, to spell out what the dispositions in question are dispositions to do, but the natural affinity of *dispositions* and *abilities* in this context must strike one. One thing that one might think that the two new Marys can do is imagine what seeing red is like and (pseudo) remember what the experience they never had was like. It looks here as if we have come close to the 'abilities hypothesis' of Lewis and Nemirow. This was the second option that we cited as possible routes for the opponent of the KA. Insofar as Dennett's position is coherent, and does not give an illicit priority to the first-person perspective, it seems to be no different from the abilities hypothesis. We will move on to considering how that option fares in the next chapter.

2.3   A coup de grace: is MBB even relevant?

Everything in this chapter and in Dennett's strategy depends on his claim that MBB, supported by SM and RM, refutes KA by showing that Mary could work out which experience she would be having. But the 'blue banana' example in fact changes the topic. The issue raised by KA is whether Mary is able to know the nature of certain experiences – what they are like – on the basis of knowledge of physical facts alone. Dennett, in MBB, is arguing that Mary could, on the basis of such knowledge, predict which experience she was going to have. These are not the same thing. It is uncontroversial that if Mary had a machine which displayed to her what the states in her optic nerves were, she would be able to see that she was in a state that normally people went with seeing blue, so she could infer that the banana must be a blue one. This in no way shows that it would be possible for her, from the physical information alone, to work out what blue looked like; she can merely tell 'oh, that must be blue'. What blue actually looked like would still be new to her. So even if there were a route by which Mary could work out which colour it must be that she was seeing (and I doubt that she could do this without particular knowledge of her own current brain state), this would still not be a way of inferring *what it is like* from the physical information. The assumption behind Dennett's strategy would have to be that if she could say what colour it must be, that could only be because she already knew, or had the resources to know, what that colour was like. But that does not seem to be how Dennett's Mary works. It is consistent with Dennett's story that Mary infers what colour it must be because she knows that that colour (or its perception) is correlated with certain physical facts that she also knows. So MBB, even if successful, would only show that Mary need not be surprised by what colour it was that she was shown, and not being surprised does not entail that she already knew what it would look like.

This carries over to Dennett's remarks on Mary's thoughts. Even if the banana prompted the thought 'that's blue' (as I have argued it would not), and, on this basis, she could work out that it must be blue, that would not show that it was not new to her that things that were blue, and looking blue, looked like *that*.[1] So MBB misses the point. And so do SM and RM, because they only explain (even if successful) how Mary might come to be in the same state as someone who had had the experience, not how one might work out what having such a state would be like, on the basis of scientific, third-personal knowledge.

---

[1] This last point was raised by Aakash Patel in a seminar at Central European University, and this prompted the argument in the preceding paragraph.

2.4   Dennett's behaviourism and the dubious relevance of Mary's scientific knowledge

I have argued that Dennett's rival thought experiments do not undermine KA, but I think that there is also a deeper and more revealing tension within his strategy, and, before moving on to the *abilities hypothesis*, I want to consider this. In doing so, the argument will not be purely *ad hominem*, because I think it brings out a more general problem concerning the relation between behavioural and functional approaches and the philosophical relevance of internal, neural structures.

In a second footnote in his (2007) Dennett argues as follows.

Robinson (1993) also claims that I beg the question by not honouring the distinction he declares to exist between knowing '*what one would say and how one would react*' and knowing 'what it is like'. If there is such a distinction, it has not yet been articulated or defended by Robinson or anyone else, so far as I know. (16)

This quotation seems to embody a more or less straightforward behaviourism – which is not surprising from Dennett, who claims to derive his philosophy of mind from a synthesis of Ryle and Quine. I admitted in Robinson (1993a) that KA would not work against a thoroughly resistant behaviourist or functionalist. That is to say, if someone is prepared to stand by the view that Mary, when she leaves the room, simply acquires certain dispositions – mainly discriminatory – that she has not previously possessed, and that she could, of course, whilst in her room, know what these dispositions are in others and would be in her, then there is no problem. For these purposes, behaviourism and functionalism are not significantly different. But this raises an interesting problem. Given that a large proportion of physicalists are functionalists, why should KA be thought to be generally effective if a determined adherence to functionalism can resist it? The answer must be that, in some way, the argument is meant to force us to recognise that functionalism is counter-intuitive in a way and to a degree that amounts to denying obvious phenomena: it is a way of forcing one to recognise just how radically counter-intuitive functionalism is, when applied to 'raw feels' and the 'hard problem' and not just to propositional attitudes and informational states. The argument seems to run as follows:

(1) If functionalism were true, then Mary would know what to expect – what it would be like – when she first saw a chromatic colour.
(2) But it is obvious that she would not know this.
(3) So functionalism is not correct.

The argument stated in this way serves to drive the physicalist away from functionalism and what Chalmers calls type-A materialism, into some type-B form – one that allows for the 'explanatory gap'. Viewed in this light, the argument is simply a way of focusing and heightening the intuition that functionalism and other similar 'causal theories of mind' plainly miss something out. But for Dennett, this is just an 'intuition pump' that begs the question. He denies (2).

There is a problem here for behaviouristic theories. If the behaviourist/ functionalist is going to allow that there is such a thing as 'what it is like', he is going to have to identify it with the behavioural disposition or causal readiness to make certain discriminations. But what discriminations?[2] Typically, for red it will be to classify certain things with tomatoes, fire engines, post boxes, etc.; for green, with grass, leaves, granny smith apples, etc. But when Mary sees her first chromatic colour she has no idea which colour it is and so has no idea what classificatory group to put it in. We shall see in Chapter 3 how difficult it is to state the relevant capacities or dispositions without begging the question.

But there is another way of stating the problem.

(4) If functionalism were true, there would be no intuitive problem in seeing how Mary could work it out in principle.
(5) Everyone agrees there is such an intuitive problem – even Dennett concedes, as we saw above, that his theory is 'counter-intuitive'.

Therefore

(6) Functionalism is not true.

As it stands, (4) is not true. What is true is

(7) For anyone who does not find functionalism seriously counter-intuitive, there is no problem in seeing how Mary could work it out in principle.

(7) and (5) together give

(8) Everyone finds functionalism counter-intuitive – i.e. it does not seem to be the case that experiential states are just functional.

One might then be tempted by

(9) If functionalism were true, there is no reason why it should seem counter-intuitive.

(7) and (9) together give (4).

Dennett agrees that denying (2) is counter-intuitive and so must agree that functionalism is counter-intuitive. Why does he think this latter? If his view were correct, why would it seem so counter-intuitive? I think it is because he thinks that we cannot really imagine what it would be like to have all the information that Mary has, so we cannot see how it adds up to

---

[2] I will discuss how a functionalist should handle the identity of the dispositions in Chapter 3, after showing that the abilities hypothesis, as stated, will not do.

knowing what it is like; our projection from the case of our relative ignorance leaves us unable to see how this can be possible. When challenged to say how Mary could do it, he replies:

It wasn't easy. She deduced it in a 4,675 step proof (for red – once she'd deduced what red would look like to her, green fell into line with a 300-step lemma, and the other colors, and all the hues thereof, were relatively trivial extensions of those proofs). (2007: 16)

When challenged that this is just made up, Dennett defends himself as I say above, by saying that this is just a thought experiment, so 'I get to make up all sorts of things'.

But once one moves to a behavioural/functional position it is not clear that Mary's scientific omniscience is relevant to the issue. The argument of (iii) is relevant here. One can see how scientific detail might be necessary to work out what state she would be in under certain speculative conditions, and so would be relevant to the tasks of the Marys in MBB and RM, but why should it be necessary for Mary if there is no difference 'between knowing "what one would say and how one would react" and knowing "what it is like"', as Dennett claims? Careful and astute observation would surely serve the purpose then.

Imagine a variant on Mary, Extremely Observant Mary. She lacks chromatic vision and has no special knowledge of science, but is very acute at observing people's reactions. Would she come to know what it is like to see chromatic colour? Her degree of astuteness is not beyond the range of our imagination, as many people are able to be like that. Suppose that one were to say that she could, on the grounds that she could know how people react to objects she knows to be of certain colours and, in knowing these dispositions of theirs, thereby knows *what it is like* for them. If it seems credible that she might be able to do this, change the example and move to the deaf-from-birth scientist whom I introduced in Robinson (1982). He knows all that there is to know scientifically about the process of human hearing. I assume that the breach between hearing and other senses (or between the different senses in general, excepting, perhaps, taste and smell) is greater than that between visually experiencing chromatic and non-chromatic colours. Could the deaf scientist, from observing people's responses to sounds – in ordinary life and in concerts – construct what it is like to hear? Could a bat expert, from close observation of bats (no bat neurology required), come to grasp what echo-location experiences must be like? I do not deny that someone logically could dig their heels in and insist that, in all these cases, a grasp on the dispositions to react tell you all there is to know about *what it is like*. But such a claim seems totally incredible – and even if one can believe it, it would render the 4,675 steps, and the detailed knowledge of physiology, in general, completely irrelevant.

Notwithstanding, what is the status of the feeling of incredulity in response to the behaviourist account? Is it just an intuition, like the 'intuition' that Dennett cites that if one burps, farts and coughs at the same time, one will die? There seem to me to be, if not two notions of intuition, at least two poles of the idea. At one end, an intuition is a kind of intellectual hunch; a sort of theoretical speculation that has a hold of one. Someone who has an intuition of this sort will probably admit that it is a reaching out after something, a shot in the dark. Sherlock Holmes, or a scientist with a hunch he wants to try out, has an intuition of this sort. At the other end there is what is expressed by the idea that something is 'intuitively obvious'. Here there is the idea that something forces itself on you – it does not present itself as an insight, a speculative discovery, but as a fact that you cannot ignore. Dennett's example of the burp, etc., is meant to imply that there is no significant difference between these two: something can strike one as 'intuitively obvious' that is a more or less arbitrary belief. No doubt there can be people in that condition, but the clarity of a direct experience is not obviously just the same as an *idée fixe*. It is 'intuitively obvious' that having one's foot stamped on is unpleasant, and, a little more speculatively, that a life dominated by sensations of that sort is not a pleasant one. It is also intuitively obvious that the way green looks is different from the way red looks and that sounds are generically different from colours in a way that is greater than the difference between colours, even if this is difficult to explain or fill out. Any science that tried to tell us that red and green look just the same could not be right. A real-life analogy is with the difference between reflected colour and luminescent colour. They are very different physically but look similar. If a scientist who had a simple realist view of colour were to insist that we were simply wrong to insist that they looked similar, he could not be right.

It also seems 'intuitively obvious' in a similar way that *what it is like to seem to see red* is not just a disposition to react to a certain kind of stimulus, nor equivalent to a whole stock of neurological knowledge. In other words it goes with, or is much closer to, the *intuitively obvious* rather than the speculative hunch or would-be insight. Someone might reply that it has intellectual content, so goes on the other side, but, though it is a thought experiment and involves imagination these concern *what experience is (actually) like* and so go most naturally with the red–green cases.

Indeed, the claim that the phenomenal just is a disposition seems even to be a category mistake. Why is this so? The doctrine – much favoured by physicalists – of transparency explains this. *What it is like to seem to see red* and *what red is (visually) like* are two sides of the same coin.[3] The same applies to *what it is like to seem to see square*: that is, this is not a fact attached only to secondary qualities. Now the idea that *red* (or *square*), as it figures in our pre-scientific, common-sense or manifest image conception of the world, *is* a collection of *our* dispositions to react makes no sense at all. A behaviourist/functionalist account of experiencing together with its subjective contents (and without the latter there is no experience) loses the world altogether. I shall be spelling this argument out in more detail in the Section 3.5.

The '4,675-step proof' shows that Dennett would explain the counter-intuitiveness of his position by saying that we cannot imagine what it would be like to know as much as Mary and so cannot appreciate how she might come to grasp unexperienced 'what it is like'. I have claimed that, perhaps, on his own behavioural principles, the scientific knowledge ought not to be relevant. How might he resist this last claim?

One might give a rationale to the 'intuitive' position as follows. We can see that behavioural knowledge of the kind Extremely Observant Mary might have, augmented by the sort of neurology we can know at the moment, is not enough. If it were enough, then it would not seem to the well-informed and reasonably observant person now that there was a problem. But the idea that careful observation of behaviour and a little bit of science would not tell someone in Mary's position what colours looked like seems to be a universal thought. And presuming that greater neural knowledge is 'more of the same kind' – not either a 'conceptual breakthrough' or a move to some sort of 'neutral monism' – it is difficult to see how 'more of the same kind' could make any difference. Dennett seems to be forced into a 'quantity into quality' position. This is why the original thought experiment has a rationale and MBB does not. The rationale of the former is that more of the inefficacious same will not help and Dennett's response is 'let's just assume that it does'.

Does it help if all the neural details are thought of as micro-discriminations, contributing to the complexity of the functional state, and 'knowing what it is like' involves appreciating this complexity? One might put the question as follows: from a behavioural/functional point of view, why should more detail – and what sort of detail – amount to an account of *what it is like*? *What it is like* just is a highly detailed response readiness. But why is the detail necessary and not just the outline of the kind of response, such as we all know? What one cannot say, of course (though one may be tempted to think this unwittingly), is that *what it is like* is *what it is like* **to be in** such a detailed response state. But this would not help Mary, who

---

[3] See Chapter 1, Section 1.4 and Chapter 8 *passim*.

does not know what it is like to be in that state – she just knows the nature of that state. If the behavioural/functional account is correct, *what it is like* just is the behavioural disposition, not some further *what it is like to be in* that disposition. To bring in such a state is to give a priority to the first person that the scientific view is supposed to render redundant.

So Dennett's account, in terms of the unimaginable extent of Mary's knowledge, of why his theory is counter-intuitive is not convincing. If functionalism (or behaviourism) were true, it could seem counter-intuitive only if experiential states 'presented themselves' in some other way than as being functional (or dispositional). Jackson, in his later work, when he has abandoned the KA (Jackson 1998/2004), tries to give an explanation of why a complex functional state might be represented as simple and so not as functional, and we shall discuss the problems with this when we consider Jackson's change of mind in Chapter 4. Kirk's theory, which is discussed in Section 3.6, does something similar, as does the phenomenal concept strategy, which is the topic of Chapter 5.

2.5   The tension between structural and functional criteria for the identity of mental states

The previous section pointed to a tension between Dennett's belief that it is Mary's scientific 'omniscience' that outruns our imagination, and his commitment to the behaviourism that he inherits from Ryle and Quine. Dennett's predicament, however, is only one instance of physicalists' attempts to have the benefits of both a behavioural/functional and a central state approach to the analysis of mentality, when these are in fact quite generally in tension. Lewis's account of 'mad pain and Martian pain' is also a case of this (Lewis 1983b). He wants to preserve the concrete internality of sensations, as the identity theory requires, whilst recognising the possibility of multiple realisability, as functionalism or any causal criterion requires, and does so by insisting on type identity within species, but not universally. As has been shown (Shoemaker 1981, Robinson 1989), this is not a viable combination. The boundaries of species or kinds is uncertain (especially if one includes robots, as the causal analysis requires) and the stipulation that type identity must be maintained within these limits turns out to be an ad hoc attempt to preserve the intuition behind the identity theory.[4]

Robert Kirk also stipulates that not just any creature that is functionally similar to a human will count as possessing similar mental states to us. It is

---

[4] See also Section 1.3 for a discussion of Lewis's mad and Martian pains.

necessary that it also have inner workings of a similar structure, so that the processes that lie behind our behaviour are mapped, as well as the behaviour be mirrored. A property dualist can easily motivate this requirement: he will believe that the particular brain states (or at least ones of a given structure) are what *cause* the mental states. This is particularly salient when the state is a conscious one. But if mental content and consciousness simply consist in dispositional or functional appropriateness, then the stipulation that the 'right' structure must be present is an artificial device to preserve an intuitive plausibility on which causal and functional approaches have no claim. If a state counts as mental simply in virtue of its causal role, how those outputs are produced must be irrelevant, by definition.[5]

2.6 Conclusion: the shape of Dennett's failure

Dennett's approach fails because

(i) the thought experiments, MBB, SM and RM do not suggest paths by which someone without the experience could come to know what the experience was like, without making it at least *as if* they had had the experience in question. This knowledge is not achieved through third-personal scientific knowledge.

(ii) There is a tension between Dennett's behaviourism and his claim that Mary's ability to work out what the experience would be like rests on the vastness of her knowledge. According to Dennett, it is our inability to imaginatively grasp this vastness that gives KA its intuitive appeal, but this knowledge ought not to be relevant – or, at least, not central – if the behaviouristic approach is correct.

The best sense that can be made of Dennett's position pushes it into the 'abilities' approach, which we discuss next.

---

[5] That the identity theory, combined with the causal analysis fails in its attempt to provide an account of consciousness that is less abstract or ethereal than a purely dispositional or functional theory is the main purport of Chapter 4 of *Matter and Sense*. (Robinson 1982: 51–78) The importance of this failure does not seem to me to have been recognised.

3 The abilities hypothesis and other functionalist strategies

3.1 Introductory remarks

We have seen that Dennett's attempt to show that Mary could work out what it would be like to see chromatic colour on the basis of scientific knowledge alone is a failure. The most that could be rescued from his argument is that perhaps what Mary acquires when she leaves her room is some sort of disposition or ability. In Section 3.2 we will investigate the abilities hypothesis (AH), as found in Lewis and Nemirow, followed, in Section 3.3 by Stalnaker's attempt to refute the knowledge argument (KA) by appeal to Lewis's attack on the idea of phenomenal information. As these fail we will then consider in Section 3.4 what a fully functionalist response would have to say. In the remainder of the chapter I will consider other functionalist strategies: first I shall argue that analytical functionalism when applied to first personal experience is self-refuting; then I will consider Robert Kirk's argument that a form of functionalism that is not analytic can be demonstrated via a proof of the inconceivability of zombies.

3.2 The abilities hypothesis: what is it a theory about?

Dennett is one of the few philosophers who explicitly claim that Mary could, in principle, work out, when confined in her black-and-white room, what seeing colours would be like. We have seen that he cannot justify this unless he equates 'what seeing colours would be like' with some disposition or ability. This shrinks the distance between his view and the AH, which concedes that Mary initially lacks something, but what she lacks is only some set of abilities that are acquired on having the experience. According to this view, what Mary initially lacks is some kind of knowledge *how* and not knowledge *that*. The main contentious premise in the original argument was

(2) Unlike those who have normal visual experiences, Mary does not know the phenomenal nature of chromatic colour (what it is like to perceive chromatic colour).

If we gloss this with an 'abilities' interpretation, this would give us

(2b) Unlike those who have seen colours, Mary does not have the ability to *F*.

From this nothing threatening would follow, provided *F*-ing does not including knowing some fact. This is the line taken by the AH associated with Nemirow and Lewis. The issue is what one should substitute for *F*. This proves to be far from straightforward and much less so than I imagined in 1993a. I then imagined a deaf scientist who knew all the physical information about hearing but did not know what it was like to hear. Adapting that to Mary, we would imagine her as chromatic colour blind, not just lacking colour experiences as a result of her constrained circumstances. The temptation is then to say that, if Mary's proper functioning was restored, she would acquire the *ability* to see colour and that this is the ability in question. So modified (2) would run

(2c) Unlike those who can see colours, Mary does not have the ability to see them.

This is the ability she gains when she is 'cured' of her colour blindness. But, though it is true that she would acquire this ability, this is not to the point, for the ability to see colour or colours is not what she acquires *on the occasion of her first actually seeing a particular colour*. Mary, in Jackson's version, where she is not colour blind, lacks no obvious sensory *capacities* at all, only some actual experiences, and it is not easy to equate these with abilities.

This brings out a serious tension in AH. Gilbert Ryle is often thought of as a paradigm analytic behaviourist, but he is quite clear about the impossibility of equating occurrent experiences with things of a dispositional kind, including abilities. For Ryle, perception (or 'observation' as he prefers to call it) is an occurrence, the psychological or conscious character of which is given by what it is a perception of. And sensations are described on analogy with perception, in terms of a public object – the sensation is *stabbing*, even though no knife is actually involved (1949: 202). Ryle's overall objective was to exorcise the 'ghost in the machine', and his dispositionalism was only a part of his total strategy. For many psychological concepts, he removes their ghostly association by analysing them dispositionally, but it never occurs to him to make such an approach completely general. Characterisation in terms of external objects, as in direct realism, or by analogy with such, for sensations, is, he believes, enough to avoid talk of an 'inner life'. Ryle's discussion of sensations in Chapter 6 of *The Concept of Mind* is elusive in many ways, but he seems to be clear (i) that sensations are occurrent, not dispositional states; (ii) that one can do such things as notice or attend to them (one is just not allowed to say that one *perceives*, or *observes* them); (iii) that noticing and attending are occurrences and not simply dispositions. The thorough-going behaviourist or functionalist cannot be contented with this halfway house, but Ryle's caution should give one cause to reflect: he does not believe that an occurrent experience can easily be equated with the acquiring of a disposition. Finding an appropriate content for such a disposition is something which, I shall argue, the proponents of AH fail to do.

It is in fact less clear than one might have thought, what AH is a theory of. It is obviously meant to be an answer to whatever problem KA raises for the physicalist, but what exactly is that problem? The answer to this appears to be straightforward: it is that Mary did not know *what experience of colour was like*, though she knew all the physical facts, so what is the nature or status of the 'feel' or 'what it is like' of such experiences? But in fact there is another approach, which is to put the emphasis on the question 'what does Mary first learn when she leaves her room and sees chromatic colours?' It is natural to answer this question by saying that she was ignorant of *what it is like* to see colours (how colours look to us), so what she learns when she leaves the room is something that remedies her ignorance of *what it is like* to see colours (how colours appear to us). Indeed, this appears to be what Lewis thinks he is explaining. At the beginning of (2004) he cites Mary's plight as an instance of what he is trying to explain, and says 'But she does not know what it is like to see color', so it would seem he wants to explain what it is like to see colour. But this is not what AH does. This shows in the accounts of Lewis and Nemirow.

Lewis (2004: 98) quotes Nemirow with approval.

Some modes of understanding consist, not in the grasping of facts, but in the acquisition of abilities ... As for understanding an experience, we may construe that as an ability to place oneself, at will, in a state representative of the experience. I understand the experience of seeing red if I can at will visualize red. Now it is perfectly clear why there must be a special connection between the ability to place oneself in a state representative of a given experience and the point of view of the experiencer: exercising the ability just *is* what we call 'adopting the point of view of the experiencer' ... We can, then, come to terms with the subjectivity of our understanding of experience without positing subjective facts as the objects of our understanding. This account explains, incidentally, the linguistic incommunicability of our subjective understanding of experience (a phenomenon which might seem to support the hypothesis of subjective facts). The latter is explained as a special case of the linguistic incommunicability of abilities to place oneself at will in a given state, such as the state of having lowered blood pressure, and the state of having wiggling ears.

Nemirow elsewhere says:

For purposes of [the Abilities Hypothesis], the ability to imagine a color experience amounts to the ability to see a color in the mind's eye – to visualize it. (2007: 33)

If one were thinking that AH was meant to be an explanation of what the 'feel' of experience consisted in, then this would strike one as an odd item to include because imaging, as naïvely conceived, involves something very close to having appropriate qualia. In other words, unless one provides an appropriately 'abilities' (i.e. functional/behavioural) account of imaging (or imagining), one would be no further on. 'Internally visualizing' and 'seeing a colour in the mind's eye' are naturally construed as 'Cartesian theatre' events, unless a more functional or behavioural paraphrase of them can be given. This is perhaps made clearer by spelling out what the suggested abilities come to. 'Visualizing', 'imagining', 'seeing in the mind's eye' are all said to be equivalent to 'reactivating what the experience was like'. How can this be an illuminating account of the 'what it is like' of experience?[1] If the state of undergoing an experience with phenomenal content is mysterious, so is the ability to reactivate it, for what you are reactivating is a mystery.

So 'Learning to re-activate the experience of seeing colours' does not seem to fit the bill of explaining the 'what it is like' of experience, for what it is like to see red can hardly amount to being able to re-activate the experience of seeing it. So at least one response which looks like a response to 'what does she learn?' will not function as a reply to the question 'what was she ignorant of?' if this latter question is given the

---

[1] It is not only AH theorists who put emphasis on the role of imaginative re-creation of the experience in explaining the difference in Mary. Papineau, who opposes AH and supports the phenomenal concept strategy thinks that 'imaginative re-creation' constitutes 'an obvious alternative materialist story' to Jackson's property dualist account of what is happening.

Here is the obvious materialist explanation. Suppose that imaginative re-creation depends on the ability to reactivate some of the same parts of the brain as are activated by the original experience itself. Then it would be scarcely surprising that we can only do this with respect to types of experience we have had previously. We can't form replicas, so to speak, if external stimulation hasn't fixed a mould in our brains. Less metaphorically, we can only reactivate the parts of the brain required for the imaginative re-creation of some type of experience, if some actual experience of that type has previously activated those parts. (Papineau, 2002: 56)

This seems to ignore the basic question of how, from a physicalist, 'third-person' perspective, there could be anything special revealed from the first-person perspective. Why should reactivating a physical state tell you anything about that you cannot discern by examining it in a scientific manner? The phenomenal concept strategy attempts to explain the *illusion* that it tells something extra. We shall see in chapter 5 that it does not even explain why it should *seem* to present something extra.

initial answer 'the *what it is like* of experience'. If one interprets 'what is she ignorant of?' so as to allow the answer 'how to reactivate the experience', one seems to have by-passed reference to the *what it is like* (WIL) of experience (or 'what colours look like to us'). In fact, with the AH approach, an account of experience is taken for granted: the physicalist knows what experience is – a physical process – and Mary has learnt to reactivate it. AH presents an account of *knowing what it is like* to see colour in what one might call a hyphenated sense ('knowing-what-it-is-like') which does not include as a part an account of the what it is like – the current 'feel' of the experience, as one is having it.

This seems to show that AH is not attempting to analyse or explain the 'what it is like' of experience, but only what Mary initially lacked, and then gained on seeing colours. Lewis's article is, after all, called 'What experience *teaches*', not 'What experience *is*'. So the 'feel' of experience does not consist in acquiring an ability, rather, *as a result of experience* one acquires an ability. It is not a behaviouristic account of experience, but a behaviouristic account of the difference experience makes for the subject.

Michael Tye (1992) makes a similar objection to AH. He argues that when Mary is actually viewing a colour she is not exercising these abilities: in other words, AH does not provide an account of WIL as it occurs in the experience. Nemirow (2007) replies that if Mary did not have the ability to discriminate the colour she was seeing from others, then she would not know what it is like. This may be true, but it is inadequate as a response because the ability to discriminate is different from the ability to re-live the experience. The former can be represented as is a purely behavioural notion, the later falls into circularity by saying that the character of experience is given by the ability to repeat it.

In fact Lewis does have an explanation of the 'feel' or 'what it is like' of experience, as he makes clear in 'Mad Pain and Martian Pain' (1983b). In that article, Lewis presents a species-relative version of the identity theory of sensations. He ends the article in the following way:

Pain is a feeling . . . A theory of what it is for a state to be a pain is inescapably a theory of what it is like to be in that state, of how the state feels, of the phenomenal character of that state. Far from ignoring questions of how states feel in the odd cases we have been considering, I have been discussing nothing else! Only if you believe on independent grounds that considerations of causal role and physical realization have no bearing on whether a state is pain should you say that they have no bearing on how the state feels. (130)

There are two closely connected fatal objections to this, in the context of KA and AH. First, it creates a kind of asymmetry between his accounts of the nature of the 'feel' of experience and of *knowing* the 'feel'. The former is identical to the functional role of a species-specific brain state, but the latter consists in being able to reactivate that same state. But should not knowing the feel consist in knowing the brain state and its functional role, for that is the feel? If one were to reply that knowing the brain would indeed constitute knowing what it is like, but that is not the only way of knowing it – being able to reactivate it is another – then one meets the second objection. I argued in Section 1.3 that one of the problems with the topic neutral account was that Mary should have *better than* topic-neutral knowledge of the experience, so she should be the one with supreme knowledge of the 'what it is like' of experience. Lewis seems to be saddled with an ambiguity in WIL. As a component of experience, it is a brain state, as it features in an account of what Mary does not know then learns – so to speak in the hyphenated idiom 'knowing-what-it-is-like' – it is an ability.

Lewis may seem to take this on when he discusses what he calls the *Identification Thesis* (Lewis 1995; 1999: 328). This is the thesis that we can identify introspectively the intrinsic nature of our qualia. This, he thinks, is inconsistent with materialism.

A materialist cannot accept the Identification Thesis. If qualia are physical properties of experiences, and experiences in turn are physical events, then it is certain
that we seldom, if ever, identify the qualia of our experiences. Making discoveries
in neurophysiology is not so easy! ... I may know *de re* of a certain physical
property that it is among the qualia of my present experience, but without
identifying the property in question. (1999: 329–30)

Thus ignorance of *what it is like* is not peculiar to Mary, but is a condition common to us all. It is easily recognisable as the doctrine that our know-ledge of our qualia is topic neutral. The similarity to Smart's original position is reinforced by what he has to say about what we do know about the nature of our experiences. He says:

Though I do not know the essences of various qualia of my experiences, I do know
what relations of acquaintance I bear to these qualia. (330–1)

The only sense I can give to this latter idea is that *it is the kind of experience I have under circumstances such and such*: that is contextual and circumstan-tial facts by which I identify the otherwise unknown qualia. So overall, Lewis's thesis is that our knowledge of our qualia is topic neutral, for experience or introspection does not reveal what they are really like, but reveals only the kinds of context in which they typically occur.

So what does Mary's own peculiar ignorance consist in, for it is agreed that she is, in some way, worse off than the rest of us? The question is, what is it that a normal perceiver has when she sees a colour which Mary does not have by knowing the science of the situation? Obviously, she does not have the experience, but what does that mean, concerning the time of the experience itself and not some later capacity? It clearly means that she lacks some internal brain event that the normal perceiver lacks, but this, on its own, is not enough. If Mary were an expert on kidney conditions and herself lacked a painless condition about which she knew the science, it would not occur to anyone to class this as any kind of ignorance. The only answer to this question that Lewis's topic-neutral functional account allows is that the normal perceiver spontaneously acquires certain discriminatory responses just by looking that Mary cannot get in this way. Being able to report the onset of these is what the *what it is like* consists in, as far as the ordinary perceiver is concerned.

The shocking truth is that Mary is less ignorant about the real nature of qualia than we are. Lewis says that discoveries in neuroscience do not come as easily as having ordinary experiences, but Mary has the knowledge gained from neuroscience, so she knows what the qualia are like. This was an argument I used in Section 1.3 against the topic-neutral analysis. I acknowledged that I had, in *Matter and Sense*, thought that what was later called the KA set up the problem for the physicalist and that Smart-Armstrong's topic neutrality was an attempt to answer it, but it is now clear that the topic-neutralist approach does not touch the KA, because Mary has fuller than topic-neutral knowledge of the neural states, so she can hardly be ignorant of the real nature of experience: we are the ones in that situation. The paradoxical situation appears to be that the rest of us are ignorant about the nature of our qualia, but Mary the scientist knows it all! So ignorance cannot be the explanation of her limitations.

It looks as if, from the AH point of view, Mary's deficit when still in her room must consist in the fact that she cannot reactivate a state she does not yet possess, but of which she has total scientific knowledge. Is this a plausible account of what Mary is lacking by never seeing a colour? Perhaps Mary cannot waggle her ears, as some people can, though she knows exactly the physiology of how they do it. This does not seem to threaten physicalism because it would not occur to anyone to think that this was a form of factual ignorance. There must be lots of states that Mary cannot reactivate because she never had them in the first place, and these would not even seem to present themselves as factual ignorance, because they do not involve anything being revealed in experience. If the claim was that Mary *did not know what it felt like* to waggle her ears, then we would be back to the original problem.

A non-tendentious abilities account would have to make explicit how the abilities in question are purely functional. The fact that we cannot say that what Mary acquires is the ability to discriminate chromatic colours leaves us with no obvious abilities characterisation that does not leave an 'untreated' experiential element. The question remains what abilities, purely functionally conceived, you acquire when you exercise a perceptual discriminative capacity for the first time. It is no accident that Ryle did not try to apply his analytic behaviourism to such occurrent states.

There is, of course, an obvious and, in other contexts, wholly uncontroversial answer to what someone learns when they experience a kind of sensible feature, such as a colour, for the first time, namely, they learn what that feature is like. I am not talking about *what it is like* to *see*, e.g., red, but *what red itself is like*. This does not apply only to secondary qualities. It is by looking that one sees e.g. what square things are visually like or look like. In other words, if the *what it is like* jargon is put in terms of the sensible quality perceived, not the experience, to say that what you acquire by perceiving some quality for the first time is *what that quality is like* seems uncontroversial. Indeed, we can see Ryle as doing this. Furthermore, that this is so follows from the doctrine of transparency, favoured by most physicalists, according to which the *what it is* like of experience is a direct function of the nature of the things perceived: *what red looks like* and *what it is like to seem to see red* are just two sides of the same coin, as I said when introducing KA.

There are those who, like Ryle, think that direct realism of this sort presents a way round the mind-body problem. They follow U. T. Place (1956) and others in thinking that all one needs to do is avoid the *phenomenological fallacy*, which is the supposed fallacy of treating the contents of experience as internal, mental objects. I shall explain why direct realism is not, of itself, any help to the physicalist, in Chapter 4. This strategy is not, however, the one that the AH follows. Indeed, if one allowed that Mary discovered something new about the physical world when she first saw a colour, it would still follow that science, which she knew thoroughly, could not reveal all the truths about the physical world as it appears to us.

Now someone might reply to this that, although it is true that perception tells you what sensible properties are like, science can also tell you the same thing. But this is obviously not true. Even if it is true that, in some sense, science tells you what a colour *is*, it is not true that it tells you what it looks like; and the same for a shape. The upshot is that, if one is going to explain away the apparently qualitative nature of experience ('qualia'), one must do the same for the qualitative nature of the 'manifest image' or common sense world, for they are not qualitatively independent.

3.3   Stalnaker and Lewis on the knowledge argument and 'phenomenal information'

Robert Stalnaker rejects the KA, in a way that depends entirely on Lewis and therefore in a way that fails along with Lewis (Stalnaker 2008). His strategy is not a version of AH, but his reliance on Lewis makes this a convenient place to discuss his opposition to KA.

Stalnaker is a *phenomenal externalist*: he believes that the nature of all mental states, including phenomenal ones, depends on factors outside the subject. This conflicts directly with the idea that a subject can tell directly *what an experience is like* and, therefore, he can tell whether two experiences (putting problems about memory aside) are *similar to each other* simply by introspection. Stalnaker calls the idea that we can discriminate in this way *the principle of phenomenal indistinguishability*. He objects to this on the grounds that it leads to a belief in *phenomenal information*, a notion which he believes David Lewis to have discredited. *Phenomenal information* is information about what the phenomena are. Lewis, quoted by Stalnaker, puts it as follows.

Besides physical information there is an irreducibly different kind of information to be had: phenomenal information. The two are independent. Two possible cases might be exactly alike physically, yet different phenomenally. When we get physical information we narrow down the physical possibilities, and perhaps we narrow them down all the way to one, but we leave open a range of phenomenal possibilities. (Lewis 2004: 84, quoted Stalnaker 2008: 77)

Stalnaker continues:

Lewis goes on to argue that the issue about this hypothesis is not really materialism or physicalism; he notes that no assumptions about the substance of a materialist or physicalist theory play a role in Jackson's argument. To bring this point out, Lewis invites us to suppose that some dualist theory is true: suppose there were spiritual fluids, or noetic forces, or irreducible, immaterial qualia, or whatever. Presumably we could write down a true theory about them (in black and white print), and let Mary read all about it. But this won't help her to know what it is like. The restriction that Jackson's thought experiment puts on Mary's education, Lewis persuasively argued, has nothing to do with the content of her information, but depends only on the form in which she receives it. So if the hypothesis of phenomenal information is correct, the upshot must be that this particular kind of information is for some reason incapable of being communicated.

This is, I think, a completely mysterious argument. The information that Mary initially lacks concerns *what it is like* to have certain experiences. There is no reason whatsoever to think that this can be written down 'in black and white' so that she can come to know it. Lewis's argument seems to resemble one of Churchland's (1989c), when he argues that the KA would work just as well against dualism, because a thorough theoretical account of mental substance would still not tell you *what it was like* to have a certain experience. This presupposes what one might call the 'ectoplasmic' theory of dualism, where the mental entity is just a weird kind of stuff made of immaterial atoms. Stalnaker's talk of 'spiritual fluids or noetic forces' might seem to suggest this. But he has no right to bring 'immaterial qualia' into this grouping, as if they had an essence hidden behind their experiential content. The whole point of the KA is to bring out the fact that the surface *what it is like of experience* cannot be caught in the physicalist net, and that Mary gains new information about this.[2]

Lewis has four arguments against phenomenal information. One is the Churchland-like argument repeated by Stalnaker quoted above. The others are (i) an argument that such information would entail either epiphenomenalism or the abandonment of physical closure and that neither of these are acceptable. (ii) An argument that, even accepting interactionism, an unacceptable element of epiphenomenalism still remains. (iii) The claim that the alternative to phenomenal information is the abilities account of 'what Mary learns' and this is preferable in its own right. I have already argued that the AH fails to unpack into abilities of a relevantly physicalistic kind. The other arguments have the role of softening us up to accept AH. If they are not convincing, we would have even less reason to accept AH. As we shall see, they are not convincing.

(i) It is true a belief in phenomenal information forces one to choose between interactionism, with a consequent abandonment of physical closure, and epiphenomenalism. I also agree that epiphenomenalism is unacceptable. So my discussion of this option focuses on Lewis's arguments against interactionism. He argues as follows.

Making a difference to what [Mary] does or says means, at least in part, making a difference to the motions of the particles of which she is composed ... For how could she say or do anything different, if none of her particles moved any differently? But if something non-physical sometimes makes a difference to the motions of physical particles, then physics as we know it is wrong. Not just silent, not just incomplete – wrong. Either the particles are caused to change their paths without benefit of any force, or there is some force that works very differently from the usual four. To believe in the phenomenal aspect of the world, but to deny that it is epiphenomenal is to bet against the truth of physics. (2004: 95)

Many physicalists seem to take this view, namely that it is constitutive of physics that it purports to give an account of how *everything* in the world

---

[2] This is, of course, the essence of Kripke's argument that you cannot assimilate experience to cases of a posteriori identities.

works, rather than of how the material part (which may or may not be everything) works when left to itself. I can see no non-question-begging reason for adopting this view. And it seems never to have occurred to Newton that he was committed, by the nature of his enterprise, to a total account of all the causation in the world.

(ii) Lewis believes that even an interactionist is saddled with an implausible epiphenomenal component. Putting it rather more directly than Lewis, the argument is that different qualia might have done the same job (just as in the way you might see red as I see green and vice versa) so the intrinsic nature of the quale is itself irrelevant and so epiphenomenal.

> The alleged difference between [such] possibilities does nothing to explain the alleged physical manifestation ... It is in that way that the difference is epiphenomenal. That makes it very queer and repugnant to good sense. (2004: 85)

But this argument is too strong and would work equally against Lewis's own identity theory. Different intrinsic brain structures might have performed the same mentally relevant role (this is multiple realisability) so the particular structure that fills the role is epiphenomenal. But it is precisely these structures that Lewis wants to identify with/as mental states. But a state is not made idle and hence epiphenomenal just because something else might have done what it does – it still does it.

3.4   What would a truly physicalist AH need to say?

The attack on phenomenal information is a failure, and so, as a consequence, is Stalnaker's argument for phenomenal externalism. Furthermore, the account of the AH given by both Nemirow and Lewis fails to be adequately physicalist. This leaves one wondering what a truly physicalist AH would need to say. Originally, the second premise of KA was

(2) Unlike those who have normal visual experiences, Mary does not know the phenomenal nature of chromatic colour (what it is like to perceive chromatic colour).

Someone starting from a behaviourist or functionalist orientation could definitely affirm the following to replace (2).

(2d) Unlike those who have seen colours, Mary has never directly responded to them.

This is true, but all that then follows about Mary when she leaves her room and sees colours is

(2e) Mary has now responded directly to colours.

What purely behavioural or functional abilities does this give her?
One might try the following

(2f) Mary has gone through the procedure of discriminating objects with respect
       to their chromatic colours and she can remember (with respect to some of
       them at least) which of them resembled which, and to what degree.

What this means is that she has gained factual information about objects,
directly and without the aid of science or reporting, which was unavailable
to her before in that way. Her knowledge gain is restricted to particular
information gained directly – '*that* object is red' – but this involves no
deepening or extending of her knowledge of what colours are or are like,
or of what it is like to see them, nor the gaining of any generically new
ability.

There is, however, what one might think of as a more direct beha-
viourist/functionalist response. It is to bite the bullet and say that
'knowing what it is like' is just another way of saying 'having had
the experience'. 'Knowing what it is like to be a bat' is simply having
had the experience of responding to a certain kind of echo-waves,
which no human has done. 'I know what it is like' is just 'been
there, done that!' We do in fact have a use of 'know what it is like'
which is very like that. If someone says that they know what it is like to
be let down by a friend, for example, they need not be recalling
specifically what it *felt* like. Mary's coming to know what it is like to
see red is just her having had the experience – and remembering that
she has had the experience of seeing red (without invoking imagining
or reliving the experience in one's account of remembering). She has
now begun to discriminate chromatically coloured things for herself.
In the case of Swamp Mary, who has not had the experience but is in
the brain state of someone who has, she falsely believes that she has
seen red and anticipates that if she sees another red thing it will strike
her as familiar, which it will.

This is no doubt rather counter-intuitive, but a behaviourist or functionalist who can swallow the idea that being in pain is no more than being
disposed (or internally caused) to behave in a certain way has nothing
extra to lose intuitively by taking this line in this case.

There are, I believe, two ways of showing the inadequacy of any
behaviouristic or functional treatment of experience. One of them I
shall present in the next section and it concerns the analytic versions
of these theories. The other, to which Chapter 8 is dedicated, argues
that no theory which rejects the KA can accommodate the essential
role of experience in giving us our conception of the manifest world,
which is itself essential to our scientific conception of the world. Until

these arguments are accepted, there still remains the issue of why physicalists who are functionalists should be worried by KA at all. My suspicion is that KA brings to the fore the revelatory role of experience, and we know that this is something we cannot do without. But to see this we need to await the arguments that are to come.

3.5   A general argument against analytic behaviourism and functionalism

There is an intuition that behaviouristic analyses are viciously third-personal – 'viciously' in the sense that they cannot accommodate the first-personal perspective. It is a serious challenge to turn this intuition into an argument. First we must develop the intuition a little further. My sense of how it works is that if we take our own understanding of the world for granted, then we can parse the understanding of others – or of rats or pigeons – in terms of how they act within that world, but that we cannot play the same trick on our own understanding; I cannot think of my own understanding as just some sort of disposition or functional state, except by presupposing an intuitive grasp on the empirical world, when it is precisely that grasp of which I am trying to give an analysis. The challenge is to turn this intuition into a proper, non-question-begging argument. I believe this can be done, and tried my hand at it in Robinson (1993a; 1994).

The argument against analytical behaviourism and analytical function-alism can be put as follows.

The concept of a disposition to behave (or a functional state ultimately related to behaviour) presupposes our normal battery of physical world concepts – e.g. the concepts of body, space, movement and time – for dispositions of the relevant kind are, or, at least involve, the movement of a body through space and in time.

If either analytical behaviourism or analytical functionalism is correct, then *what it is to understand*, or *possess*, for example, the concept 'body' or 'space' etc. will be analysed as the possession of a disposition to behave in some particular way.

If a philosophical analysis is correct, one can, in principle, replace the *analysandum* with the *analysans* without cognitive loss (if not without loss of convenience).

For example, if the justified true belief account of knowledge be correct, then instead of saying 'S knows that P' one could say 'S justifiably believes that p and p is true'.

One cannot similarly replace 'I understand (or possess) the concept "body" (or "space", etc.)' by 'I am disposed to behave in manner M', because this latter analytically presupposes an understanding of the concept 'body' ('space' etc.). It is equivalent to 'my body is disposed to move in manner ... through space'. This would give the analysis of 'I understand (or possess) the concept "body"' as 'I am disposed to move my body in a certain way through space'. Here I am deploying the concept my grasp on which I am trying to explain in the explanation of it. The contrast with the third-person case is clear. In that case I locate the subject I am analysing in the manifest world of my first-personal experience.

I think that there is only one possible response to this argument and it runs as follows. Someone would object that the behavioural or functional analysis is intended as an analysis of *understanding*, or of concept *possession*, not of the concepts understood, so the implicit presence of 'body' (etc.) in the *analysans* of the psychological state, understanding (or possessing) the concept 'body' does not matter.

This objection is misconceived. If analytic behaviourism or functionalism is correct, then there will be a different analysis for each mental state, not just for generic types of mental state. This, in Robinson (1994: 130) I called the *entrapment of content*, because mental content is not – for a physicalist, at least – something to which a generic mental state (such as understanding, thinking, believing) is related; it is a mode of the mental state itself. Thus the disposition associated with possession of the concept 'body' must be different from those associated with possession of 'space', 'horse', 'electron' etc. and the content of the state is given by the content of the disposition. The dispositional analysis, therefore, does not just cover *understanding* 'body', but *understanding 'body'*. And what I understand *by* 'body' – that is, what I think bodies to be – is not separate from what *understanding 'body'* is.

This general argument, I think, spells out the intuition that behaviouristic analyses are viciously third-personal. I could replace all reference to my *knowing* with reference to my having *justified true beliefs*, eliminating the concept 'knowledge' from my conceptual repertoire, but I cannot replace reference to all my thought about *bodies, space,* etc. by reference to my dispositions (to move my *body* through *space*) and eliminate the content of my 'body' thoughts etc., from my repertoire. I can only understand what I think or mean by the notion 'body' by presupposing a concept of the manifest world which is prior to this supposed interpretation of my understanding. My picture of the world is internal to my mental states, and an account of those states that either presupposes or eliminates that picture cannot be a correct account of my mentality.

I want to make two connections for this argument, which, I think, give it support. The first concerns a tension which Armstrong brings out within all behaviouristic or functionalist theories. Such theories emphasise stimulus and response, input and output, in characterising mental states. In most cognitive states it is the behavioural output that is most relevant to individuating the state. I can come to believe that Paris is in France in many different ways. I can read it, be told it, see it on film or in a map, but the informational value of the state is independent of these and – though difficult to pin down – constant. I can forget how I learnt it (as indeed I have) but if I lose the relevant dispositional capacities, I have forgotten the information itself. Philosophers are not disposed to treat perceptual states in this way. Armstrong characterises mental states as:

> The concept of a mental state is primarily the concept of *a state of a person apt for bringing about a certain sort of behaviour* ... In the case of some mental states only they are also *states of the person apt for being brought about by a certain sort of stimulus* ... (1968: 82)

It is perceptual and sensational states that he has in mind in the second clause. It seems to me, however, that if the behavioural/functional theories were adequate, this should not be the case. Suppose that whenever S experiences a square he was disposed to react as if it were a circle, so that, for example, he attempted to fit square wheels on his bicycle, we would think he hallucinated square things as round. Or if he reacted to elephants as if they were mice (supposing, in both cases S seemed otherwise quite sane) we would think that somehow, he saw elephants as looking like mice. Why do physicalists, despite this, feel the need to change from emphasising response to emphasising stimulus in the case of perception?

There seem to me to be two reasons. The first is phenomenological. This is presented as an analysis of perceptual *experience* and the experience is of *what seems to be out there in front of me*, not of *what I feel disposed to do about it*. In the case of ordinary conscious beliefs, the phenomenology is much more elusive – indeed it was usual until recently to deny that there was such a thing. And one does naturally think about such information in terms of what you can do with it, rather than how you get it. But the second point is even more fundamental and connects with the argument I have given in this section. Perception is fundamental to how we form our conception of what the world is like: propositional beliefs about the world depend on this prior perceptual input. So the notion of *what I am disposed to do about objects I confront* cannot replace my sense of contact with the objects themselves, on pain of losing the world.

This latter point is connected to the argument in Chapter 8. I argue there that what the KA shows is that science cannot capture the qualitative nature of experience at all, and that this is not just a corner of our mental life, but is at the core of our manifest image of the world, without which we could have no non-abstract conception of the physical at all. The argument above shows how analytic reductionism loses the world on which its scientific realism is based.

If the argument of this section is correct, it has the consequence, I think, that a conceptual role semantics is self-defeating, for such a theory gives an account of concepts and meanings in terms of the role that certain states or representations play in connection with each other and with our behaviour. In so much as these functional roles are meant to be the content or meaning of our concepts, the theory is a form of analytical functionalism and falls to the argument.

The only resort open to the functionalist if the above argument is correct is to claim that his theory is not meant to be analytic: mental states are in fact functional states, but that is not the source of the meaning or contents of our thoughts.

Analytic functionalism is normally contrasted in the literature with psycho-functionalism, which starts not from our 'folk-psychological' concepts, but from the theories of cognitive science. Most psycho-functionalists are not eliminativists; they accept the validity of the general body of our ordinary psychological concepts, and they believe that what those concepts designate are shown by science to be functional states, but that this fact cannot be revealed either by introspection or conceptual analysis. This raises an obvious problem: how are we to understand our ordinary concepts – what is the mode of presentation to the conscious subject of these hidden functional states, if they are not presented functionally? This raises the question of how a functional state comes to present itself in another mode, so that it does not manifest itself, under analysis, as functional. The phenomenal concept strategy attempts an account of this for phenomenal states of the kind Mary first lacked then acquired, and we will discuss this in Chapter 5, but it is difficult to see how a line similar to that deployed in the phenomenal concept strategy could be taken with cognitive, as opposed to phenomenal, states. The phenomenal concept strategy clears the decks by denying that there is any mode of presentation, in the ordinary sense, for phenomenal states; the concepts that capture them are rather like indexicals. But a similar tactic makes no sense for concepts in general, for, by definition, descriptive content is precisely what they have. So, when considered as a philosophical account, and not just as a fact about cognitive science, psycho-functionalism is something of a mystery.

Nevertheless, there has been a sustained attempt to prove that a form of non-analytic functionalism must be correct and we must next consider that.

3.6   Kirk, zombies, epiphenomenalism and physicalism

In the two previous sections, I have argued that the AH, as found in Lewis and Nemirow, does not work and that neither does a more thorough analytical functionalism. In this section I shall consider Robert Kirk's attempt to prove that some form of functionalism *must* be correct, but that it is not analytical functionalism. If Kirk were correct, KA could not prove what its supporters claim, because he will have shown that functionalism must be true.

Kirk is not an analytic functionalist, because he does not think that functionalism can be proved a priori, even by the deepest sort of conceptual analysis. On the one hand, he shares with the non-reductive physicalist, such as the supporter of the phenomenal concept strategy, the view that the nature of experience cannot be shown to be physical, or ontologically topic neutral, by philosophical analysis. On the other hand, he is what Chalmers calls a 'type A' physicalist, because he believes that functional facts are 'logico-conceptually' sufficient for psychological facts. Normally, type A physicalists believe that the truth of their position can be proved a priori – at least in the sense that functionalism can be so proved, even if the realisation of these functions in matter is contingent – but Kirk eschews this a priori element. In fact, Kirk admits that the relation between the functional essence of our mental states and their experiential 'surface' is something of a mystery (as do the followers of the phenomenal concept strategy), but he believes that he has a demonstration of the truth of functionalism.

The outline of Kirk's argument in his (2005) and (2013) is the following.

(1) If functionalism is not true – that is, if an appropriately sophisticated functional system is not 'logically and conceptually' sufficient for the existence of phenomenal and other consciousness – then zombies (as he understands that term – see below) are possible.

(2) If zombies are possible, then a creature that is physically just like the zombie, but which has, in addition, epiphenomenal qualia, is possible.

(3) Epiphenomenalism, as here required, is not logically possible, however.

Therefore

(4) An appropriately sophisticated functional system must be logically and conceptually sufficient for the possession of phenomenal and other consciousness; that is, functionalism is true.

First it is necessary to clarify both what is, for Kirk, the relevant notion of appropriately sophisticated functionalism, and also what he means by a zombie.

Kirk does not believe that superficial functional isomorphism with a human being is sufficient for consciousness. The inner functional system must broadly mirror the kind of processes that subserve human and animal action and decision processes. He calls this 'decision plus' functionalism. This could perhaps be realised in a silicone-based system, as well as it is in a carbon-based one, but the kind of complexity must be similar. A functional system that delivers the right behaviour, but lacks appropriate inner structure, will not do, Kirk contends.

By 'zombie', Kirk means any system that possesses this kind of sophisticated functional system, but lacks consciousness. This marks the point where Kirk's argument diverges from, and is more comprehensive than, Jackson's revisionary anti-KA stance. Jackson assumes that physical closure must be true in our case, in the actual world. This implies that any non-physical qualia would have to be epiphenomenal in our case, in the actual world. This view he held in his (1982), but he then held that epiphenomenalism was acceptable. He later came to think that epiphenomenalism was incoherent, and so was obliged to think that there could be no non-physical qualia in our case, in the actual world. Kirk does not want his argument to rest on the assumption that there is closure in the actual world, so he does not want to rely on the idea that, if qualia were removed in the actual world, the result would be zombies that behaved just as they did when the qualia were present, for this would beg the question against dualist interactionism. Kirk wants his argument to run from the mere logical possibility of zombies. So his strategy is to argue first, that the falsehood of functionalism would entail the logical possibility of zombies and that this mere logical possibility entails the possibility of epiphenomenalism, which, he then argues, is incoherent.

One might be unconvinced that a functionalist has any right to demand the kind of 'decision plus' inner sophistication that Kirk insists on, but, putting aside such a worry, it seems that one might challenge the argument at any of three points. One could claim that the falsehood of functionalism would not entail the logical possibility of zombies. One might deny that the possibility of zombies entails the possibility of epiphenomenalism, or one might challenge the claim that epiphenomenalism is incoherent.

Some of these points would take one into deep questions that it makes no sense to pursue here, but I will indicate them. One could challenge the claim that the falsehood of functionalism entails the logical possibility of zombies in the following way. The logical possibility of zombies entails that a non-conscious machine might pass the Turing Test, and one might hold that no purely syntactic engine – one lacking a grasp on meaning as such – could do that. I think that this is correct, but trying to defend it would take us into distant and deep waters, so this is not a profitable strategy at the moment.

The challenge to the second – denying that the possibility of zombies entails the possibility of epiphenomenalism – would go as follows. Kirk argues that, if a zombie world is possible, then there is possible a world physically like it, except that, by 'nomological dangler' laws, e[piphenomenal]-qualia are produced. Kirk claims that, even if the actual world is an interactionist world in which the physical is not closed, this makes no difference to the logical possibility of an e-qualia world.

Now someone might be tempted to argue against this by denying the coherence of laws which do not follow from the nature of the things they 'govern'. If they argued in this way, then a physical system could not have the power to produce a non-physical state. Kirk says that the contingency of causal relations is enough to guarantee the possibility of e-qualia 'zombies', but a complete division between natures and causal powers is not obviously correct. Again, I have sympathy with this thought but pursuing it would involve us in an extensive and doubtless inconclusive discussion of causation.

The final and more directly focused point concerns the inconceivability of epiphenomenalism. Kirk's argument there is that, if conscious states make no impact on the body (and, by definition, if epiphenomenal, they do not), then the person could have no 'epistemic contact' with them. What exactly does this latter claim mean and why is such contact impossible? Kirk makes the following claim.

(E5) Human beings are able to do such things as notice, attend to, think about, compare and (on occasion) remember their e-qualia. In short they are in epistemic contact with their e-qualia (2013: 183).

But all these processes involve things that do not happen in consciousness itself – they involve unconscious physical processes that one might loosely label 'brain traces'. But as qualia are epiphenomenal, they cannot be responsible for these physical effects, so they are not traces of the qualia. Kirk concludes that, as the e-qualia do not bring about any traces in the brain, the epiphenomenally conscious creature cannot be in 'epistemic contact' with his experiences, in the way we are.

Kirk reinforces this point by making an analogy with the case of imaginary 'cranial currents', which, he says, are in a parallel case to e-qualia.

Suppose the complex electro-chemical processes inside our brains which constitute perceptual processing induce, without themselves being affected by, isomorphically patterned electric currents in their vicinity. If that were the case, would our cognitive processing be about those patterned electric currents? Would we notice or attend to them? Would we be able to compare them, or stand in any sort of epistemically intimate relation to them? Obviously not, given we know nothing about such currents and they have no effects on our cognitive processing. There is nothing to make it the case that our thoughts would be epistemically relevant to such electrical activity. (2005: 46)

Kirk's point is that such by-products of the system cannot count as *objects* of the system (or as being something the system is somehow *about*), however much they may map features of the system.

This analogy is, however, seriously defective. Suppose that one has a typical physicalist account of the epistemic states; this would be a functionalist account. What the analogy with cranial currents misses is that the functional response in the case of a quale will be appropriate to, for example, seeming to see something red, not appropriate to there being some activity in one's brain. There will be something that makes the quale an intentional object of the response. Kirk says nothing about there being an appropriate response in the case of the cranial currents. If there is no functional response appropriate to the currents, then they are not the objects of any epistemic state or process. What an appropriate response could or would be in this case is not clear – perhaps scratching the head in an appropriate place, but differentiating behaviourally different parts of the brain is not easy. By contrast, the responses appropriate to seeming to see something red are varied, but well known and easily recognised. There is nothing, that is, to make the cranial currents the *intentional object* of the epistemic states, whereas there will be reasons to take the phenomenal content as the intentional object. The object of a functional state (standardly, at least) will be that to which it is the appropriate response.

Being the intentional object does not necessarily involve having a direct or uncomplicated causal relation. Suppose that brain state B^1 causes epiphenomenal quale Q and that, five minutes later, another brain state B^2, of which B^1 was a significant causal antecedent, causes the thought 'I had an experience like this: "Q", five minutes ago'. (The quoted 'Q' means that the thought involves a memory image.) It will seem to the subject just as it seems to us in such memory situations. One could argue that, because the causal relation is not as direct as one might have hoped, it does not count as a memory, but the information in it is correct ('I had an experience like this, "Q", five minutes ago'), and, at worst, it might be classified as a deviant memory of some sort, but, as subjects, we would be none the wiser. A similar line of thought will apply to noticing, attending etc. Brain state B produces Q and also produces or is accompanied by B^3, which is the conscious act of attending to or noticing Q. Q will still be around and will form part of the mental complex produced by B and B^3, which consists of Q and attending to it.

Kirk's analogy with cranial currents is, therefore, ineffective. *Direct* causal influence is not necessary to make something the intentional object of epistemic assimilation. The causal relation can be indirect, as it is in the case of epiphenomenalism; this is not harmful if the response is appropriate. So Kirk fails to prove the incoherence of epiphenomenalism.

4 Why Frank should not have jilted Mary

The inadequacy of representationalism as a strategy against KA

4.1 How Jackson has changed his opinion

As is now well known, Frank Jackson has abandoned the knowledge argument (KA), of which he was the most famous protagonist. In this chapter I want to investigate the reasons and rationale that he gives for this notorious volte-face, and discuss the representationalist challenge to KA that he sets up. The reasons Jackson gives for his apostasy are to be found in two papers, 'Postscript on qualia' (1998) and 'Mind and illusion' (2004). The outline of his overall argument, found mainly in the former, is as follows.[1]

A. Jackson's overall argument:

(1) If the KA is sound and physical closure (PC) is correct, then there are qualia which are epiphenomenal.
(2) Epiphenomenalism about qualia is incoherent.

Therefore

(3) Either KA is not sound or PC is not correct. (1, 2, MT)
(4) The success of science obliges us to believe that PC is correct.

Therefore

(5) KA is not sound. (3, 4 DS)

The argument is valid. The premises are (1), (2) and (4). (1) is plainly true if over determination is excluded and I do not want any resistance to Jackson to rest on over determination; so I shall take (1) to be true. (4) is something to which Jackson is committed by the form of his belief in science. He does not argue for it, but merely asserts it:

> We know that our knowledge of what it is like to see red and feel pain has purely physical causes. We know, for example, that Mary's transition from not knowing what it is like to see red to knowing what it is like to see red will have a causal explanation in purely physical terms. (Dualist interactionism is false.) (418)

I do not share Jackson's faith in science as the true metaphysics, but this is not the point at which I wish to challenge his argument. If my challenge is

---

[1] References to these Jackson articles are to page numbers in Ludlow *et al.*

successful, however, it will follow that his kind of scientific naturalism must be false.

The issue, on which Jackson has changed his opinion, is (2). In 'Epiphenomenal qualia', he had claimed that epiphenomenalism was respectable. His argument for abandoning epiphenominalism is as follows.

B. Argument for $A(2)$:

(1) Reference to any x involves causal influence from x to the referential act.
(2) If x is epiphenomenal then it has no causal influence on anything, *a fortiori*, not on any referential act.

Therefore

(3) If x is epiphenomenal then it is something to which we cannot refer (1, 2, Trans., HS); therefore
(4) If qualia are epiphenomenal then they cannot be objects of reference. (3, UI)
(5) Qualia (if they exist) are what are referred to by using our phenomenal concepts.

Therefore

(6) If qualia exist and are epiphenomenal then they can and cannot be objects of reference. (4, 5, Conj.)
(7) Epiphenomenalism about qualia is incoherent. (6, RAA)

I had in Robinson (2008) said that I thought this argument was sound, but the above considerations raised against Kirk in Section 3.6 can be made to apply to Jackson's reasoning. One needs to distinguish between the two following claims.

(i) If S's qualia are epiphenomenal, then no sentence uttered by S can refer to his qualia.
(ii) If S's qualia are epiphenomenal then S cannot think about them.

This distinction shows that there are two kinds of referential act, one a verbal utterance and one a thought. The application of phenomenal concepts is an act of thought rather than a verbal report, so the argument would have to go through under interpretation (ii) and it would have to show that phenomenal concepts do not capture qualia in thought in the way required to make the situation coherent.

The arguments against Kirk show that (ii) is not true in any interesting sense, because it can be for S just as it seems to be for a non-epiphenomenal thinker. Whether one wants to say that S would *really* be thinking about his qualia does not matter. It would seem to him as if he were and that is all that is required to show that epiphenomenalism is not an incoherent position. It is a perfectly general and explicit feature of epiphenomenalism that the subject seems to himself to be active in ways that he actually is not. How does this leave (i)? This can be expressed as follows.

(iii) If S's qualia are epiphenomenal, then it can be to S as if he were thinking about them and S utters a sentence that seems to report that he is thinking about (or aware of) them.

Once again this looks like a coherent account of what would actually be going on if epiphenomenalism obtained. There is nothing to show that this is an impossible state of affairs.

But even if Jackson's argument against epiphenomenalism were sound, it would not necessarily matter. Kirk's argument was a threat because he claimed not only that epiphenomenalism is incoherent, but also that anyone who denies functionalism is committed to the coherence of epiphenomenalism, and we have seen that this rests on a contentious understanding of what it is for causal relations to be contingent.

Putting aside the menace of epiphenomenalism, we face a straight choice between accepting PC and accepting the KA. The rejection of epiphenomenalism is not itself a direct attack on the KA, for that argument does not make any appeal to epiphenomenalism. It is only that if you accept KA and PC then you are committed to epiphenomenalism. The title of Jackson's original paper 'Epiphenomenal Qualia' (1982) was, in a sense, presumptuous, for he had not presented any argument to show that qualia are epiphenomenal, only that they exist and are not physical. It was a presumption that they must therefore be epiphenomenal. Jackson's rejection of the argument is not direct but, as one might put it, transcendental: it is a presupposition of the closure of physics that *something* must be wrong with the argument. This does not of itself tell us what is wrong with it. If it cannot be faulted, Jackson will be in an impasse.

If one looks at the argument as it is presented in Sections 1.5 and 1.7, it is plain that there is nothing about epiphenomenalism, interactionism or PC employed directly in the argument itself. If the contrast between Mary and others, or between Mary before and after, is a genuine one, then property dualism is established and one must adjust one's views accordingly. If epiphenomenalism is not an available option, interactionism must replace the dogma of PC.

It is interesting to see at what point Jackson now rejects the argument. He denies premise (2) – the claim that Mary did not initially have the resources to work out what it would be like to see chromatic colours, and he attempts to explain both how she can and why it intuitively seems she could not, by invoking the representational nature of experience. Trying to follow Jackson's explanations here is no easy task! In order – I hope – to make things clearer, I shall begin with a general discussion of how representationalism and physicalism might relate and then return to Jackson to see how his strategy fits in with these general points.

4.2   Pure representationalism and experience

It might not at first sight be wholly clear why anyone should think that representationalism in perception would avoid the KA. The recent use of the term 'representationalism' in the philosophy of perception is likely to cause confusion for the more traditionally minded. The traditional 'representative theory of perception' is closely allied to the sense-datum theory and rests upon the idea that there is, in perception, some introspectable vehicle which represents, but is not a part of, the external world. This invocation of an introspectable *vehicle* is absolutely the opposite of what modern representationalism asserts. Now the claim is that experience itself is, as it is put, *wholly transparent*. This, too, is not without ambiguity. Hume, in his failure to find either *act* or *subject* of perception, only ever discovering its *object*, treated experience as transparent, because nothing was introspectable except what it was *of*. But, for Hume, this object of experience was not a feature of the mind-independent, external world, but an impression or sense-datum. *Transparency*, now, signifies the idea that there is nothing introspectable in experience other than the external, physicalistically respectable, objects that it is supposed to be of. This is often expressed by saying that experience is purely intentional. ('Intentional' and 'representational' are in fact used more or less as synonyms.)

The simplest way in which representationalism might be supposed to help the physicalist cope with Mary would be, I think, as follows.

C. Simple representationalism:

(1) When Mary leaves the room, she acquires a state the nature of which, *qua* experience, is wholly accounted for in terms of the properties it is *of*.
(2) The properties it is *of* are physical properties.

Therefore

(3) When Mary leaves the room, she acquires a state the nature of which is wholly accounted for in terms of physical properties. (1, 2, =)
(4) Mary already has complete relevant knowledge about the nature of physical properties.

Therefore

(5) When Mary leaves the room she acquires a state the nature of which is wholly accounted for in terms of properties the nature of which she already completely knows. (3, 4, =)

Therefore

(6) Mary does not learn about any new properties when she leaves the room. (5 and meaning of 'new'.)

Therefore

(7) Her original total physical knowledge was not incomplete with respect to knowing the nature of experience. (6, principle that if nothing new needed, old is complete.)

We must look at the possible grounds for rejecting *C*. The premises are (1), (2) and (4). (4) is *ex hypothesis*, so the argument focuses on (1) and (2). There are two paths for disputing (1). They are by claiming either or both of:

(a) representationalism about experience is not adequate as a complete account;
(b) representationalism is not, on its own, physicalistically respectable.

And one can dispute (2) by arguing:

(c) the *objects* of perception, in the case of secondary qualities, are not physicalistically respectable.

The best way of considering these issues is to look closely at the nature of representationalism, and how it relates to physicalism. This will be our concern for the rest of this chapter.

4.3 What is representationalism?

The notion of representation is part of the common currency of the contemporary debate on perception. Nevertheless, I find myself less than clear about what is involved in a state's being representational. I shall attempt to distinguish various propositions that might, on their own or in various combinations with each other, be thought of as representing the core idea of representationalism.

The weakest statement might be

(1a) All experiences with phenomenal content *can be taken as* representing the world as being some way or another; that is, they can be taken as having an intentional object.

A slightly stronger version would be

(1b) All experiences with phenomenal content *are naturally taken as* representing the world as being in some way or another; that is, *are naturally taken as* having an intentional object.

Both (1a) and (1b) talk of phenomenal content being *taken as* representing the world, and this might suggest that the representational contribution is not intrinsic to the phenomenal content, but comes, for example, by interpretation. This might be thought to undermine the essential point of representationalism, because it suggests that there is something not essentially representational in itself, which is being interpreted as a representation. To avoid this limitation, one might suggest:

(1c) All experiences with phenomenal content *naturally represent* the world as being some way or other; that is, naturally present a certain object intentionally.

A sense-datum theorist might (though, for reasons I am about to present, need not) accept either (1a) or (1b). (1c) is, perhaps, therefore, the only version of (1) that a genuine representationalist could accept. (1c), however, does not present what one might call a *complete* representationalism, for although it says that all experiences with phenomenal content are representational, it does not say that every phenomenal aspect of the experience must be representational. This latter is necessary if representationalism is to present itself as a complete account of phenomenal content. It can be stated in ways that combine with any version of (1), though, for the reasons I have given, only that which is modelled on (1c) is probably of interest. That version runs as follows:

(2) There is no phenomenal aspect of experience which does not naturally represent the world as being some way or other.

This does not give us the full force of representationalism, however. Representationalists emphasise the *transparency* of experience. This means that the nature of experience comes entirely from the nature of its intentional object, not from the nature of the experiencing itself. This idea, however, is not entirely unambiguous, for it might be read as neutral on what contributes to the nature of the object, *qua* object of experience. For example, one could hold that the nature of the experience of seeing red is entirely a function of the nature of the redness of the thing perceived, but agree that secondary qualities such as red are what they are because of the way that objects interact with our sense organs. In so far as the objective of the representationalist is to account for the nature of experience by reference to the nature of what it is *of*, such a compromised position is not adequate. What is needed is:

(3) There is nothing in the 'act' of having an experience with phenomenal content, except what is contributed by the nature of the object, which nature is wholly independent of what it is like to experience it.

This is required to make it clear that the character of experience is entirely conceptually derivative from something external to and independent of experience itself.

(3), however, would have been acceptable to Hume, because he believed that the 'impressions' which were the objects of experience could, in principle, exist outside mind. This strange doctrine is, of course, a consequence of his 'bundle' theory of the mind, rather than of his account of consciousness. And it is not clear whether an impression of red that were to float out of its mental bundle would not then still constitute an experience, rather than an 'unsensed sensibilium'. These matters are all clarified from the representationalist and intentionalist perspective, without entering into discussion of these Humean niceties, by insisting that, because experience is essentially *of* its object, it is not itself characterised by instances of the properties attributed to the object. Hume's impressions and all traditional 'sense-data', constitute the subjective contents of the experience, and are themselves instances of the basic sensible qualities the experiences are of. To avoid this, the representationalist must insist upon the intentional inexistence of the object, as represented by:

(4) None of the subjective phenomenal contents of experience is an instance of any of the properties the experience represents: for any F, such that the experience represents the world as being F, there is no instance of F constituting the content of the experience, other than that represented as being in the external world. The experience itself, and its subjective constitution, can only be characterised as being *of* F.

The purpose of representationalism, in this context at least, is to deny that individual experiences possess any features that they do not borrow from the world of which they are experiences. This has some initial plausibility for veridical perception, of which the content may seem to be things in the external world and their properties. But hallucinations and even what are traditionally called 'illusions' – things not looking exactly as they really are – may seem to cause a problem. Their contents would not seem to be straightforwardly identifiable with features of the external world, and so would seem to constitute a challenge to the attempt to deny experience any ontological baggage that cannot be identified with physical reality. It is to overcome this problem that representationalists affirm:

(5) In so far as the intentional object of an experience cannot be identified with an actual physical thing or state of affairs, it has no positive ontological status.

A representationalist with Jackson's physicalist ambitions must affirm:

(6) What it is to represent the world, including experientially, can be given a purely naturalist account.

Whether (6) adds anything to the other propositions, or whether they constitute such an account, might be an issue. We shall see that they do not, on their own, constitute a naturalistic account, but require to be set in the context of such a theory as Dretske's (1981) informationalism, or a purely functionalist account of consciousness and mind. This of itself might seem to leave problematic what representationalism itself contributes to the argument.[2]

If we take (1c) as defining the starting point for any intentionalist or representationalist theory of perception, it can be filled out or strengthened in the following ways. First, I think that (4) is essential if the contrast with a sense-datum theory is to be made firm. (1c) and (4) together constitute an intentionalist theory of perceptual content, whilst leaving open the option that some phenomenal content might not be representational (and so not perceptual) but, as one might say, purely sensational. Provided that nothing that the naïve realist would wish to impute to the external, physical world is included in the category of sensations, but within the representational, these two propositions together are enough to satisfy someone who is an intentionalist in perception, but is not interested in deploying representationalism as part of a physicalist strategy. If the latter is the programme, then (2) is necessary to bring all phenomenal content within its purview and (3) is necessary to ensure that no phenomenal residue is contributed by the mind (as I explained above on introducing (3)). (5) is necessary to sweep up the contents of non-veridical experiences.

Because I am here concerned with the use made of representationalism by physicalists, I am not going to concentrate on (1c) and (4), except for the following important point. (1c) could be interpreted either as

(1c′) All experiences with phenomenal content, *taken individually*, naturally represent the world as being some way or other.

or

(1c″) All experiences with phenomenal content, *taken as part of the general flow of experience*, naturally represent the world as being some way or other.

The point of this distinction is as follows. If the property of being representational is an intrinsic feature of phenomenal content as such, then it ought to apply to each occurrence of such content in its own right. That is, (1c′) ought to be true. But it seems to me that (1c″) is the only one that is plausible, and even that it is plausible only given that the flow of experience has a certain structure. My reason for saying this can be brought out by considering the following case. Imagine someone born blind, who, because of internal activity in his brain, occasionally has experiences of a

---

[2] That representationalism leaves Mary's problem untouched is one of the conclusions of Alter (2007).

kind that we would recognise as being of flashes of colour, and even coloured shapes. These do not form any structure in their own right, nor do they correlate with any tactile or other sensory experiences. I can see no reason why the subject of these odd experiences should have inclination to take them as representing any reality, either external, nor (as some philosophers want to say about bodily sensations) as apparently representing something going on in the body – presumably, in this case, the head. Representationalism as a whole ignores Hume's insight, which is that the claim of experiences to be about the world depends essentially on the ordering and patterning of those experiences.[3] If they were wholly chaotic and fragmentary, there is no reason to believe that their qualitative nature would, of itself, point to anything beyond them.

Putting aside this general difficulty, from which representationalism suffers even when freed from the physicalist burden, I shall now consider problems facing (2), (3) and (5).

4.4 The plausibility of (2)

The question of whether representationalism can be extended to all phenomenal content comes down, in the end, to the issue of whether sensations can all be treated representationally. Thanks to Ned Block, I think, this issue has focused on the question of whether the phenomenal content of orgasm can be wholly understood in perceptual and representational terms. He thinks that it cannot, for he thinks that it is clear that the experience contains something phenomenal that is not purely cognitive. Michael Tye (1995) disagrees. He says:

In this case, one undergoes sensory representations of certain physical changes in the genital region. These changes quickly undulate in their intensity. Furthermore, they are highly pleasing. They illicit an immediate and strong positive reaction. (118)

Then he adds, presumably in case this seems too intellectualised an account:

It is important to stress . . . that the representations of bodily changes involved in orgasms are nonconceptual.

The issue is not whether Tye is right that one locates the sensations and associates them with certain bodily events. The issue is whether characterising the sensations as being of those events, whilst those events are to be understood in a physicalist manner (that is, no irreducible secondary

---

[3] *Treatise*, Bk I Pt 4 sect ii, 'Of scepticism with regard to the senses'.

qualities present), entirely exhausts the experiential content of the sensation. The addition that they are 'highly pleasing' only obfuscates the matter. Is this pleasingness itself a quality of the sensation, in which case an extra phenomenal residue has been imported? Or is it unpacked in the notion of a 'strong positive reaction', that is, is finding something pleasing only a matter of behavioural response? If it is the latter, then the experience of orgasm is being reduced to non-conceptual cognition of bodily changes, plus behavioural reaction of, for example, an 'I want more' type. One must not be deceived into thinking that calling a representation 'nonconceptual' somehow qualifies it as experiential. We shall see this more clearly when discussing Dretske's use of 'analogue representation' – a close cousin of the non-conceptual – below. But, in the jargon of the informational theorist, mindless nature is full of 'representations', and they are all non-conceptual and non-experiential.

What seems plain is that Tye's attempt to extend representationalism to brute sensations commits him to a radically reductive account of the experience itself. It is information inflow, plus behavioural reaction. Representationalism, unless treated in this way, does not complete the job. It seems that (6) is required if representationalism is to do the work the physicalist asks of it.

4.5   Physicalism and (3) and (4)

The difference between (3) alone and (3) and (4) together is the difference between the form of direct or naïve realism now known as *relationism*, and the more standard form of the representational or intentional theory. Proponents of the former deny that representationalists are really direct realist, whereas representationalists, I think, claim that they are. For present purposes, it is enough to see how both (3) alone and (3) and (4) together relate to physicalism.

Just how reductive (3) must be, if interpreted physicalistically, can be seen by considering how it relates to secondary qualities. The most natural form of direct realism for secondary qualities is what is often dubbed *naïve realism*, which treats the phenomenal version of those qualities as objective features of external objects. This runs into difficulty with physicalism in two ways. First, there is the fact that science has never found a place in the external world for the secondary qualities, as naïvely conceived. This point is too obvious to need labouring. Second, and irrespective of the problem of secondary qualities, is the fact that it is a mistake to think that physicalism can accommodate the kind of *sui generis* awareness relation that non-reductive naïve realism involves. The idea that naïve realism is respectable from a physicalist viewpoint seems to rest on the mistake of thinking that physicalism is safe provided only that there are no subjective contents of awareness. This is plainly mistaken, however, because to postulate an irreducible awareness relation between perceiver and external world is to postulate something that is as inconsistent with the physicalist world picture as are subjective contents. The 'torch beam' view of consciousness is anti-physicalist, whether it falls on something external and physical or internal and mental. The 'transparency' of experience is not sufficient on its own to allow it to be an open empirical matter whether it simply be a state of the brain or not.

These two problems together mean that (3) alone – naïve realism – is helpful to the physicalist only if he can provide both a reductive account of secondary qualities and a reductive account of the perceptual relation (that is, condition (6)) in addition to the bare direct realism.

But (4) is also needed to accommodate those many experiences when the world does not look exactly as it is, even by naïve realist standards. This includes not only hallucinations, but all cases of what are standardly classed as 'illusions', in the sense required by the 'argument from illusion'. In these cases, the phenomenal content of the experience must be an intentional object, in the sense of not being an instance of the property that is apparently present, otherwise one will be related to properties that are not physically realised in the environment or in one's head. How hallucinations are handled by physicalists, we shall see in the next section.

4.6   The physicalist need for (5)

In order to see how representationalism relates physicalism to perceptual experience, we can ask how representationalism is supposed to capture the particular 'feel' of such experience without invoking anything that the physicalist cannot accept. How he might think it does this can be shown by the following two questions and answers.

Qu.1. What gives experience its 'feel' – its 'what it is like'?
Ans. to 1. Its intentional object – what it seems to be of.
Qu.2. What specific ontology is involved with intentional objects?
Ans. to 2. None because *either*

(i)   the intentional object = a physical object, or facet of the same. This covers the case of genuine (veridical?) perception;

or

(ii) the intentional object is a kind of non-entity, and so cannot be an ontological liability. This covers hallucination (and 'illusion'?).

(i) and (ii) together constitute (5).

We have seen in discussing (3) some of the serious problems that face the physicalist, even for straightforward cases of perception, but I am concerned now with the case where the intentional object is not veridical and so cannot be simply identified with something external. As my way of stating (i) and (ii) shows, there is an ambiguity in the intentionalist position concerning whether the contrast is between *perception* and *hallucination* or between *veridical perception* and *non-veridical perceptual experiences*, where the latter category includes what was traditionally classified as 'illusion', as well as hallucination. The arguments we are going to consider are all stated as concerning hallucination, but one should also bear in mind that there is, or may be, a parallel problem for the intentional objects of misperceptions; what, for example, is the ontological status of the blue involved in a white wall's looking blue, as well as the ontological status of the blue wall if one simply hallucinated such a wall.

There are two strategies falling under (ii) for dealing with either or both of these cases. The first consists in claiming that intentional objects are abstract entities and that, as such, do not exist in the spatio-temporal world of objects, whether mental or physical. The second attempts to analyse the contents of hallucinations and non-veridical perceptions solely in terms of their indiscriminability from veridical perceptions, thereby avoiding invocation of their contents at all. I discuss the former here. The second, which is M. G. F. Martin's theory, I discussed in detail in Robinson (2008) and (2013).

Dismissing the ontology of hallucination etc. on the grounds that it is abstract seems to be the line many representationalists take. The idea seems to be that, in so far as an experience is veridical, its intentional object is a thing, or facet of a thing, in the external world; and in so far as its intentional object is non-veridical, though phenomenologically quite real, any question of its ontological status can quite simply be dismissed.

Dretske (2000), for example, explains the status of the contents of hallucination or misperceptions in the following way. He says that 'the properties we are aware of in achieving this awareness (being universals) exist nowhere' (160). He follows this up by saying:

Awareness of colors, shapes, and movements, when there is no external object that has the property one is aware of, is not, therefore, a violation of [the principle that experience involves no internal phenomenal properties]. A measuring instrument (a speedometer, for example) can (when malfunctioning) be 'aware of' (i.e., represent) a speed of 45 mph without any object's (inside or outside the instrument) having this magnitude.

The idea that a malfunctioning speedometer and an hallucinating person both 'hallucinate', in a similar enough sense for the analogy to be of any use in providing a physicalist model for hallucination, is bizarre enough. But it also seems to carry the implication that crude analogue representing devices do actually experience what they represent – they just have rather limited experiences. This seems to me to be a *reductio* of this approach.

Lycan's (1987) view is similar:

I take the view . . . that phenomenal individuals such as sense-data are intentional inexistents *a la* Brentano and Meinong. It is, after all, no surprise to be told that mental states have intentional objects that do not exist. So why should we not suppose that after-images and other sense-data are intentional objects that do not exist? If they do not exist then – *voila* – they do not exist; there are in reality no such things. And that is why we can consistently admit that phenomenal-color properties qualify individuals without granting that there exist individuals that are the bearers of phenomenal-color properties. (1987: 88)

The cavalier attitude to intentional objects does indeed seem to be Jackson's approach, as is shown by what Jackson says.

Intentionalism means that no amount of tub-thumping assertion by dualists (including by myself in the past) that the *redness* of seeing red cannot be accommodated in the austere physicalist picture carries any weight. That striking feature is a feature of how things are represented to be, and if, as claimed by the tub thumpers, it is transparently a feature that has no place in the physicalist picture, what follows is that physicalists should deny that anything has that striking feature. And this is no argument against physicalism. Physicalists can allow that people are sometimes in states that represent that things have a non-physical property. Examples are people who believe that there are fairies. What physicalists must deny is that such properties are instantiated. (2004: 431)

There are at least three problems with this cavalier approach to intentional objects. First, to say that they are abstract and so not part of the ontology of the empirical world leaves untouched the question of how, for a physicalist, an abstract, immaterial entity is supposed to constitute the content of a physical state; what is it for the brain to be aware of an abstract object? Second, the emphasis on the possible non-existence of intentional objects does not seem to be a fair account of the actual nature of a mental state – absence is not what gives a state the phenomenological nature it has. (This sounds rather too reminiscent of Sartre's characterisation of intentionality as 'nothingness'.) Third, the difference between intellectual states and sensory ones is not given enough attention. The idea that phenomenal redness might simply not exist, in the way that fairies do not exist, hardly seems adequate. You can stop believing in fairies, but you cannot stop things looking red. It is a bedrock fact that that is how things appear. Even the psychological event of someone's exercising their belief in fairies does not consist wholly in an absence. Something actual and real – say, saying some words to oneself – constitutes the phenomenology of it. The phenomenology of seeming to see something red must be constituted by something empirical and actual.

4.7   Standard physicalist accounts of representation

Suspicions might be raised by the fact that I have not explicitly discussed the standard kind of physicalist account of representation. According to that account, some internal state represents an external one if it causally co-varies with it in some appropriate way. This theory is not easy to state exactly and has many variants, but these are not the reason why I have not discussed it and do not presume to do so in any detail. The reason is that these theories are primarily theories of propositional attitudes and pay no serious attention to consciousness itself. Fodor, for example, who admits to being a 'qualia freak', has no idea how consciousness fits into the mind and thinks that the sort of computational account to which his theory belongs makes no call on consciousness to explain how his representationalism works. Other representationalists who are not qualia freaks have either to deal with consciousness as Dretske and Lycan do above, or in some other way say that a pure functionalist account is adequate for phenomenal consciousness. All of the first part of this book can be seen as giving reasons why this is not so.

4.8   Jackson's use of representationalism

I have argued that neither representationalism, nor the more naïve form of direct realism, is of any help to the physicalist. How do my general arguments relate to Jackson's own theory? In fact, his position is the fully representational, and not naïve realist, one that I follow above.

First he accepts the diaphanous nature of experience – its so-called transparency. But he denies that this is to be understood on the act-object or relational model, because this picture cannot accommodate illusion and hallucinations without falling into the sense-datum theory, which is inconsistent with physicalism. (There are no suitable red, square patches in the brain.) He notes that this puts him on the side of 'common factor' theorists, not disjunctivists. Denying the relational theory and adopting a common-factor representationalism means that the contents of experience are intentional objects. Because intentional objects are intentional, they are not actually instances of the properties they appear to present, so one need not worry about the location or ontological status of these apparent property-instances, for they have none. This leaves one with the problem of what it is that gives the experience the peculiar feel that it has and which leads us to think that Mary learns something new, for this cannot be accounted for simply by appeal to something that does not exist – the experience is real. It is here that the account becomes most hard to follow.

Jackson says (I have added the Roman numbering):

I now think that the puzzle posed by the knowledge argument is to explain why we have such a strong intuition that Mary learns something about how things are that outruns what can [be] deduced from the physical account of how things are. I suggest that the answer is the strikingly atypical nature of the way she acquires certain relational and functional information ... (i) The most plausible view for physicalists is that sensory experience is putative information about certain highly relational and functional properties of goings on *inside us* [italics added]. (ii) As it is often put nowadays, its very nature is representational: ... (iii) sensory information is a quite unusually 'quick and easy' way of acquiring highly relational and functional information ... Sensory experience in this regard is like the way we acquire information about intrinsic properties ... But, very obviously, it is not information about intrinsic *physical* nature, so the information Mary acquires presents itself as if it were information about more than the physical. (2004: 419)

The key points in Jackson's explanation of the 'illusion' of knowledge acquisition are that: (i) experience represents states which are (a) highly complexly relational and functional and (b) internal; (ii) such experience is purely representational; (iii) experience does this in a 'holistic' or 'Gestallt-like' way, so that the complex seems like a simple or intrinsic property; (iv) because there is obviously no such physical property, it seems to be a non-physical one.

Putting aside for the moment the virtues of a representational theory of perception from a physicalist point of view, there are at least two problems here. The first concerns the fate of the supposed transparency of experience, if the phenomenology is to be explained by appeal to the simplified way in which the *representing*, rather than the property *represented* is presented in introspection. What we introspect is an internal, complex functional state – that is not a transparent grasp on the apparent object. The second, and more directly devastating, is why such a simplified informational form should present itself as an *experience* at all. (See Alter (2007) for this point clearly made.) Jackson replies to Alter by emphasising that his theory is *strongly representationalist*, where that means that every feature of the experience is representational. It is completely opaque to this reader – and to Alter – how this fact is supposed to make any difference.

4.9   Conclusion of the argument

Representationalism in general, and in Jackson's form, does not help physicalism unless: (i) it can cover all phenomenal properties, not just those that are naturally regarded as perceptual, and this is not plausible; (ii) it is associated with a reductive account of secondary qualities, and such accounts are not convincing; (iii) it can provide an account of phenomenal contents in hallucinations and other cases of non-veridical experiences; so far, no account provided is plausible.

5 The phenomenal concept strategy
More enigma than argument

5.1 Trying to understand the phenomenal concept strategy

The normal approach to adopt when discussing and criticising a position is to begin by giving as lucid an account as possible of the theory under discussion, so that the target is clear. For reasons that, I hope, will become plain in the course of this chapter, I find this extremely hard to do in the case of the PCS, for despite the fact that many subtle philosophers have defended this line of argument, I still find it difficult to pin down exactly how it is meant to work. I shall, therefore, start with two long quotations, one from its originator and another from one of its most resolute defenders.

In an article often thought to be the origin of the strategy, Brian Loar argues as follows.

We have to distinguish *concepts* and *properties*, and this paper turns on that distinction. Anti-physicalist arguments and intuitions take off from a sound intuition about concepts. Phenomenal concepts are conceptually irreducible in this sense: they neither a priori imply, nor are implied by, physical-functional concepts. Although that is denied by analytical functionalists [Levin 1983, 1986], many other physicalists, including me, find it intuitively appealing. The anti-physicalist takes this conceptual intuition a good deal further, to the conclusion that phenomenal qualities are themselves irreducible, are not physical-functional properties, at least not of the ordinary sort. The upshot is a range of anti-reductionist views: that consciousness and phenomenal qualities are unreal because irreducible; that they are irreducibly non-physical-functional facts; that they are forever mysterious, or pose an intellectual problem different from other empirical problems, or require new conceptions of the physical.

It is my view that we can have it both ways. We may take the phenomenological intuition at face value, accepting introspective concepts and their conceptual irreducibility, and at the same time take phenomenal qualities to be identical with physical-functional properties of the sort envisaged by contemporary brain science. As I see it, there is no persuasive philosophically articulated argument to the contrary.

This is not to deny the power of raw metaphysical intuition. Thoughtful people compare phenomenal qualities and kinds of physical-functional property, say the activation of neural assemblies. It appears to them to be an evident and unmediated truth, independent of further premises, that phenomenal qualities cannot be identical with properties of those types or perhaps of any physical-functional type. This intuition is so compelling that it is tempting to regard anti-physicalist arguments as rationalizations of an intuition whose independent force masks their tendentiousness. It is the point of this paper to consider the arguments. But we will also present a positive account of the relation between phenomenal concepts and physical properties that may provide some relief, or at least some distance, from the illusory metaphysical intuition. (1997: 597–8)

There seem to be three salient claims here. First, is the claim that anti-physicalist arguments, such as the knowledge argument, involve confusing conceptual irreducibility and property irreducibility. Second is the assertion that this is what prevents us from seeing how phenomenal qualities could be identical to neural, functional states. Third is the admission that, somehow, this mistake has tremendous intuitive pull – it does not disappear simply on being pointed out, as do most simple confusions. One thing that will continually recur in our discussion is the problem of how a mode of conceptualising can be responsible for the emergence of apparently distinctive (from physical-functional properties) phenomenal *qualities*. The core of my argument will be that this is never explained.

The first move in trying to reconcile these three claims is to re-locate the problem away from phenomenology and into the relation of explanatory schemes. Loar continues:

In recent years the central problem with physicalism has been thought by many to be 'the explanatory gap'. This is the idea that we cannot *explain*, in terms of physical-functional properties, what makes a certain experience 'feel like this', in the way we can explain what makes a certain substance a liquid, say. It is concluded that physicalism is defective in some respect, that there cannot be a (proper) reduction of the mental to the physical. Before we consider this explanatory gap, we must first examine, in some detail, a more basic anti-physicalist line of reasoning that goes back to Leibniz and beyond, a leading version of which is called nowadays the knowledge argument. Answering this argument will generate a framework in which to address anti-physicalist concerns in general. (598)

Katalin Balog throws more light on the strategy by making more explicit the nature of its target.

A number of anti-physicalist arguments have been proposed during the last two decades that start from a premise about an *epistemic, conceptual or explanatory* gap between physical and phenomenal descriptions and conclude – on *a priori* grounds – that physicalism is false . . . Phenomenal descriptions feature phenomenal concepts that refer to token phenomenal experiences or phenomenal properties, i.e., *qualia*. Phenomenal experience is characterized by the fact that there is something *it is like* to undergo it, something one can normally introspect, e.g., there is something it is like to feel my body against the chair I am sitting in. Anti-physicalists conclude that phenomenal facts – e.g., the fact that I feel the pressure of the chair against my body right now – are absent in a purely physical world.

Physicalists have come up with various different strategies to counter these arguments. The most promising physicalist line of defense, in my view, is based on the idea that these epistemic and conceptual gaps can be explained by appeal to the nature of phenomenal *concepts* rather than the nature of non-physical phenomenal properties. Phenomenal concepts, on this proposal, involve unique cognitive mechanisms, but none that could not be fully physically implemented. If this project is successful, it amounts to a powerful reply to the anti-physicalist arguments. I will call this project – following Stoljar (2005) – the Phenomenal Concept Strategy (PCS). (2012b: 1)

I think that Balog's understanding of the problem throws much light on PCS. She follows up Loar's citing of the explanatory gap as the crucial problem to be overcome by the physicalist, by broadening this by saying that there is 'an *epistemic, conceptual or explanatory* gap'. The assumption is both that these terms capture essentially the same problems and that what they capture is the 'hard problem' of consciousness. But all these expressions seem to concern how we can know or think something, rather than how can there *be* something – a phenomenal quality – that is, to all appearances, different from the physical properties of the brain.

In the following chapter I shall be arguing that PCS fails because it fails to address the central problem, and it makes this equivocation because the issues of the 'hard problem', the knowledge argument, the 'explanatory gap' and the 'possibility of zombies' are treated as if they were exactly the same issue (as opposed to a set of closely interrelated issues) all concerned with the difficulty of making a certain conceptual transition.

In order to justify this last claim, I must try to unravel what is going on in the PCS, and that is what I shall try to do in the following sections of this chapter.

5.2   Phenomenal concepts, dualism and physicalism

Almost everyone believes in phenomenal concepts – most especially dualists. Phenomenal concepts are those concepts that can only be fully understood by a process of ostension, because they designate features of the world as they are revealed only in experience. Paradigmatically, these concepts include secondary quality concepts, concepts designating sensations, such as pain, moods, feelings, and the like. It used to be the case that dualists were the only people who believed in these concepts, because accepting them seemed to commit one to accepting special referents of a 'logically private' or 'privileged access' kind, that fall outside the range of the public, physical world. The qualities which can only be ostensively defined, it was thought, belong to an inner, Cartesian world.

But then a strange thing happened. Physicalists discovered phenomenal concepts, and, in the context of 'the phenomenal concept strategy', began to talk as if they had discovered some previously ignored conceptual phenomenon, recognition of which enabled one to understand why physicalists appeared to have problems accommodating the apparent privacy of experience. The strategy, as most generally expounded, consists in some way of claiming that phenomenal concepts contain the experience within themselves; generally this is conceived on the model of indexicals or of quotation. The result is meant to be that the 'explanatory gap' and all that goes with it, cease to be challenges to physicalism once one realises that these things are merely the by-products of the difference between physical and phenomenal concepts, and not a difference between public and private properties or qualities.

This is very strange in at least two ways. First, it is strange because, as traditionally understood, phenomenal concepts have their content because of the experiential qualities that they designate, and it is precisely these qualities – what Mary did not initially know about and what she learned about when leaving her room – that seem to fall outside the physicalists' remit. One challenge, therefore, facing PCS as a physicalist strategy is to explain how these concepts work and why they are needed if they do not designate special 'private' qualities. Second, it is strange because the quotational-indexical model mimics dualism in a further way. Katilin Balog (2012a) describes this theory as 'speculative', by which, I think, she means to include 'innovative', but the quotational-indexical model is simply a version of Russell's semantic of logically proper names, according to which that with which one is acquainted (restricted, for him, to sense-data and the self) itself figures as part of the content of the thought which is the recognition of its presence. So in a proposition such as 'that is red', indicating a sense-datum, the datum itself figures as part of the proposition. So PCS is not presenting a new kind of concept or strategy; it is boldly claiming that semantic features originally regarded as specifically designed to cope with the peculiar features of dualistic inner life can be transferred wholesale to a physicalist account. But, as I shall argue below, this semantic transfer is not the only or main challenge facing PCS, for it is also necessary to explain how PCS solves 'the hard problem' of the nature of qualia or sensations. Or if it does not solve this problem, at least to say how it relates to this problem, and how it could still be interesting as a physicalist strategy if it leaves the 'hard problem' untouched. For, after all, the hard problem is *the* problem for the physicalist.

5.3 Why I have difficulty understanding the PCS

There is a sense in which PCS is not dealing with 'the hard problem', as are other physicalist theories of consciousness.

Why do I say this? First, what is 'the hard problem'? No doubt it can be expressed in various ways, but it is roughly as follows:

How can a physical state – presumably neural – taken as being just the way that physical science understands it, be the same thing as the 'what it is like' (WIL) – the phenomenal, subjective, qualitative nature – of experience?

Chalmers states the problem in similar terms.

We can say that a mental state is conscious if it has a qualitative feel – an associated quality of experience. These qualitative feels are also known as phenomenal qualities, or qualia for short. The problem of explaining these phenomenal qualities is just the problem of explaining consciousness. This is the really hard part of the mind-body problem. (1996: 4)

Why does this seem to be a problem? As physicalists like J. J. C. Smart and others acknowledged from early on in the contemporary discussion, it is because the properties ascribed to neural states by science and the qualitative properties revealed in the WIL of experience seem entirely different, and, by Leibniz's Law, things with different properties cannot be identical.

So the problem can be put as follows: The physicalist claim that phenomenally conscious states are identical to, or in some other way 'nothing over and above', physical states or processes, seems to run up against Leibniz's Law. The challenge for the physicalist is to say what, if anything, it could be about a physical state or process that constituted it as, or made it count as, or made it to be, an experience with phenomenal character without imputing to it the kind of non-physical property that lead to the Leibniz Law problem.[1]

Traditional physicalist theories, such as behaviourism, functionalism and the topic neutral analysis, are clearly attempts at direct answers to this problem, and they do so by arguing that the phenomenal data are not what they seem be (or have seemed to certain philosophers to be), namely the transparent presentation of phenomenal qualities. Thus a behaviourist says that the WIL of experience is just some sort of behavioural readiness to respond, grounded, no doubt, in neural structures. The functionalist says more or less the same thing, namely that 'WIL' is just being in a functional

---

[1] Kati Balog in her (2012a) gives eight versions of 'the traditional puzzles about consciousness', but none of them is put in this explicit LL form, and so, in my opinion, none does justice to the hard problem, neat, so to speak.

state, realised in the brain and characterised in terms of the discriminatory responses appropriate to the stimulus in question. The topic neutralist (who is normally simply trying to improve on one of the above two) says that there is no problem because 'WIL' states don't reveal their nature, only their similarity/dissimilarity relations to other internal states that occur when prompted by certain stimuli. Thus there is no Leibniz Law clash because the 'WIL' states do not make manifest properties of a kind different from those ascribed to physical objects.

These answers may be judged radically inadequate, but it is intuitively clear how, if they were correct, they would constitute a solution to the problem they are intended to address: their relevance is not in doubt, only their adequacy to the apparent data of experience. My main difficulty with PCS is that it is not clear how it is meant to address the traditional problem in the first place. In other words, how does the fact that phenomenal concepts are in some sense discontinuous with physical concepts show how a physical state can manifest itself (or seem to do so) as a phenomenal quality?

In fact supporters of PCS are divided on how to express the theory themselves. The disagreements are not about details but about how to state the core of the theory. In fact PCS is not so much a particular general theory – as even behaviourism or functionalism might be thought to be – but a framework for a theory; *somehow* the special ostensive nature of phenomenal concepts should explain the explanatory gap and, with it, the 'hard problem'.

5.4   The problem facing PCS

One cannot deny that prima facie at least, there are three things in the game. (i) There is the neural state, as represented in science. (ii) There is the WIL/the phenomenal quality, which is how it seems to the subject. (iii) There is the phenomenal concept.

The core of what is obscure and problematic in PCS, I think, turns on how it handles (ii). The fundamental issue is what it is for/how one explains the fact that/a neural state is experienced as a phenomenal quality. The physicalist and PCS-ist say this is just the neural state as it is present (or presented) in experience, but the whole problem is to explain this latter notion. This is the root of the Leibniz Law problem: how can the standard neural properties and what appears to be a quite distinct phenomenal quality be identical?

Loar, who inspired the PCS, says nothing which is both plausible and illuminating on this point. He says that

What [Mary] lacked and then acquired ... was knowledge of certain [physical] properties *couched in experiential terms*. [Italics added] (599)

What can this latter expression mean? Something is usually 'couched' in words. Here it obviously contains the idea of expressing itself experientially but what – if anything – it could be for a physical state to do this is what is at stake. Given that it is not verbal, the 'terms' in which it is 'couched' can, in this context, only be concepts. Loar is similarly unilluminating in the following passage.

Odd though it may sound, the properties these conceptions phenomenologically reveal are physical-functional properties – but not of course *under physical-functional descriptions*. [Italics in original] (602)

The implication would appear to be that the physicalist can help himself to some such notion as phenomenal mode of presentation and treat it as primitive, in the sense that it is only by appealing to this notion that one can express the idea that some brain state is an experience, whilst, at the same time, claiming that ontologically one need only admit the physical-functional properties that science ascribes to the brain. This leaves completely untouched the question of how we are to explain how certain brain states manifest themselves phenomenally, unlike the rest of the physical world.

There seem to me to be four ways of tackling this. (a) The first is to say that certain physical states manifest themselves phenomenally simply by being conceptualised in the way that PCS suggests; stated bluntly, a brain state is 'turned into' an experience simply by our thinking of it in a certain way. (b) The second is to accept that it is just a brute fact that some neural states are experiences, and that is that! (c) The third is to say that some neural states are experiences and this is a brute fact, but why this seems so mysterious is somehow connected with the fact that experiences are conceptualised by phenomenal concepts. In other words, if [*per impossible?*] they were not conceptualised in this way, there would be no explanatory gap. (d) The fourth is to explain how a neural state is presented as an experience by saying it is presented topic neutrally, so that the way it comes across in experience reveals nothing about its real nature.

My impression is that both (a) and (d) are positions most PCS theorists want to avoid, though they cannot avoid saying things that seem to suggest them. (b) is often adopted but usually with some gesture to (c). I shall discuss these positions in turn.

5.5 Taking option (a): phenomenal concepts are what present brain states as experiences

Option (a) has the advantage that it is clear how it makes PCS relevant to the hard problem: it makes the phenomenality of experience simply into a way of conceptualising certain brain states. But it purchases this relevance at a great price. The idea that, for example, a neural spiking frequency is rendered as an experience by being conceptualised in a certain way seems to hover between the radically implausible and the barely intelligible. It at least seems to put into the notion of conceptualisation a very special kind of content. It seems to put on the physicalist the obligation to provide an account of conceptualisation, which is both consistent with physicalism and able to perform the trick of rendering a physical state as an experience, giving it WIL quality. Without something like this, it would just be the suggestion that one 'turns a brain state into' an experience by conceptualising it – thinking of it – in a certain way and this makes even behaviourism look intuitively plausible: think of your brain in a certain way and it will seem to you like an experience! I do not see how this is improved by saying (as supporters of PCS usually do) that the relevant brain state is actually part of or quoted in the phenomenal concept. It is wholly opaque how including a spiking frequency within a concept could bring it to phenomenal life. I do not believe that supporters of PCS want to say anything as bizarre – or as straightforward – as this; but, on the other hand, they often seem to be falling back on a move of this sort. If one says, for example, that there is only one property present, namely the spiking frequency, but two ways of conceiving of it, one as a spiking frequency and one as a phenomenal quality (and I have often come across this formula in discussion, at least), then I think one is falling back on (a), for it seems to say that when one conceives of, say, a spiking frequency using a phenomenal concept, the frequency manifests itself as a phenomenal quality.

The idea that the 'hard problem' can be thought of as essentially a conceptual problem has, I think, the following source.

The 'hard problem' can be broken down into two parts. One is the apparent Leibniz Law problem, namely, how the experiential state and the neural state can be the same, given the apparent manifest difference in their properties. But there is a second problem waiting in the wings, namely, given the answer (whatever it is) that one gives to the first problem, why should it seem so intuitively obvious that these states instantiate different properties? Suppose, for example, that one thought that WILs were neuro-functional states; why should it seem that they were something completely different – for example, the presentation of simple qualities? The PCS approaches the 'hard problem' through this second problem – it attempts to explain why any physicalist solution to the Leibniz Law problem is so counter-intuitive. It does this by claiming that there is a discontinuity between the concepts of science and those involved in recognition of our own phenomenal states and that this makes impossible an intuitive grasp on the ontological affinity of what they are conceptualising. So PCS is trying to answer the question 'if physicalism is true, why is it so counter-intuitive?' It is not trying directly to answer the question, 'given the apparent facts, how can physicalism be true and how can a physical state be, or constitute, a phenomenal state?' The thought behind PCS, then, seems to be that if PCS can explain away physicalism's counter-intuitiveness, then rational resistance to physicalism will have been overcome. Accepting for the moment this strategy, the question then becomes 'does explaining the misfit of the two kinds of concepts actually explain why physicalism seems so counterintuitive?' This is, I think, the point at which the failure of PCS to address the fundamental Leibniz Law problem comes in. If you think that the correct focus for the problem facing physicalism is the explanatory gap, then conceptual misfit could plausibly seem to be the answer. But if you think that the problem is to explain how a physical state can do the job of being a phenomenal state without invoking non-material properties, then explanatory relations between concepts do not seem to get to the heart of the question.

Some protagonists of PCS argue that it is not concerned with the hard problem, but with the knowledge argument, the explanatory gap and the conceivability of zombies.[2] This presupposes that there is a serious difference between the hard problem, as exposed by Leibniz Law, and the knowledge argument. The explanatory gap is, it can plausibly be said, about the relation between two sets of concepts, the physical and the phenomenal, not about how a brain state can also be an experience. Similarly, the conceivability of zombies is also about the conceptual separability of these groups. But which of these two issues – conceptual distinctness or the hard problem – does the knowledge argument concern? It seems to me that the problem facing Mary when she has her first chromatic colour experiences is not best expressed (let alone only expressed) as 'why could I not previously derive this conceptual characterisation of this situation from the conceptual characterisation of it I received from science?' Rather her puzzlement would be in the form 'how can *that* quality/property I am now experiencing be the same property as those that were exhaustively characterised by the science I already knew?' The problem is a *de re* not a *de dicto* one: the problem is how to explain physicalistically the phenomenal quality that figures in the experience, not just to explain the role of the concept that characterises it.

The explanatory gap and the conceivability of zombies are consequences of the hard problem, whereas the knowledge argument is a way of focusing on the hard problem itself. The transferring of discussion from

---

[2] This point was made in discussion to me by David Papineau.

the hard problem and the knowledge argument to the explanatory gap and the conceivability of zombies seems to me not to be helpful when trying to evaluate the adequacy of physicalism as an account of phenomenal consciousness.[3]

In fact, this way of misconstruing the knowledge argument dates back to Brian Loar's initial statement of PCS (1997). He reports it as follows:

> The knowledge argument is straightforward on the face of it. Consider any phenomenal quality and any physical property however complex. We can *know that a person has the physical property without knowing that she experiences the phenomenal quality.* And no amount of a priori reasoning or construction can bridge this conceptual gap. That is the intuitive premise. The conclusion is drawn that the phenomenal quality cannot be identical with the physical property. The argument is equivalent to this: since physical and phenomenal conceptions can be connected only a posteriori, physical properties must be distinct from phenomenal properties. (598: italics added)

The idea is that the separateness of the concepts misleads us into believing in a separateness of properties. Notice that there is nothing here about Mary's first-personal perspective. We are presented with something rather like the other minds problem, because Loar sets the issue up in terms of our not being able to infer a priori from someone's physical properties that they are phenomenally conscious. This approach is closely connected to the conceivability of zombies: if zombies were not conceivable, we could not doubt whether other people had minds – at least if we were allowed to examine their brains as well as their outer behaviour. This approach says nothing about how the content of her experience strikes Mary when she sees chromatic colour, and how different that quality seems from the properties about which science had told her: the approach is entirely third-personal and this enables it to by-pass the real issue, namely the Leibniz Law problem of the seemingly total difference between the qualities revealed directly in first-person consciousness and those revealed by third-person scientific observation. This problem can only emerge when one focuses on the first-person perspective, which knowledge argument does, but the 'zombie' argument does not; neither does Loar and this seems to have led his followers down a blind alley.

Barry Loewer has suggested to me that my way of describing the situation in terms of properties and Loar's in terms of concepts are just two ways of characterising the situation and that Loar's has the advantage of not leading directly to dualism. It is important to my position that

---

[3] This is certainly the way I intended and understood my version of the knowledge argument when I used it as a way of setting out the challenge facing physicalism, at the opening of (1982).

Loar's way is actually defective, and does not constitute another empirically adequate theoretical framework. It is important that Loar actually misses something out. He misses out on the qualitative nature of the experience *unless* that can be characterised solely in terms of how the brain state is conceptualised by phenomenal concepts. But that this is the way in which experience is 'manufactured' is what seems to be a completely hopeless position.

This conclusion is reinforced by a consideration which will be invoked in the next section, namely that if this were true it would be difficult to see how qualia and WIL could play the vital role they do in forming our conception of the world. I shall be taking this theme up more fully in Chapter 8, but it is useful to pursue it briefly here, because it links closely with the transparency of experience, which physicalists usually think it helps them to emphasise.

5.6   Phenomenal qualities, transparency and our conception of the physical world

The following doctrine of *weak transparency* should be, and probably is, uncontroversial. It might be expressed as follows.

The principal phenomenal qualities that characterise experience in our major sense modalities are the qualities that we prima facie and naïvely take to be the qualities/properties that characterise the physical world at the macroscopic level. These are such qualities as colour, shape as presented in vision and touch, hardness/solidity as presented in touch.

This is transparency because it takes central features of experience – the features that characterise the WIL of experience – to be essentially the same or similar to the features we attribute to the common sense or manifest image world. It is a weak version of this doctrine because it does not claim (or deny) that all the features of experience or qualia can be treated in this way, both because it does not try to apply this idea to sensations, such as pains or itches, nor does it claim that every feature of perceptual states such as visual experience can be so dealt with. It only claims that it is true for certain central features. It is also weak because it does not claim that even these features *actually are* features of the external world, only that they *purport to be* and are features of our *naïve* or *manifest image* conception of the world. It is because of the minimalness of my claim that I take it to be uncontroversial. Though uncontroversial, it is not, however, inconsequential.

It follows from this limited transparency that *what it is like to see red*, for example, and *what red, as naïvely conceived, is like* are two sides of the same coin. This applies not only to secondary qualities, for *what it is like to see square*, and *what square, as naïvely understood by the sighted, is* are similarly linked by the transparency relation. This has serious consequences for any attempt to give a physicalist reduction of the WIL of experience. If the WIL of experience is a reflection of what the qualities of our manifest world are like, then no account of WIL that deprives them of this world-constituting nature will be plausible. For example, if one were to claim that different WILs were really *just* different spiking frequencies of neuronal electrical activities, one would be at a loss to see how our picture of the world could be merely a transparent projection of such frequencies: I do not experience the world as an externalised set of electronic firings, nor as a set of my own behavioural dispositions or functional states. This is not, of course, to say that the experience does not causally depend on such physical states, but it does mean that, if anything like identity is asserted to exist between the qualitative states of experience and their neural grounds, then an explanation must be given of how such a thing can be that out of which our manifest world is (to a significant extent) constructed.[4]

This point is salient because the discussion about WIL and qualia is conducted as if it simply concerned certain intra-mental phenomena – things that leave one's conception of the external, physical world untouched. These qualia are embarrassments to be somehow accommodated into one's independent conception of the world. If they were all like itches and pains – sensations that do not form part of our construction of external reality – this would be fine. But this is not so. Qualia must be construed in a way that makes sense of their world-constructing role. Given transparency, qualia must be construed in a way that enables them to retain such a quality of 'mental paint' that they paint not only avowedly subjective experience, but our manifest world as well.[5] Now it is hard to see how they could do this unless qualia (or WILs) really possess some qualitative features that stand in an appropriate relation to the qualities of

---

[4] I attempted to show how behavioural/functional accounts of experiential states lose our grasp on the world in Robinson (1994: 128–36), and also in Chapter 3 and Section 5.5 above.

[5] Lycan (1996: 75–7) distinguishes between the qualitative content of experience – the qualia – and WIL, on the grounds that the latter is higher order: our experience can have qualitative content without our noticing this, and in such a case there will be nothing it is like for us, according to Lycan. Even if this is correct, it would not follow that the quality is not the object/content of WIL, just as it is the object/content of the experience, noticed or not. When you are in the higher-order state of noticing what your experience is like, it is still the lower-order content – the quality – that you are coming to notice – perhaps plus the fact that you are noticing it. So even if Lycan is correct about the difference between qualia and WIL, this does not affect my point that phenomenal red and what it is like to see phenomenal red are two sides of the same coin.

our manifest world, so that what is, in some sense, a projection of those features can constitute our lived world. I believe that development of this theme shows how radically mistaken orthodox physicalist accounts of experience must be. This is the thought that I shall develop in Chapter 8.

5.7   Options (b) and (c): identity is given but PCS explains away the mystery

Options (b) and (c) are normally taken together. Consider first the idea that one can assume that phenomenal states and brain states are identical. This, after all, is the physicalist hypothesis, so how can it be wrong to take it ex hypothesis in the present discussion?

There are in fact two different positions in this vicinity. One is exemplified by Block and Stalnaker (1999) and by Searle (1992). According to this view, all identities in science suffer from an 'explanatory gap' which is bridged simply by the fact that the best theory requires one to posit the identity; the properties belonging to the two 'levels' always seem to be different. In this respect, the identity between a brain state and an experience is no different from that between liquidity or heat, on the one side, and various kinds of molecular motion on the other. It is not clear why someone who took this line should need PCS, any more than such an account is needed to justify or explain the other identities posited in science.

The other view, exemplified by Papineau, Balog and most supporters of PCS, accepts that there is no explanatory gap in cases other than that of the mind-body relation, and that PCS is needed to explain it in that case. Nevertheless, they hold, it is not question-begging to take the identity *ex hypothesi*. The issue for this theory is to make clear how PCS relates to the hard problem and the Leibniz law problem; whether it somehow dissolves them, if so, how, and, if not, whether PCS is much help to the physicalist in facing the major challenge which they constitute. Unless it makes a significant contribution to these issues, assuming identity will simply be question-begging.

An example of someone who seems to take this latter line is David Papineau. Reporting his 2002 views, he says the following:

To have a phenomenal concept of some experience, you must be able introspectively to focus on it when you have it, and to re-create it imaginatively at other times; given these abilities, you can form a term with the structure the experience: –, in which the gap is filled either by a current experience or by an imaginative re-creation of an experience... (2007: 112)

Here the idea that certain brain states are experiences is simply taken as primitive. Of course, as I have conceded, physicalists believe that certain brain events are experiences, but the challenge they face is to explain what it is about a brain process that makes it an experience, not to take their theory as needless of an explanation. This potentially question-begging position remains in his later theory.

[The new] model of phenomenal concepts as a species of perceptual concept retains one crucial feature from my earlier quotational-indexical model, namely that phenomenal references to an experience will deploy an instance of that experience, and in that sense will use that experience to mention it. (2007: 123)

Once again, the fact that certain brain states are experiences is taken as a given and unproblematic, and phenomenal concept is explained in terms of how these experiences are deployed in concepts. This transfers the answer to the 'hard problem' away from the nature of phenomenal concepts to certain accounts about the constraints on property identity. If the idea that certain brain states are experiences is essentially unproblematic, then it might seem that there was no 'hard problem' in the first place.

The supporter of PCS can try to bring together the ideas behind (a) and (b) – namely, the idea that phenomenal concepts create experience and the idea that the experiential status of certain brain states is essentially unproblematic – by uniting them in (c). They might argue that identity between phenomenal states and physical states only seems bizarre because of the explanatory gap (EG), and it is the discontinuity between the different kinds of concepts that causes explanatory gap: so, if there were no explanatory gap, which is caused by the conceptual structure, one would not find the identity strange. This just seems completely false. The identity is strange because of the apparently manifest difference between the phenomenal quality as it is presented in experience and neural states as they are characterised by science or external observation. It is the fact that the quality as presented in experience can only be accessed by the subject that gives phenomenal concepts their different and discontinuous status.

The suggestion that this radical discontinuity cannot be explained simply from the conceptual features of phenomenal concepts can be seen by considering those features and the other places in which they occur.

Phenomenal concepts are what pick out phenomenal qualities, whether primary or secondary. In fact most of our initial empirical concepts are given content for us wholly or largely by ostension – that is, by experiencing their instances. I think that this generates a problem for PCS. Consider the concept of liquidity, or the concept of flowing, as it applies to liquids. It would be very difficult to get these notions without experience of liquids and their typical behaviour. 'A liquid is that sort of thing' – 'flowing is behaving like that – get it – you see what I mean?' But if ostension, which involves quoting or reactivating, or some such, the WIL of the experience itself, is what creates the explanatory gap between the physical account and experience, why do we not feel any problem in understanding the behaviour of liquids as being adequately explained by the behaviour of molecules? If the manifest world is, as I argued in the last section, just (or largely) WIL plus transparency, why is there not an explanatory gap between physical science and the world of common experience, in its primary as well as its secondary qualities? The only reasonable conclusion is that the conceptual features picked on by PCS are irrelevant to the real hard problem, which is founded on the Leibniz Law problem.

Ned Block appears to accept that there is some genuine feature in experience which is only accessible to the subject and which is not an artifact of conceptualisation, but that this is no threat to the physicalist because such properties are 'thick' and the neural structure is their hidden nature, just as H_2O is the hidden nature of water. So the subjectively available feature can be identified with the 'deeper' physical structure, as water can be with H_2O. Kripke has argued, seemingly convincingly, that this model cannot be applied to experiential states. How does Block respond to this?

I agree that the two terms of the identity 'Q = cortico-thalamic oscillation' Pick out the referents via different aspects of that referent, different MMoPs [Metaphysical Modes of Presentation]. And I also agree that the aspect used by the mental term of the identity is available to the first person whereas the aspect used by the physical term is not. But it does not follow that the aspect used by the mental term is thin. It is true that no neurological property is explicitly part of the first person route, but that does not show that it is not part of the first-person route, albeit ontologically rather than explicitly. The MMoP of Q is stipulated to be phenomenal and may be taken to be the property of being Q. But being identical to Q, on the physicalist view, is both a thick property and available to the first person. Being identical to Q is a physical property (being identical to cortico-thalamic oscillation) but is nonetheless distinct from the MMoP I have been supposing for 'cortico-thalamic oscillation', which has to do with the oxygen uptake that functional magnetic resonance scanners use to identify it. On the physicalist view, the feel and the neurological state are not different aspects of one thing: they are literally identical. If they are aspects, they are identical aspects. But the MMoP of the right-hand term of the identity is still different from the MMoP of the left-hand term. (2007: 292–3)

This will work if we accept Block and Stalnaker (1999) on what is involved in scientific claims that two seemingly different properties are really the same. Block and Stalnaker maintain that there are explanatory gaps between every explanatory level.[6] The properties associated with liquidity, for example, do not follow from those of the molecules making up the liquid. The identification is made simply on grounds of theoretical neatness and unity. In this case, a resilient prima facie difference and actual identity are both preserved, giving a 'thick' property, so property identities can then follow the model of 'stuff' – e.g., water = H_2O – identities. But the claim that there is an explanatory gap in cases such as liquidity is hard to maintain. So it seems to be generally accepted that the case of phenomenal qualities presents an explanatory gap in a unique way. It would undermine the plausibility of Block's claim that property identities can be thick if the phenomenal quality-brain state cases were the only ones to which it applied. So if thickness is general but the explanatory gap is unique, thickness must be independent of whether there is an explanatory gap. It would have to be the case that all cross-level property identities were thick, but explanatory gap existed only when there was the kind of conceptual breach created by phenomenal concepts.

Now it might seem that liquidity is a 'thick' property, because there might be different mechanisms in different possible worlds – or even in the actual world – by which it is realised. But they will still all manifest liquidity, because that is a behavioural property. In other words, there is no way that that very ostensively identifiable feature could be essentially dependent on a certain realisation. If you allow this same fact for, e.g. red qualia, namely that they could be multiply realised and add the fact that, unlike liquidity, this is not a behavioural property, then you reach the real problem, which is that one cannot see how this property – phenomenal red, as opposed to liquidity (the latter being a behavioural property) – can be wholly implemented – sufficiently explained – by the mechanism that underlies it. Moreover this difference cannot be explained by the unique nature of PCS, as I argued above against Papineau: PCS is not unique to the intra mental case, but applies also in the case of liquidity and similar, where there is no explanatory gap. Given that the Block and Stalnaker theory, in so far as it depends on taking liquidity and the like as thick properties, does not explain why there is an explanatory gap in the phenomenal case, and that PCS cannot assist it, it seems that the Block and Stalnaker theory is no help to a physicalist who wants to appropriate phenomenal qualities.

---

[6] It might come as something of a surprise to note that Block and Stalnaker's position on this is not significantly different from Searle's (1992). In both cases it is maintained that throughout the sciences (i) the lower level remains closed (ii) there are explanatory gaps between the levels, and (iii) these together do not entail epiphenomenalism for the higher level or over determination. Searle does not talk of identity between the levels, but given (i) to (iii), this is a verbal difference.

So taking the identity of experiential and neural states as primitive begs, rather than answers, the question.

5.8 Option (d): the topic neutral approach

The fourth, topic neutralist, option seems to be how Janet Levine interprets PCS when she says that phenomenal concepts 'aren't supposed to characterize phenomenal properties at all' (2007: 105). She is also against the 'quotational' approach and the idea that phenomenal concepts are partially constituted by the experience or that one can speak of 'acquaintance'. Her conception of the concepts, therefore, seems very neutral. But resorting to topic neutrality takes the whole issue back to Jack Smart's theory of 1959 – which is to admit that no serious progress has been made by physicalism in the last fifty years!

This, though correct, is not the most serious objection to the topic neutral approach. If normal experience gives us topic neutral knowledge of our inner workings and Mary already has topic-specific knowledge, then she already knew more before she had colour experience than can be acquired by having it. Neither Levine nor anyone else can give a plausible account of why such topic neutral knowledge should present itself as something new, in addition to the detailed information Mary already knew, or why she should seemed to have lacked anything whilst still in the room. One would have to combine the neutral interpretation of PCS with, say, an abilities account of these things, or Jackson's appeal to the simple representation of something complex, but we have already seen that these do not work.

5.9 A more general objection to PCS as a whole

All the above versions of PCS take for granted the idea that a physicalist can contrast the physical system with the way it is conceptualised, in such a manner that Mary might know all about the former whilst being in some kind of ignorance about certain important features in the latter. This itself can be disputed.

PCS is essentially a version of Churchland's early response to the knowledge argument. Churchland argued that what knowledge argument showed was not that Mary learnt something new on leaving her room but that she gained a new way of knowing something she had already known. PCS is just an attempt to fill out how this 'new way' works. I argued in (1993b: 165–6) that if this 'new way of knowing' was itself a physical process then it had to be included in what Mary already knew.

The idea behind the 'mode' theory is, presumably, that if the phenomenal is merely another mode of access to respectable physical facts, then it does not itself constitute an extra fact: it is not an addition to ontology, but an extra mode of access to part of the previously accepted ontology. A moment's reflexion will, however, show this to be sophistical. Call the set of physical facts P and the scientific modes of access which [Mary] has to these facts S, and the experiential mode of access [she] lacks H. If we regard S and H as external to P, then the addition of a new mode of access will not alter P. But the physicalist hypothesis is that everything relevant is included in P: modes of access to physical facts are themselves simply physical processes and are included in physical facts. Therefore, if [Mary] knows all the relevant members of P, [she] should know all the facts about H, including the fact of what that mode of access is phenomenally like.[7]

The same applies to the PCS, which is just a version of the 'different mode' theory. Chalmers uses a similar, but fuller, argument. Papineau summarises it as follows.

Let C be the thesis that humans possess phenomenal concepts. As Chalmers sees it, type-B physicalists require both (a) that C explains our epistemic situation with respect to consciousness and (b) that C is explicable in physical terms. However, Chalmers argues that there is no version of C that satisfies both these desiderata – either C can be explained in a way that makes it physically explicable or in a way that allows us to explain our epistemic situation, but not both. (2007: 136)

Papineau claims that one can do both as a full physical account that still leaves an epistemic gap. Mary works out how phenomenal concepts work physically, but she is still mentioning them, not using them, so she still does not know them in the phenomenal concept way.

This response is sound if we are allowed to take the fact of identity as a primitive that overcomes the explanatory gap by force, so to speak. No amount of physical conceptual knowledge entails phenomenal conceptual knowledge, just as (if the primitive identity theory is correct across the board, as Block and Stalnaker, and Searle, claim) no amount of description of molecules entails that there is a liquid present. But all the weight is now on defending that theory of property identity: PCS alone cannot explain how it is true of consciousness and not – against Block, Stalnaker and Searle – of other cases.

Katalin Balog (2012a: 22) puts herself into a similar position to Papineau. She gives as one of the puzzles facing physicalism:

---

[7] When I first discussed what is now known as 'the knowledge argument', in Robinson (1982), I introduced a deaf scientist who played the counterpart to Jackson's Mary. I was still keeping to this practice in 1993, so I have modified the quotation to substitute Mary for references to the deaf scientist.

Only subjects who have undergone or who are currently undergoing the relevant phenomenal states can token the corresponding phenomenal concepts. This underlies Jackson's 1982 Knowledge Argument and is widely accepted.

The verb 'token' here is somewhat evasive. The question is whether Mary in her room should, if physicalism were true, have been able to understand what colour was like, not whether she was in a position to deploy colour concepts recognitionally. Now the response might be that one cannot understand these concepts unless one can apply them recognitionally, but on what grounds could a physicalist say this? Mary can observe exactly how these concepts work in others and can recognise that experiential neural states (of a kind she has never had) constitute part of them. If she can understand other things that people are thinking, not by empathy – i.e. by having had the same thoughts herself – but by studying their brains, why cannot the same obtain in this case? No orthodox physicalist can retreat to the position that there is any state of which you cannot have complete knowledge unless you are, or have been, in it yourself, or can imaginatively recreate what being in it is like; the third-person perspective must command everything. There will be certain things you cannot do unless you are in the state yourself, but that will be strictly knowledge how.

Perhaps one might claim that someone cannot understand a concept unless you can deploy it, but this is not necessarily true. It may often be the case that someone cannot deploy a concept *because* they cannot understand it, but it is possible to understand a concept and not be able to deploy it because you are not in a situation that makes deployment possible. I cannot myself deploy the concept 'solemnising a marriage' in a first-person way because I am not a legal registrar of marriages, but I understand it perfectly well. Mary cannot deploy the concept 'recognising red' in a first person way because she never has the experience that licenses its use. I can, of course, deploy the concept 'solemnising a marriage' in a third-personal sort of way, but so can Mary deploy 'recognising red' in such a way, for she can know when others are doing so. So appeal to 'deploying the concept' is irrelevant against Chalmers's objection.

5.10 Papineau and the Leibniz Law problem

David Papineau in effect challenges the Leibniz Law problem by characterising it as 'the intuition of distinctness' (2007: 139). In other words, the sense that there are clearly different properties involved is deemed to be an 'intuition'. I think that the use of the word 'intuition' here is likely to be misleading. In fact the word as used in natural language and in philosophy has, if not two senses, at least two poles. On the one hand it means something close to intellectual hunch or putative insight. On the other it means something that seems plainly and obviously true; a blatant fact that cannot be ignored because it is a datum of experience. Philosophers who denigrate something as an intuition are assimilating both kinds to the former. The former is the sense behind Dennett's powerful metaphor of the intuition pump, and also behind his citing as a case of an 'intuition', in a relevant sense, the belief that if you fart, burp and cough at the same time you will die. I have the intuition that the world could not be infinitely old and that Cantor and Hilbert were right in thinking that their logico-mathematical treatment of infinity cannot be empirically interpreted, only formally. This is an intuition in the first sense and I may very well be completely wrong in this belief. One person's insight is another's prejudice. But if you show me a red patch, a blue patch and play middle C on the piano, it is intuitively obvious to me that these are qualitatively different phenomena. This is not a speculative hunch or a putative insight. If there is such a thing as experience at all, I am plainly right. The claim that phenomenal red is the same property as electrical activity between neurons, as these are characterised in physical science, is intuitively obviously false in pretty much the same way as it is intuitively obviously false that phenomenal red is the same quality or property as phenomenal blue, or as the sound of middle C. This is why Smart and Armstrong desperately tried to magic away the positive content from the phenomenal side with their topic neutral analysis.

5.11   Conclusion

It looks as if PCS has no plausible way of either meeting the 'hard problem' or of explaining away why physicalism is so counter-intuitive. I said at the opening of Section 5.3 that there are three things in play: (i) there is the neural state, as represented in science; (ii) there is the 'WIL'/ the phenomenal quality, which is how it seems to the subject; (iii) there is the phenomenal concept. And that it is (ii) that PCS does not seem to tackle. I have looked at all the strategies by which they might try to do this and found them all wanting. There is, however – as I hinted in Section 5.5 – another vital feature of WILs or qualia that PCS and other responses to the knowledge argument fail to take properly into account. This is the role of the transparency of experience – a feature often supposed to favour physicalism, but which is in fact completely opposed to it, because it requires that experience be qualitatively rich, if it is to paint our world, as well as our subjective experience. This is the theme of Chapter 8.

6 Davidson, non-reductive physicalism and naturalism without physicalism

6.1 Donald Davidson and non-reduction

Donald Davidson played a major role in a particular strain of 'non-reductive physicalism'.[1] He influenced many philosophers, including John McDowell, who developed his ideas in the direction of what one might call 'naturalism without physicalism'. It is this line of thought that I want to investigate in this chapter. It is an important part of my argument that Davidson's notion of the *non-reductive* is both unclear and regularly misunderstood. In fact his theory is reductive, according to certain natural understandings of that term. My discussion of reductionism in this book occurs in Chapter 9 because of its role in Part II, but it might help readers with my discussion of Davidson if they were to read Sections 9.1 and 9.2 of that chapter before proceeding now.

It seems to me that the discussion of 'non-reductive materialism' has been conducted under the shadow of an ambiguity in the sense of 'reductive'. One sense is specific to the philosophy of mind, and here the reductive tradition is marked by the attempt to give an account of the mind in behavioural or functional terms, without remainder. The other sense derives from the philosophy of science, and it concerns the possibility of giving some kind of systematic account of 'higher' sciences in terms of 'lower' ones, and, ultimately, in terms of physics. I shall argue that failure to distinguish these senses in Davidson's 'Mental Events' has led to serious confusions in the discussion of 'non-reductive materialism' and in the attendant notion of 'supervenience'. Davidson in 'Mental Causes' has clarified the confusion, but in a way that makes his original contribution much less interesting than it seemed to be.

6.2 The two senses of 'non-reductive'

Story 1. In order to vindicate a materialist theory of the mind it is necessary to show how something that is a purely physical object can

---

[1] I give a more extended treatment to Davidson and his 'non-reductive' theory than I can fit in this chapter in Robinson (2001).

satisfy psychological predicates. Those features of the mind which seem to be, prima facie, incompatible with this physicalism – such as consciousness and the intentionality of thought – must, therefore, be explained in a way that purges them of their apparently Cartesian elements, which would be incompatible with materialism. Overt behaviour is expressive of mentality and is a purely physical phenomenon, so it is necessary to provide some kind of analysis, or looser gloss, of psychological predicates which shows how they need be no more than dispositions to behave – or, more probably, functional states defined by their ultimate contribution to behaviour: in this way, it can be shown that there is no principled objection to physicalism.

Story 2. In order to vindicate a physicalist theory of the mind it is necessary to integrate psychology into a unified science resting on physics. Such a *scientific reduction* requires that there be bridging laws relating the properties or concepts of any science higher than physics to those of the science below it, until nomological correlation with physics itself is achieved. In the case of psychology, this means that, at the first stage, there be laws connecting psychological states with neurological states.

Story 3. Reductionism never looked plausible. Fortunately, a materialist theory of the mind requires only that each mental event be also a physical event. This will be so if a given mental event and a given physical event have all and only the same causal relations. Nothing is required in the way of reduction of psychological predicates or properties to physical ones.

Question. Is the reduction that is *not* required for materialism according to *story 3* the analytic reduction advocated in *story 1* or the scientific reduction of *story 2*, or both, and does it make a difference whether it is understood primarily in relation to one of them or to the other?

6.3   Confusing the two senses

The analytical reductionism of *story 1* is the approach to the mind-body problem associated with analytical behaviourists, such as Ryle is normally interpreted as being, with Australian central state materialism, with analytical functionalism, and with the computational theory of the mind. It is analytical because there is an explication of the possession of particular mental states in terms of the kinds of behaviour paradigmatically associated with them, and it is reductive because it purports to show how, through the behavioural connection, mental states need be no more than – 'nothing but' – physical states, contrary to one's Cartesian intuitions: the mind is ultimately its contribution to behaviour, and nothing more.

The scientific reductionism of *story 2* is part of the logical positivist program to produce a unified science: one rationale for it is the belief that such nomological reduction is necessary if the different sciences are to be thought of as being genuinely true but different ways of talking about the same subject matter, namely the one physical world.[2] I argued in Chapter 1, Section 1.1, that this distinction in approaches to the philosophy of mind and in the understanding of 'reduction' marks a difference between British and Australian philosophy on the one hand and American on the other. It is remarkable that Davidson does not, I think, give anywhere any serious attention to sensations or 'raw feels' and, therefore, entirely bypasses the issues with which this book is mainly concerned.[3]

What I have called *story 3* represents, of course, Donald Davidson's (1970) non-reductive physicalism. Many of Davidson's readers including, I would hazard, most, if not all, of his British ones, understood his theory to be non-reductive in the sense of avoiding analytical reductionism, as well as scientific reductionism (if they gave that issue any thought). It was, for them, an alternative to the counter-intuitive theories of Ryle, Smart and Armstrong. Thus, David Charles has written:

In his writings [Davidson] sought to support the conviction that the mental is dependent on the physical, while at the same time holding that the mental need not, and indeed should not, be reductively defined in terms of the physical or functional. (1992: 265–6)

Nor does Charles make this attribution carelessly. He quotes Davidson on the kind of supervenience his theory involves. Davidson says:

Supervenience of this kind does not entail reducibility through law *or definition.* [my italics] (1970: 88)

Nothing would seem to be plainer than that Davidson is disowning reductionism as it appears in both *story 1* and *story 2*. My argument is that, despite this apparent avowal, Davidson is actually concerned only with forms of nomological reduction, and that his theory positively requires analytical reduction; and that this fact is brought out by the

[2] This rationale might seem rather too ontologically based to be the positivists' reason. Carnap's reason, at the end of his (1955), is that we could not apply a variety of sciences to one problem – as we often need to do – if there were not a strict unity of the laws of the various sciences. This, I think, is only a *de dicto* way of making the same point.

[3] It is worth remarking, whilst abusing Davidson, on the contrast between his approach and Dennett's. One the one hand, they both focus on propositional attitude states, and, importantly, take an interpretationalist approach to them. But Dennett finally recognised the need to deal with phenomenal states, and devoted a large book, packed with science and arguments, to the topic. Davidson, on the other hand, seemed to think that this issue was unworthy of his attention.

way he defends his doctrine in 'Thinking Causes'. If one is interested in developing a 'soft materialism', free from the counter-intuitive rigours of functionalism and similar theories, Davidson is no ally.

If this is true, how can he say what Charles quotes him as saying? Shortly after the passage quoted, Davidson considers, as an example of the *reduction by definition* that he eschews what he calls 'definitional behaviourism'. He asks '[w]hy are we willing ... to abandon the attempt to give explicit definitions of mental concepts in terms of behavioural ones?' He illustrates what such a programme would be committed to by citing an attempt to analyse having a certain belief in terms of having the disposition to utter certain *sounds*. The goal is the explicit definition of the mental in terms which contain no mentalese; it is the matching of a mentally characterised type of behaviour with behaviours that are types in purely physical terms. Reduction by explicit definition is not, therefore, something different from nomological reduction, but is a strengthened version of it: it replaces mere nomological correlation with definitional correlation, which entails nomological correlation. Twenty three years later, in 'Thinking Causes', he still has the same notion of reduction.

Supervenience ... obviously applies in an uninteresting sense to cases where [some higher level vocabulary] p is ... *explicitly* [my italics] definable by means of the predicates in [some more basic vocabulary] S, and to cases where there is a law to the effect that the extension of p is identical with the extension of a predicate definable in terms of the predicates in S. The interesting cases are those where p resists any of these forms of reduction. (1993: 4–5)

The definitional reduction of mental predicates to explicitly physical ones, so that the mental predicate can be identified in meaning with some kind of physical process, characterised in wholly non-mental terms, is associated with Carnap, but not with an analytical behaviourist such as Ryle, with the topic neutral analyses, nor with any functionalist, nor computational approach. Ryle's emphasis on the 'multi-track' nature of psychological dispositions (1963: 42ff) rests on his belief that the manifestations of those dispositions need possess no unity as physical kinds, thereby ruling out nomological reduction, and, hence, explicit definition in terms of bodily movement. Putnam (1975b) introduced the term 'functionalism' as explicitly non-reductive in Davidson's sense; and one of the toughest analytical functionalists, Sydney Shoemaker (1994: 56), has described his position as 'radically "nonreductive"', meaning that the functions can be multiply realised, and, hence, are neither nomologically nor definitionally reducible. These latter theories might be called 'token behaviourism' and 'token functionalism', in contrast with 'type behaviourism' and 'type functionalism', because they identify each individual expression of a mental state with physical behaviour, or some other purely physical change, but do not identify types of mental states with types of physical process. The *topic neutral* analysis of the mental, such as that provided by Smart and Armstrong, is devised precisely to avoid defining the mental in *explicitly* physical terms, substituting instead terms that leave room for the *possibility* of wholly physical realisation. But can it be denied that these topic neutral analyses are reductive analyses? As far as I can tell, Davidson shows no awareness of the existence – or, at least, the special relevance to his project – of such theories, yet they constitute paradigms of reductionism *in the philosophy of mind.*

6.4 Davidson's theory, naïvely and sophisticatedly understood

As naïvely and naturally and usually understood, Davidson's theory involves a kind of property dualism that is sufficiently dualistic to render any kind of functionalist understanding of mentalistic concepts unnecessary. The theory seems to be presented as if no kind of analytic preparation of our psychological concepts is required as a preliminary for the type of token identity theory that Davidson is giving. This is because the identity in question is not between mental and physical states or properties, but between mental and physical events; where the identity of events seems to place no constraints on the nature of any monadic qualities or properties involved in the event, because it is entirely a function of causal relations.

This theory of event identity might be pictured as the 'flagpole' theory of events. The same event can be thought of as possessing or instantiating quite different properties, just as two or more quite dissimilar flags could be flying from the same flagpole at the same time. The same event could instantiate some neurological property, and also be having of a deep red quale, with the latter conceived in as 'qualia-freakish' way as one likes, or be having of some fully self-conscious thought content; the only requirement is that the causes that bring about the having of the quale, or the conscious thought, and the occurrence of the neural event are the same, and so are their consequences.[4] The identity of the event is no more

---

[4] It might be objected that it is wrong to bring qualia and similar creatures of consciousness into this debate, for Davidson is only concerned with propositional attitudes. There are two reasons for rejecting this objection. First, if Davidson's strategy does not apply to such conscious states, it hardly represents a general physicalist approach to mind. (Perhaps Davidson, like other post-positivist Americans is an eliminativist about qualia, and this is essential to his overall strategy. If so, it is something we should know.) Second, as Galen Strawson (1994) has reminded those mesmerised by our neo-behaviourist tradition, thoughts can be just as much conscious states with introspectable contents as can qualia.

dependent on, nor does it impose constraints upon, the nature of the non-causal properties involved, than the identity of a flagpole depends on or constrains the colour or shape of the flags it flies. In property and state terms this theory permits full-blooded dual aspect theory.

It is this theory, when combined with his doctrines of the nomological nature of causation and the anomolousness of the mental, that has left Davidson's theory open to the accusation that it entails epiphenomenalism. This accusation is put in two ways. First it is claimed that the irrelevance of mental states or properties to causal explanation is itself constitutive of epiphenomenalism, for interaction involves causal explanatory relevance. The second ground for the accusation is that, given the strict causal monopoly he allows to the physical, the world would have followed just the same path if the mental had been absent. There is a possible world physically and nomically just like this without the mental. It follows that the presence of the mental makes no difference and so it is epiphenomenal.

The first ground for the charge of epiphenomenalism is rendered inconclusive in two ways. First, there is a clash of intuitions concerning what interaction requires. It is possible to insist that it is mere causal relatedness that is relevant, not explanatory relevance.[5] But, second, and more importantly for our purposes, in 'Thinking Causes' (1993: 9ff) Davidson explains what he means by 'strict causal explanation' in a way that radically alters the situation. Most readers seem, rightly or wrongly, to have read 'Mental Events' as saying that there was nothing worth calling proper causal explanation, such as applied in the physical world, operating in the mental realm. The thesis, however, turns out to be rather more specialised than this. It is that strict causal explanation operates only at the level of physics, not 'only at the physical level'; it is the science of physics itself that supports the rest. Davidson says:

> Whatever might be the contribution of causal relations to giving thoughts their content, that content, however derived, is a monadic property of the mental event.

[5] There is another argument employed by Cynthia and Graham Macdonald (1986). They argue that the mental property cannot be idle if the physical property is active, for given the token identity of the mental event with the physical event, the instance of the mental property is identical with the instance of the physical property; so anything one does is done by the other, for they are the same instance. This argument seems to me to confuse two senses of 'instance'. The fact that the same particular – be it event or object – instantiates two properties does not entail that the two property *instances* are identical. If, for example, a ball is red and round, it does not follow that the instance of redness is the same thing as the instance of roundness: the property instances that are realised in an object are not simply all identical with the object itself. It is, therefore, perfectly possible for the instance of one property in a particular to be causally relevant and the instance of another to be causally idle: the ball rolls because it is round, not because it is red. What is true of objects as particulars is also true of events.

I made clear that what I was calling a law in this context was something that one could at best hope to find in a developed physics: a generalization that was not only 'law-like' and true, but was as deterministic as nature can be found to be, was free from caveats and *ceteris paribus* clauses; that could, therefore, be viewed as treating the universe as a closed system. I stressed that it was only laws of this kind (which I called 'strict laws') that I was arguing could not cover events when those events were described in the mental vocabulary. I allowed that there are not, and perhaps could not be expected to be, laws of this sort in the special sciences. Most, if not all, of the practical knowledge that we (or engineers, chemists, geneticists, geologists) have that allows us to explain and predict ordinary happenings does not involve strict laws. The best descriptions that we are able to give of most events are not descriptions that fall under, or will ever fall under, strict laws. (1993: 8–9)

What we have here is a residue of the positivist doctrine of the unity of science. Davidson does not believe that science need be unified in the strong sense, with all sciences nomologically reducible to physics, but he does believe that only physics (and, perhaps, consequently, those sciences that are strongly unified with physics – that is, reducible as in *story 2*) is the strict bearer of causal explanations. There are looser forms of causal explanation at higher levels, including the psychological, and so it becomes just as proper to explain causally human action by reference to human thought as it is, for example, to explain the destruction of a village by reference to the force of a hurricane, given that meteorology is not nomically reducible to physics. In neither the psychological nor meteorological cases are there strict causal explanations – nothing wholly deterministic or as probabilistic as nature allows – but there is what we intuitively recognise as causal explanation. If Davidson's theory allows our mental states to be causally on a par with hurricanes, it would not seem just to accuse him of epiphenomenalism. We shall see below why nobody had read him originally in this way.[6]

The second ground for the accusation of epiphenomenalism is also affected by the new interpretation of his theory, if not quite so obviously. The suggestion that the world would have followed just the same path if the mental had been absent only gets a hold if there is a possible world physically and nomically just like this without the mental. Denying the argument naturally involves, therefore, denying that there could be a world physically but not mentally like this. Davidson says that the mental

---

[6] Davidson's indignation in his (1993) at having been misunderstood is exceeded only by his critics' – Kim (1993a), McLaughlin (1993) and Sosa (1993) – incredulity at his protestations of injury. It seems to me that, apart from his blatantly misleading denial of 'nothing but' materialism, his (1970) is entirely consistent with his later interpretation; but his critics' misreading is entirely due to their having believed that he was saying something of relevance to avoiding reductionism as then found in the philosophy of mind. If I am correct, they flattered him in their error.

supervenes on the physical, in the sense that a mental difference presupposes a physical one, but seems to apply this only to the actual world. If there is a genuine absence of property reduction, it is difficult to see how it could apply to all worlds: though it might be a brute fact that the mental supervenes in a given world, it could hardly be a brute fact that it supervened in all – a rationale would be required. Token functionalism would provide such a rationale, but that is a form of reductionism in the sense of *story 1*. In fact Davidson requires the truth of some such theory as functionalism if the relation between psychology and physics is to be like that between physics and other sciences that are not reducible to it. Let us suppose that meteorology is such a science. There is no logically possible world which, at the level of physics, is just like one in which a hurricane is destroying a village, but in which there is not a hurricane destroying a village: the physics base is a priori sufficient. There is no need to invoke some *elusive* conception of supervenience here: in the broadest sense of 'logically possible', there is no possible world with the same physical base as the given one and no hurricane; the relation is one of entailment in the strongest sense. Also, the hurricane is strictly constituted by the things physics describes, and that is why there is no problem about attributing causal power to hurricanes. A hurricane is *nothing but* the action of physical particles, though talk about hurricanes is not nomically reducible to physics. It is because Davidson's readers took him to be claiming that mental properties are irreducible in a stronger sense than this that they feared he was in danger of epiphenomenalism.

The sophisticated reading of anomalous monism, which only becomes clear on reading 'Thinking Causes', is, therefore, as follows:

Strict causal laws only apply in physics and in those sciences – if any – nomically reducible to physics. All other special sciences – and that includes psychology – employ only loose causal explanations that depend on the potential availability of the tight account provided by physics. Psychology is irreducible just in the way that geology or meteorology is irreducible, and its properties are causally explanatory to a similar extent.

But this parallel with the other special sciences requires some such theory as token functionalism to preserve the conceptual sufficiency of the physical base that characterises the relation in those other cases. If this feature of the parallel with the other special sciences is lost, the monism is lost; mental properties lose the appropriate involvement in the causal explanatory network, for it becomes at least logically possible, in a broad sense, that the base be present without the higher properties. Hence the threat that a full-fledged property dualism leads to epiphenomenalism. There was no need for the long and ultimately fruitless literature on supervenience, or the attempt to dragoon Kripkean *de re* necessities into the mind-brain relation, both of which were meant to facilitate the combination of full-fledged property dualism with a dependence strong enough to frustrate the charge of epiphenomenalism; for such an impossible relation was never required by Davidson's programme.[7] It does not face the danger of epiphenomenalism for mental properties are not, in the image used above, independent flags at the same mast as physical properties; they are just high-level descriptions of the array of physically present signals. Davidson's supervenience is constituted by the anomolous logical sufficiency of physics. In his own limited post-positivist project, Davidson is quite successful. He shows how there can be different descriptions of the same subject matter that are not nomically related to each other, without this rendering any of them wholly otiose in causal explanations and without impugning the unity of the subject matter. This was not, however, perhaps generally controversial.

Davidson does nothing to show that this general model can plausibly be applied to the mental, for he does not discuss whether mental ascriptions can adequately be treated in the same way as meteorology – that is, whether admitting the logical sufficiency of the physical base entails too reductive an account of mentality.

Davidson concludes, in 'Thinking Causes'

[s]o if (non-reductive) supervenience is consistent ... so is A[nomolous] M[onism]. (5)

As the comparison with hurricanes shows, this is correct only if one restricts the sense of 'non-reductive' to that of *story 2*, and positively embraces reductionism in the sense of *story 1*.

6.5   Anomolousness and normativity

It might be thought surprising that I have said nothing about the famous 'normativeness' of mentalistic language, which is supposed, in Davidson's view, to be what marks it off from the physical. This notion was relevant and important whilst it seemed that it was what explained the anomolousness of the mental and thereby explained the divide between the mental and the physical. Once we realise, however, that all or most of the physical special sciences are also anomolous, then 'normativeness', however interesting a feature of the mental it is in its own right, is supererogatory as an explanation of the mental's anomolousness; it merely

---

[7] The fruitlessness of the literature on supervenience is, perhaps, crucially admitted by Kim (1993a). An instance of the attempt to employ Kripke is Peacocke (1979). For an attempt to show that this will not work, see Robinson (1982: 22–4).

gives an extra reason for the presence of a feature that would anyway be expected in a special science like psychology.

Near the beginning of 'Thinking Causes' Davidson says that his argument 'will involve some clarification, and *perhaps modification*, of the original thesis' (3, my italics). Davidson (1987) shows these modifications being brought about. At the beginning of 'Problems in the explanation of action' (1987) he says:

I hold that there is an irreducible difference between psychological explanations that involve the propositional attitudes and explanations in sciences like physics and physiology. (35)

It is natural to jump to the conclusion, on reading such a passage against the background of his earlier work, that this particular irreducible difference between psychology and *all* the physical sciences is what makes anomolous monism possible. That would lead one to assume that anomolous monism tracked the mental-physical divide, and so was itself special to the mental. It would not lead one to think that anomolous monism was relevant to the special sciences as a whole.

Further on in the same article, Davidson reinforces the impression that the crucial theoretical divide is that between the physical sciences as a whole and psychology.

The laws of many physical sciences are also not like the laws of physics, but I do not know of important theoretical (as opposed to practical) reasons why they cannot be reduced to the laws of physics. But there *is* a reason why psychological concepts like belief, desire, and intentional action, and the laws containing them, cannot be reduced to physical concepts and laws. (45)

The in-principle reducibility of the physical sciences seems here to be important, and to be inconsistent with what he says about the irreducibility of the special sciences in the passage from 'Thinking causes' quoted in the previous section. But even on the same page of 'Problems in the Explanation of Action' he appears to have undergone a change of mind.

Explanations in terms of the ultimate physics, though it answers to various interests, is not interests relative: it treats everything without exception as a cause of an event if it lies within physical reach ... Special sciences, or explanatory schemes, take note of more or less precise correlations between effects of certain kinds and far more limited causes of certain kinds. These correlations, of the sort we find in economics, geology, biology, aerodynamics and the explanation of action, depend on assumptions of other things being more or less equal – assumptions that cannot be made precise. (45)

He then admits:

In these remarks, I have made no distinction between a science like geology and the explanatory scheme of 'folk psychology'; the big distinction came between physics and the rest. If there is a distinction between reason-explanation and the rest, it must depend on some further feature of reason-explanations. (And of course there may be a significant sense in which geology, for instance, cannot be reduced to physics.) (46)

There are two fundamental divisions: that between physics and the rest of the special sciences, especially the physical ones; and that between all the physical sciences and psychology. Davidson seems to move from believing that the divide between physics and the other physical sciences can be crossed by the relation of in-principle reducibility, to believing that it cannot. He always affirms that psychology is irreducible to any physical science. If reduction were correct within the physical sciences, the only fundamental divide would be between psychology and the rest. But if the special sciences are not reducible to physics, there remain two fundamental divides, that between physics and the rest and that between psychology and the physical sciences. The crucial question is which of these divides is doing the work in Davidson's non-reductive physicalism. What feature of psychology is it that reconciles it with physicalism; is it a feature it shares with the other special sciences, or is it something special to the mental? Davidson himself does not seem sure on the matter, but if what reconciles it are the logical features of anomolous monism and if those features are present in all or most physical special sciences, then any further properties of the mental will be irrelevant to defending physicalism – psychology must bear the same relation in the relevant respects to the physical base as that in which the other special sciences stand.

The normativeness of the mental might be sufficient to show that it is irreducible and that it is anomolous, but it does not of itself show how the mental is reconcilable to monism.[8] That task can be performed either by means of the account of event identity which, on its own, left the theory open to the charge of epiphenomenalism: or by closely following the model of anomolous monism that applies to the other special sciences, which, we have seen, is reductive. Davidson's clarification-cum-modification of his theory consists in acknowledging more plainly that, if epiphenomenalism is to be avoided, monism must be achieved by the latter route.

Davidson admits that his view on reduction and the special sciences in general is no different from Fodor's. It transpires that his difference from Fodor on psychology in particular consists in the fact that he is less of a realist about folk psychology than is Fodor.

---

[8] Ralph Walker (1993), for example, uses the ineliminability of the normative functions of reason as a ground for rejecting physicalism.

Let me make clear that in my view that the mental is not an ontological but a conceptual category ... To say of an event ... that it is mental, is simply to say that we can describe it in a certain vocabulary – and the mark of that vocabulary is semantic intentionality. (1987: 46)

It cannot be much comfort to those who wish to see Davidson as propounding a 'soft' form of materialism, to learn that his non-reductiveness rest on a kind of non-realism about the mental that places him somewhere between Fodor and Dennett.

It seems clear that Davidson makes two distinctions. One concerns the difference between, the strictly nomological science of physics, and any other sciences, if any, that are reducible to it, and all other more or less anomalous modes of explanation, which may or may not include all the special sciences. The other concerns explanations as found in physical science and *normative* explanations, which are confined to mental discourse. One can hardly fail to notice that the latter corresponds to the notorious Sellars-inspired distinction between the 'space of causes' and the 'space of reasons'. It is this aspect of the irreducibility of the mental to the physical that is taken up by John McDowell and others, who develop a form of naturalism that eschews the label 'physicalism', even with the qualification 'non-reductive'.

6.6   Naturalism without physicalism ...? (i) McDowell

There are philosophers who describe themselves as being naturalists whilst denying that they are, in the normal sense, physicalists. They are, so to speak, one step more 'liberal' than non-reductive physicalists. We must investigate whether this approach is any more successful in accommodating the human perspective without falling into dualism. There is a great variety of philosophers making such a claim and it is not clear that they all have any one thing in common, beyond their affirmation that they are 'naturalists but not physicalists'. In the following two sections I shall concentrate on philosophers who find their inspiration for this position in the later Wittgenstein, supplemented, as they think, by Davidson. Prominent amongst these is John McDowell.

McDowell's version of 'naturalism without physicalism' rests on his doctrine of *second nature*. This is a tantalising notion and peculiarly hard to explain and engage with. McDowell starts from what he regards as an Aristotelian conception of the ethical as rational and develops the notion from there.

The point is clearly not restricted to ethics. Moulding ethical character, which includes imposing a specific shape on the practical intellect, is a particular case of a general phenomenon: initiation into conceptual capacities, which include responsiveness to other rational demands beyond those of ethics. Such initiation is a normal part of what it is for a human being to come to maturity, and that is why, although the structure of the space of reasons is alien to the layout of nature conceived as the realm of law, it does not take on the remoteness from the human that rampant Platonism envisages. If we generalize the way Aristotle conceives the moulding of ethical character, we arrive at the notion of having one's eyes opened to reasons at large by acquiring a second nature. I cannot think of a good short English expression for this, but it is what figures in German philosophy as *Bildung*. (1994: 84)

This account of second nature can be regarded as a theory, in the sense that it is an attempt to come to grips with and solve a problem, namely the relation between our physical nature and our psychological nature. (Or, maybe, between physical nature as a whole and psycho-social reality.) But this understanding naturally gives rise to a demand for an explanation, in something like detail, about how the relation between these two 'realms' works. McDowell firmly rejects the demand for such an explanation. In regretting his previous use of the term 'foothold' to suggest some kind of articulable link between the two, McDowell says:

I should have restricted myself to the obvious claim that the second-nature is no less natural than the first-nature. There was no need to offer to make a connection between them beyond their both being natural. (2008: 221)

Whilst, on the one hand, this is in a sense a natural response from one who believes in 'Wittgensteinian quietism', it is not obvious that it is acceptable. One can feel a somewhat *de haut en bas* implication that if you cannot just see that there is no problem here, you are a lost case, forever caught in the maze of language. But physics and chemistry are both parts of nature, and it is obviously necessary that there be some account of how the two fit together, even if this falls short of a classic reductionism. Why is this not so for the physical sciences in general and the psycho-social? The 'human animal' is, after all, for a naturalist like McDowell, one, albeit complex, thing.

McDowell does, however, seem to have a kind of transcendental argument in hand. In discussing his use of labels such as 'Aristotelian naturalism', 'Greek naturalism', 'naturalism of second nature', 'relaxed naturalism' and 'liberal naturalism' he says the following.

Now my use of these labels ... comes in contexts in which I am considering the plausibility of theses to the effect that some region of human life exemplifies free responsiveness to reasons, with such theses understood to imply that the characteristic phenomena of those parts of human life are beyond the reach of natural-scientific understanding. And the point of these labels is captured by this thought: by dint of exploiting, in an utterly intuitive way, ideas like that of the patterns characteristic of the life of animals of a certain kind, we can insist that such phenomena, even though they are beyond the reach of natural-scientific understanding, are perfectly real, without thereby relegating them to the sphere of the occult or supernatural. (2008: 217–18)

He goes on to say that he is not denying that some things may be genuinely supernatural:

But for my purposes it is enough to consider a position that, without necessarily ruling out supernatural phenomena altogether, holds that they had better not be taken to include phenomena that are biological, in the sense that they are characteristic of the lives of animals of our species. The point of my call for a relaxation is this: the fact that such phenomena are natural, in the sense of not being supernatural, provides no grounds for supposing that the conceptual apparatus that captures free responsiveness as such must be naturalizable, in any sense congenial to scientific naturalism. (218)

I call this a transcendental argument because it is roughly of this form.

(1) We know that human beings are just natural biological entities.
(2) We also know that we are free rational beings.
(3) And we know that rationality and freedom cannot be reduced, in any sense, to natural scientific processes.
(4) It follows from this that we, as living, rational human animals, possess a nature in addition to the nature that physical science explores.

This is presented as being 'utterly intuitive', but it entirely begs the question against the dualist. It is not intuitively obvious that the human capacity for abstract thought, and for aesthetic and spiritual inspiration are 'phenomena that are biological', especially when it is being specifically denied that they can be accommodated within the natural science of biology.

Again the suggestion is that it is some sort of howler to think that there is any sort of conflict in supposing these two natures to be in the same creature in a wholly 'naturalistic' way. But this ignores the fact that the intuition that there are features of human nature that cannot be put down to our nature as animals is very common through human history.

McDowell says of the 'sphere of the occult and supernatural' that it is

a region whose extent has shrunk for us with the advent of a modern scientific outlook, in the most extreme version of the outlook to nothing at all. (217)

This seems to be an attempt to have one's cake and eat it. On the one hand the 'modern scientific outlook' has led us to believe that there is nothing about the human being that is not, in some naturalistic sense, 'biological';

on the other hand biological science cannot accommodate the most typically human phenomena.

Perhaps it is not clear what McDowell would mean by 'naturalistic', nor by the contrasting categories of 'occult' and 'supernatural' – words seemingly used more for their emotive force, rather than with any exact sense. Does naturalism allow for what others would call 'property dualism', or even substance dualism, so long as there was no question of the 'immaterial' component being able to survive the body? Is it compatible with belief in the closure under physics of the behaviour of all physical elements? I think he believes that it is not compatible with the latter and he might simply regard the former as unhelpfully ideological and theoretical characterisations of the situation.

McDowell's refusal to explain himself, and his reliance on 'persuasive definition', mean that he throws little light on how the distinctively human characteristics he calls 'second nature' can be part of nature in the secular sense.

6.7   Naturalism without physicalism ...? (ii) Price and Rorty

There are others coming from a similar orientation to McDowell, who are not so reticent about developing their position. They are explicitly pragmatist and therefore closer to the scientistic paradigm and even want to attribute such a view to the later Wittgenstein. Rorty (2010), Horwich (2006) and Price (2004) are examples of this.

Price distinguishes between two kinds of naturalism, which he calls *object naturalism* and *subject naturalism*. The former is the standard naturalist view, which is that all there is, is the world as studied by science and all knowledge is scientific knowledge. It is represented by, for example, the naturalism of Armstrong, Lewis and Jackson. Subject naturalism is less familiar.

According to this second view, philosophy needs to begin with what science tells us *about ourselves*. Science tells us that we humans are natural creatures, and if the claims and ambitions of philosophy conflict with this view, then philosophy needs to give way. This is naturalism in the sense of Hume, then, and, arguably Nietzsche. (2004: 73)

Price endorses the *priority thesis*:

Subject naturalism is theoretically prior to object naturalism, because the latter depends on validation from a subject naturalist perspective. (74)

According to Price, the problem for object naturalism is to find a way of coping with various recalcitrant phenomena within the framework of 'the world-as-studied-by-science'. He twice gives a list of such problems, which may seem to differ only by a natural abbreviation. They are as follows.

Common candidates [for 'hard problems' for the object naturalist] include meaning, value, mathematical truth, causation and physical modality, and various aspects of mentality . . . (73)

This is invoked later.

How are we to place moral facts, mathematical facts, meaning facts, and so on? (74)

Price's solution is radical. It is a mistake to think that when we worry about these things, we are worrying about *things* of a certain sort which we know from experience are there. This is the *material conception* of the problems. The alternative is the *linguistic conception*, according to which the issue concerns coming to understand how we use the term 'X' in the language, not where some object, X, fits into our ontology. So we concentrate on how the 'natural subject' deals with these topics of discourse, not where their supposed subject matter fits into a scientific ontology.

This is where Price's abbreviation of his list becomes salient, for what has gone missing is 'various aspects of mentality'. Perhaps some aspects of mentality – intentionality, for example – are as plausible as candidates for the linguistic treatment as the other things he mentions (which does not mean very plausible). But to claim that the 'hard problem' of sensations and consciousness can be treated by means of the 'linguistic conception' has no plausibility whatsoever. Perhaps it is no coincidence that none of 'consciousness', 'sensation' or 'hard problem' occurs in the index of Price's *Naturalism without Mirrors* (2011). A form of quasi-realism might stand a chance for modality or morals, but is hard to see how it can work for consciousness.

Rorty, in his defence of 'quietism', is more direct than Price and has no reservations.

For the subject naturalist, the import of Price's dictum that 'we are natural creatures in a natural environment' is that we should be wary of drawing lines between kinds of organisms in non-behavioral and non-physiological terms. This means that we should not use terms such as 'intentionality', or 'consciousness', or 'representation' unless we can specify, at least roughly, what sort of behavior suffices to show the presence of the reference of these terms.

For example, if we want to say . . . that there is something it is like to be a bat but nothing it is like to be an earthworm . . . we should be prepared to explain how we can tell – to specify what behavioral or physiological facts are relevant to the claim [otherwise] we are inventing spooks to make jobs for ghost-busters. (2010: 61–2)

Facing the suggestion that this 'emphasis on behavioral criteria is reminiscent of the positivists verificationism', he says that it is not a product of a general theory of meaning but an insistence that

rather the traditional philosophical distinctions complicate narratives of biological evolution to no good purpose. (62)

If quietists of this type have abandoned the metaphysical imperialism of scientism, they have adopted instead a cultural imperialism for science. But the linguistic conception cannot explain away 'second nature' for a further reason, namely that it presupposes it. To regard something as a language rather than as just a series of sounds and marks already sets it into a human context. Calling it 'linguistic *behavior*' does not somehow reconcile the fact that the words are just physical noises with their meaningfulness.

Rorty, of course, was one of the original eliminativists about sensations, claiming that he did not want to fight again battles that Wittgenstein had already won (1965–6: 40). If acceptance of the anti-private language argument is the price that one must pay for quietism in the philosophy of mind, then I would happily let others pay it!

One can, I think, be confident that McDowell does not want to go down the same road as Price and Rorty – even if he is sympathetic to the anti-private language argument – for their strategy is, indeed, to try to explain how the two natures are reconciled; but without some such effort I can see no reason to think that 'quietism' offers any enlightenment about how to accommodate the distinctly human features into a recognisable naturalism.

6.8   The root of the problem

In this chapter I have been investigating various attempts to be naturalist whilst disowning the label 'physicalist'. I began by looking at Davidson, who is generally classified as a non-reductive *physicalist,* but his rather confusing gestures against reduction lead finally to an emphasis on the irreducibility of the rational, and, hence, normative, dimension of human psychology. McDowell took this up and combined it with a mixture of Wittgensteinian quietism and the Sellarsian distinction between the 'space of causes and the space of reasons'. McDowell was too unwilling to explain how these two are related, but, drawing on American pragmatism, Price and Rorty developed analyses that are broadly reductionist, but in an unconventional way.

In a sense, the key modern figure behind these developments is Quine, in the shape of his attempt to combine pragmatism and scientific realism.

The human perspective – which for Quine, like Davidson, seems to mean propositional attitude states – is pragmatically necessary but not part of our ontology, which is restricted to more exact phenomena, which means the ontologies of physics, and formal first order logic. The pragmatic necessity is not *pro tem*, until we get a more complete science, but will, I think, always be required.

Why, if their ontologies are strictly not correct, should the non-fundamental perspectives be essential?

One response to this question is *eliminativism*. Quine's downgrading of the human dimension might lead a physicalist simply to scrap the human perspective – and the special sciences altogether. Or, rather, to say that they are only needed until we have a more complete fundamental theory. But this is hopeless. It means that I have never actually worried about the validity of the ontological argument or the problem of free will, or wondered whether I was about to get flu. And still, the theory of physics remains a theory held by a thinking subject. Perhaps all physicalists are forced to eliminativism, but that would only show how self-refuting physicalism is.

Quine is not strictly eliminativist, I think, because he believes that the way the human senses and faculties operate condemns us to reacting at a certain level of approximation, so we cannot help but spontaneously operate at levels that lack scientific accuracy. He does not make Churchland's mistake of thinking that what we perceive is a function simply of what theory we use to report our experiences, rather than of the actual sensitivity of our senses. So we can never abandon our strictly inaccurate theories. An analogy might be the following. Our colour perception does not map objective differences in objects, but no amount of learning the difference between reflected and illuminated red will enable us to see them as different.

Quine does not talk much about these issues – the mind-body problem seems hardly to figure explicitly in his writings. It is Dennett who develops the pragmatic angle of Quine's thought on this subject. But even to see our ordinary concepts as the product of our senses involves taking the subject's perspective as fundamental. (I shall be arguing in Chapter 13 that Dennett's attempt to reconcile the human perspective with physicalism fails.)

Nevertheless, even McDowell's theory is located with respect to Quine's. This should be less surprising if one sees Davidson as the bridge. One can see McDowell as saying that, if the human level is unavoidable, then it must be part of nature and leave it at that. One might even risk the following seemingly bizarre thought, namely that, putting aside the question of closure under physics, McDowell and Quine more or less agree.

They both hold that the human perspective is an essential feature of our existence as biological creatures, that it cannot be reduced to 'hard' science and that this has no 'supernatural' consequences and can be accepted without qualms. The difference is more or less entirely one of tone – whether one talks 'scientistically' or not. Price and Rorty, though not 'object naturalists' as Quine probably is, are more blatantly scientistic than McDowell, and might be thought to bridge the gap between McDowell and Quine.

6.9   Conclusion

The theme of this chapter has been 'naturalism without physicalism'. I believe that I have shown at least four things.

  (i) Although Davidson is usually seen as the source of this development, once one has clarified the sense of the term 'non-reductive', Davidson is barely a non-physicalist and could, for most purposes, be a functionalist.
 (ii) McDowell follows up from Davidson's rather enigmatic appeal to 'normativity', and ties it to a certain Wittgensteinian spirit of philosophical 'quietism', but fails to explain how the doctrine of second nature that is the product can be any sort of naturalism.
(iii) Price and Rorty stress the pragmatism that comes from a Quinean foundation, and thereby give a scientistic twist – but a social scientistic one – to the move away from the dominance of physics.
 (iv) Quine can be seen as a unifying factor in all the above cases, surprisingly even in the case of McDowell.

But it seems that the attempt to free naturalism from the toils of science, whether pursued along the lines originally imagined by Davidson or following the somewhat later emphasis on normativity, fails to deliver anything clear enough to be convincing.

7 Mysterianism, neutral monism and panpsychism

7.1 The mysterian option

The argument so far seems to lead to the conclusion that, as far as we can tell, phenomenal properties cannot be accommodated within a physicalist or naturalist framework. There are two obvious responses to this predicament. One is to accept that there are radically emergent mental properties, and so to become a property dualist. Another is to say that our current understanding of the physical is seriously defective: if it were not so defective, we could see how the physical could be responsible for consciousness. This chapter is concerned with the latter option.

First, I will allude briefly to the rationale for preferring this option over the other – briefly because it will be considered in more detail later. Galen Strawson (2007) argues that emergence is a bizarre and ad hoc idea. He thinks that it rests on a too radical understanding of the Humean idea that causation is a contingent relation. Causation in physical nature does not involve an 'explanatory gap'. (We have seen already in Section 5.7 that those, like Searle, and Block and Stalnaker, who think emergence pervades nature are probably wrong.) So any naturalist who does not want to invoke a kind of *deus ex machina* in his explanation of consciousness must be able to explain why it is a defect in our current understanding of nature that prevents us from understanding how it gives rise to conscious phenomena.

If one accepts this rejection of emergence, then one has two options. One is to accept that the mental is, not emergent, but imposed from outside. This is the traditional Christian doctrine of the infusion of the soul. The philosophers we are considering are not inclined to accept such a supernatural theory. Operating within a naturalist framework, then one only has the other option, namely that consciousness is produced by the physical base, in some way that we are not currently able to understand, but which, if we could understand it, we would see not to be radically emergent.

The question then is why we are not currently able to understand how this 'emergence' works. Nagel suggested in his (1974) that we need a conceptual breakthrough in order to understand this, but it is difficult to see how something analogous to the conceptual revisions that gave rise to relativity theory or quantum theory would work here. We will be looking at problems with this when we discuss Stoljar's 'explanation from ignorance'. More radically, McGinn suggested that we are so constituted that we will never be able to understand it. He puts it as follows:

The [mind-body] problem arises, I want to suggest, because we are cut off by our very cognitive constitution from achieving a conception of that natural property of the brain (or of consciousness) that accounts for our physical link. This is a kind of causal nexus that we are precluded from ever understanding, given the way we have to form our concepts and develop our theories. No wonder we find the problem so difficult! (1989: 150)

This idea of cognitive closure could take either of two possible forms. They might be described as *failure of intelligence* and *failure of sensibility*. On the former our intellectual apparatus is such that we cannot see how the connection is made: the failure is entirely on our side and is a matter of our brains not being constructed in a way that enables them to cope with this problem. McGinn argues that any apparatus that has evolved and is physical must have cognitive limitations and be able to cope only with those issues for which evolution has suited it. The other explanation of our cognitive failure places the responsibility on some to us undetectable feature of matter. We are insensitive to this feature in a way that is analogous to our inability to know what it is like to be a bat experiencing echo-location. This is not a failure of intellectual processing or intellectual imagination as such.

The difference between these two kinds of incapacity can be illustrated as follows. If our failure were entirely due to the cognitive closure of our intellectual apparatus, the following might be the case. The physical world does indeed consist of Newtonian atoms and their activity does indeed explain the presence of consciousness, *but we are just incapable of seeing how this can be so.* A creature differently constructed from us might see no problem in this. On the second account, however, we are right to think that Newtonian atoms could not explain consciousness, *so matter must possess more mysterious properties that do not show in our scientific investigations.*

This is a distinction which McGinn does not seem to notice, citing both kinds of consideration indifferently. He definitely thinks that Newtonian atoms could not do the job, whilst failing to see that, if his claim about the closure of our cognitive capacities were correct, he has no right to be confident about this; it might be that we are 'programmed' in such a way as to be unable to work out the connection. (One might suspect that the fact that he feels the need to call on the hidden property line shows that simple cognitive closure does not ring true.)

Let us look at these two different explanations of our inadequacy.

There are two kinds of argument for thinking that we might – or must – be cognitively closed in the intellectual sense for some problems. One is an argument from analogy, the other from certain physicalist assumptions.

The analogy is as follows. We know that we can think and solve problems that other animals cannot, and that some humans can solve problems – in higher mathematics, for example – that others cannot. Similarly, humans as a group might lack the kind or degree of intelligence required to solve the mind-body problem.

The physicalist argument is as follows. The brain is a physical object which has evolved, and is a kind of computer. All computational systems have limitations – as, in a sense, Godel showed. And anything that has evolved will have developed to deal with certain kinds of problem, and will be blind to others. So, on both counts – computation and evolution – we must expect to be cognitively closed to certain issues.

There are two kinds of reason for being uncomfortable with these arguments. First, and more general, the position they defend seems too indefinite. It is a kind of secular 'God of the gaps' argument – whenever we seem unable over time to solve a problem, our failure can be explained in this way. McGinn does, indeed, suggest that the fact that philosophical problems seem never to be solved is to be explained by the fact that our cognitive apparatus is unsuited to seeing the answers to philosophical problems in general (McGinn 1993). As McGinn is quite aware, this might look like preferring theft over honest toil. Why should evolution have left us bereft over the mind-body problem and yet allowed us to understand (in a certain sense) quantum theory, evolution and relativity? Surely, having a good grasp on how our physical and mental natures relate would be just as useful from an evolutionary point of view as many of the other things we can do. So there seems to be a certain arbitrariness in invoking cognitive closure on this issue. The generality of the hypothesis and the fact that it is difficult to see how one might refute it conclusively, short of solving the mind-body problem, make the cognitive closure argument difficult to discuss in detail.

Second, the specific reasons given are not as clearly sound as they might seem. Differences between ability in different humans seem to relate to kinds of complexity in the problems, but it does not seem that seeing through the mind-body problem is like the complexity of a calculation – it is not *too difficult* in that kind of way. It seems much more a matter of principle, not degree. (This point, too, will be developed when we discuss Stoljar.) In the case of animals, it is not obvious that they *understand* things in the sense in which we do. In other words, it seems to be a difference of kind, not degree. This, of course, is not an issue that I can pursue seriously here.

The argument from evolution and computation would lead us into a discussion of the nature of thought, and, again, I cannot pursue that properly here. I have argued in Robinson (2010) that, though the computational model would make the human mind into what Dennett (e.g. 1987a: 61) calls a syntactic engine, this account is not plausible. If we are not syntactic engines then it is not obvious that limitations intrinsic to computing apply to human reason. But putting that issue aside, it is an empirical fact that there is no neat tie between the reasons why something evolved and what one can do with it. Hands probably evolved to help our ancestors pick fruit and swing in trees, but we now use then for a range of activities – like writing on a word processor – that have no connection with that. Once some kind of general intelligence evolved (if it did), there would be no obvious limits on what one can do with it.

McGinn does have a general theory to explain our failure, in the form of an analogy. It is that our minds are at home with what he calls CALM – combinatorial atomism with law-like mappings (1993: 18–20). Integrating the non-spatial mind into this framework is beyond our capacity. But this is surely too simple. It is true that atomism of the kind he has in mind does seem to us to be especially clear and easy to systematise, but the suggestion that anything that falls outside it is beyond our reach does not seem to do credit to all the non-atomistic conceptions of the world that have been entertained. People who understand advanced physics are at home with a conception of the world as a quantum field, but this does not make the mind-body problem seem to go away for them.

I think that, in practice, the discussion has focused on our ignorance of some kind of 'hidden variable' in matter and not on our more systematic cognitive closure. The best focused discussion of this is to be found in Stoljar (2006).

7.2 The appeal to ignorance

Daniel Stoljar (2006) starts from the Russellian position that there is something about the nature of matter that current science cannot tell us and of which we are ignorant. He does not claim, as Russell (1927) does, that this gap is filled by the qualities revealed in experience: we are just ignorant of what this underlying feature is. He believes that this appeal to ignorance is more plausible than reifying our ignorance into dualism.

Stoljar recognises that the main opposition to the suggestion that we are simply ignorant of what it is about matter that enables it to produce consciousness comes from the conviction that, to be physical, a feature must be objective – equally available to anyone – and that no such feature could explain subjectivity – features available in a special way only to the subject who has them (153–62). The crucial part of his positive argument, therefore, consists in his attempt to show that this divide can, in principle, be crossed. He has a two-pronged argument for this conclusion.

First, Stoljar argues by counterexamples (157ff). He argues that

(i) John is in pain

is a subjective statement, and that, therefore

(ii) John is not in pain

is also subjective because it 'contains the same constituents' as (i). Moreover

(iii) John is a number

is an objective statement, but it is true that

(iv) if John is a number then John is not in pain

is a true entailment. So statements with objective subject matter can entail statements with subjective subject matter.

The initial reaction to this line of argument is to be suspicious of the way it deploys negatives. The fact that certain categories necessarily exclude each other seems not to throw light on how or whether they might positively entail each other. This suspicion is correct, for this negative strategy, if sound, would prove far too much. It is true that

(vi) if seven is a number then it is not spatially extended

It would be strange, however, to take these propositions as giving any kind of support to the hypotheses that there might be a feature of abstract objects of which we are currently ignorant which could explain how some or all of them might actually possess, or have possessed, spatial or other physical properties.

What this shows is that entailments of exclusion do not throw light on the possibility of positive entailments. So Stoljar's mistake is to treat 'John is not in pain' as a subjective statement because it 'contains the same constituents' as 'John is in pain'. But the negatives are quite different between the cases where 'John' is the kind of thing that could be in pain, and where he happens not to be, and where he is the kind of thing to which it could not apply because he is not capable of having subjective states – for example, if he is a number. In the first case it is a statement about John's subjective condition; in the second it is not, because he cannot have subjective conditions at all.

Stoljar, therefore, in my opinion, fails to vindicate materialism by an appeal to our ignorance.

7.3   A general objection to the 'hidden property' approach

There is a general problem with the 'hidden property' theory which applies, I think, to the theories of both Stoljar and McGinn. Our scientific knowledge seems to be adequate for fine-tuning the operations of matter to a remarkable degree. We can work out how to send a rocket to a distant planet so that its exact trajectory and detailed operations can be minutely planned. If there were a property in matter that we could not detect and that was not inert, surely we would find that this property, for which we could not allow, would function, at least sometime, as a spanner in the works and throw our calculations out.

There is a paradox here. If the hidden property did 'interfere' with the operations that science seemed to predict, then it would no longer be hidden. But if it does not, then in what sense is it a physical property? One possible answer to this is that it is somehow responsible for the powers and dispositional properties of the object – not just in the sense that it is their logical owner and subject, but in the further sense that its nature some-how determines the causal properties. How such a notion would work is a mystery, especially if one has a Humean view of laws of nature. This is a problem facing all 'qualitative core' theories, whether or not they are deployed, as in neutral monism, to solve the mind-body problem. It concerns the relation between the core and the dispositional properties of matter, which, I said above, it 'lies behind'. Apart from the role of being 'owner' of these dispositions, does it in any substantive sense *explain* them? On one picture, the cores could be swapped around, like an inverted colour spectrum, and it would make no difference to the causal powers. On the other, the nature of the core explains what the causal powers are: it is because electrons have the core they do that they have a negative charge. Presumably positrons have the same (but smaller) core as a proton. But could there be a monadic property that, from its nature, necessitated all the causal properties of an electron – its mass, its charge, its spin? This seems to be a total mystery and so the idea that a core might have any serious explanatory value seems to be an illusion.

Whether or not it somehow grounds the causal properties of the atoms, the only way in which its effects would be recognisably present to us would be in its producing consciousness. This pushes us directly to Russell's neutral monism: what we must be missing is something intrinsic to matter but not the kind of causal property onto which science can latch. It is most economic to think of it as an intrinsic qualitative nature which, in some sense, 'lies behind' the causal properties that science uncovers and which manifests itself in – or as – consciousness. Perhaps it could be a property that *causes* consciousness, rather than *constituting* it, but then the question would be why its causal influence was not felt elsewhere, but how it might do this would be no less mysterious than for any other physical property, unless it were itself a form of consciousness. Surely it is better to follow Russell and his modern heirs and make it to be what constitutes consciousness, rather than what causes it.

7.4   Russell and neutral monism

Neutral monism and panpsychism agree with mysterianism and ignorance theory that our scientific concept of matter misses out on a vital feature, which is the one that explains the existence of consciousness. But they do not think we are fundamentally ignorant of its nature – indeed, we are very directly acquainted with it, because it is the realm of qualities that appear in experience. This idea originates with Russell (1927), and is followed up by Maxwell (1978), Lockwood (1989),Galen Strawson (2006; 2007) and Chalmers (2003). These philosophers all agree that the scientific conception of matter is too abstract to accommodate consciousness and it must be augmented by adding phenomenal qualities.

Chalmers states this position as follows.

Russell pointed out that physics characterizes physical entities and properties by their relations to one another and to us. For example, a quark is characterized by its relation to other physical entities, and a property such as mass is characterized by an associated dispositional role, such as the tendency to resist acceleration. At the same time, physics says nothing about the intrinsic nature of these entities and properties. Where we have relations and dispositions, we expect some underlying intrinsic properties that ground the dispositions, characterizing the entities that stand in these relations. But physics is silent about the intrinsic nature of a quark, or about the intrinsic properties that play the role associated with mass. So this is one metaphysical problem: what are the intrinsic properties of fundamental physical systems?

At the same time, there is another metaphysical problem: how can phenomenal properties be integrated with the physical world? Phenomenal properties seem to be intrinsic properties that are hard to fit in with the structural/dynamic character of physical theory; and arguably, they are the only intrinsic properties of which we have direct knowledge. Russell's insight was that we might solve both these problems at once. Perhaps the intrinsic properties of the physical world are themselves phenomenal properties. Or perhaps the intrinsic properties of the physical world are not phenomenal properties, but nevertheless constitute phenomenal properties: that is, they are protophenomenal properties. If so, then consciousness and physical reality are deeply intertwined. (2003: 130)

I shall argue in Chapter 8 that what the knowledge argument shows was that the scientific conception of matter has no role for qualities at all. It is worth pausing and considering the varied roles qualities might be thought of as playing in our conception of the physical world.

7.5   How qualities might be thought of as complementing the scientific conception of matter

There are five ways in which it might be thought that quality is needed to augment science.

(i) I will argue in Chapter 8 that, without the special role of quality there could be no common sense or manifest image conception of the world, either in its primary or in its secondary quality aspects, and without this there could be no scientific image either. There could be no science without perception, no perception without sensible qualities and no grasp on them without qualia, which we have shown to be irreducible; so even if there need have been no qualitative content in the sub-atomic world (as (iii) and (iv) below insists there must) quality must figure irreducibly in the world of experience. Development of this argument must wait for the next chapter.

(ii) Quite apart from the manifest image, our conception of the scientific world must include quality in its spatial properties. We might think we proceed as follows. We form a mental picture of the web of causal powers that constitute the standard physicalist picture by imagining lines of influence and force similar to those by which we characterise a magnetic field. Then ask ourselves whether this requires supplementing by qualities, as argued in (iii) and (iv) below. But the pure causal web is imagined in a (visual) qualitative space, even if it is imagined as an ontology of pure powers. In other words, quality comes in not just as a feature of the common sense objects in space, but as an essential feature of the spatial medium itself, even in the scientific image. Space cannot be realistically conceived as purely mathematical, even in a world of pure energy and fields.[1]

These first two appeals to irreducible quality are concerned with our conception of the macro, not the micro, world. The post-Russellian tradition is mainly concerned with the role of quality at the micro level and how it can be deployed in the philosophy of mind.

---

[1] For a demonstration of this, see Foster (1982).

(iii) Some philosophers, such as Armstrong (1997) and Foster (2008: 71ff), have held that dispositional states must have categorical owners or bases: dispositions and powers are not self-standing entities. As science uncovers only structural and causal properties, these must be owned by something with further categorical properties which must be intrinsic to the objects, and, in that sense, quality-like.

(iv) The scientific account seems to construct the world from powers – forces, fields and energy – and there is a dispute about whether a world that consists purely of powers is incoherent. Those who claim that it is, argue that powers to produce powers to produce powers ... *ad infinitum,* constitute a vicious regress. The point here is not that powers must be *owned* by something categorical – pure unowned powers or fields may be a possibility, according to this objection – but that they must, ultimately, result in some effect that is categorical. Again, the only clear candidate for this is something qualitative.[2]

(v) The neutral monist or type-*F* materialist project is to appeal to the qualitative nature of matter as a way of explaining the qualitative content of consciousness. In the world of consciousness, we are simply aware of the intrinsic qualitative nature of our brains, which science, as essentially the view from the outside of mere structural and relational properties, cannot reveal.

I am not convinced of the force of (iii) – maybe there can be unowned powers – but the necessity for qualities as specified in (i), (ii) and (iv) seem to me to be conclusive, though I do not claim to have proved that here. But it is (v) which matters for the philosophy of mind. The crucial issue in the philosophy of mind is whether the appeal to qualities deployed in any of (i) to (iv), which all purport to be, in some broad sense, features of the physical world, can be deployed in the articulation of a modified kind of materialism, which can be used to solve the mind-body problem.

I do not think that anyone would suggest that the possession of a qualitative nature by space could, on its own, at least, contribute to an analysis of the phenomenology of experience: so (ii) is not central to the issue. The qualitative nature of the manifest world is taken by some direct realists as helping to dissolve the mind-body problem: if the new quality Mary experiences when she leaves her room is a feature of the external world, then it is not an internal constituent of her mental state and so does not count against that state's being physical. This, as a strategy for reconciling experience and materialism, faces three problems. The first concerns the problematic nature of attributing secondary qualities to matter as intrinsic, mind-independent features. The second concerns the plausibility of direct realism, especially when charged with the task of being deployed to cope with *all* the kinds of qualities that we perceive and not just the obviously perceptual ones. Discussion of these two points would take me too far afield from the present

---

[2] The dispute about the powers conception of reality has a growing literature. Examples are: Robinson (1982: 108–23; 2009a), Foster (1982), Blackburn (1990) and Molnar (2003).

discussion.[3] The third difficulty is that direct realism of the kind being countenanced here is surely not a materialist theory. The relation between the perceiving subject and the objects and qualities he perceives would have to be a *sui generis* relation of awareness and this is not part of a materialist ontology. Any attempt to replace this relation with something materialistically acceptable – say, some kind of purely causal relation – would leave one with a reductive account of experience: that is, if being aware of an external quality simply consists in the quality physically causing some physical process in the brain, that would seem to render the presence of the quality phenomenologically irrelevant. If A causes B in a normal physical way, the nature of B is independent of A, in the sense that B would be as it is whether or not it was A that produced it, or something else, or it just happened randomly. It is difficult to see how mere causal dependence of a brain state on some external feature could, per se, constitute the kind of awareness postulated by direct realism of that external feature.

It is not surprising, therefore, that it is the imputation of qualities to micro matter, as in (iii) and (iv), that has played a part in attempts to state type-*F* materialism.

There are at least four problems with this type-*F* or neutral monist strategy, the fourth of which has not, as far as I can tell, received serious discussion.[4] They are as follows. (i) How is one to move from the attribution of *quality* to matter, to endowing it with phenomenal *consciousness*? (ii) One must try to find a plausible account of what qualities or proto-qualities (or phenomenal qualities or proto-phenomenal qualities) can be attributed to the elementary constituents of matter. (iii) How can one account for the unity of consciousness on the basis of the phenomenal/qualitative core of individual particles or events? The neglected one is: (iv) More and more anti-reductionists seem to think that intellectual consciousness – states of conscious thinking – in addition to sensory-type experiences are irreducible. How can one apply the type-*F* strategy to these?

(i)   From quality to consciousness

At first sight, there would seem to be no reason why a qualitative core to atoms should provide any explanation of how consciousness emerges. Some defenders of neutral monism, for example Galen Strawson, try to solve the consciousness problem by adopting panpsychism. It is noteworthy, however, that earlier protagonists, such as Russell and Lockwood, thought that they could avoid compromising their

---

[3] They are discussed in Robinson (1994).
[4] This was true, I think, when the article on which this part of the chapter is based was first published, but Nagel (2012) now raises the same problem.

physicalism in this way. For Russell, the qualities themselves are equivalent to the contents of *unconscious* mental states, and consciousness of them is given something close to a behavioural analysis.

> A percept differs from another mental state, I should say, only in the nature of its causal relations to an external stimulus. 'Unconscious' mental states will be events compresent with other mental states, but not having the effects which constitute what is called the awareness of a mental state. (1927: 385)

Consciousness is, in effect, quality plus appropriate effect on behaviour. If one is not satisfied with this account of awareness, the problem of consciousness remains a major one.

Lockwood is not so behaviouristic, but his original account of awareness seems to end up having, in its application of the concept of topic neutrality to consciousness, more in common with Smart or Armstrong than one might expect from a neutral monist.

> To the extent that we have a transparent grasp on the concepts that we bring to bear on our mental lives, those concepts may be seen as capturing certain intrinsic attributes of brain states. To the extent, however, that they are topic neutral, they represent no obstacle to an identity theory anyway. Moreover, *this goes for the concept of awareness itself.* For it seems to me that we cannot be said to have a transparent conception of awareness ... If that is right, then it follows that there can be nothing in our concept of awareness, such as it is, that could debar us from identifying awareness with some kind of physical process in the brain – albeit that it remains profoundly mysterious, in physical terms, what form such a process could possibly take. (1989: 169)

These are strange remarks. If our grasp on awareness is really topic neutral, then it could be identical with any physical state that performs the right role. We may be ignorant of this but there is no reason why its nature should be 'profoundly mysterious'. Like many other philosophers, Lockwood seems to be confusing the fact that awareness is a simple, unanalysable and *transparent* relation, with the idea that our concept is an empty one, waiting to be filled by some scientific theory. If the latter were true, then one could have a straightforwardly reductive account of mind, of a broadly causal or functionalist kind.

As Chalmers points out in the quotation above, neutral monism tries to kill two birds with one stone. A crucial gap is detected in our concept of matter, and this is remedied by deploying the concept of quality that derives from our ordinary experience to fill this gap. By importing these qualities, which might be thought of as qualia, the hope is to endow matter with the resources for generating experience. But if the qualitative element is genuinely neutral between mental and physical – 'merely qualitative' – then there is no explanation of how or why this should result in conscious states: we do not think of a red patch as being per se conscious. If one is to build the consciousness into the qualitative element that one is importing into the matter, then one has lost the neutrality and moved over to a panpsychism, which makes the core of matter at least minimally conscious. Russell and Lockwood seem to want to avoid doing that, but instead seem to end up with an account of consciousness which is somewhere between straightforwardly reductive and elusive. The source of the idea that the distinction between quality and consciousness can be blurred is, of course, Hume. The hope is that impressions are sufficiently phenomenal to be the building blocks for mind, without this phenomenality presupposing mentality as a principle in addition to their qualitative content. It is fairly clear, I think, that this cannot be done.

(ii)   *Imputing (phenomenal) qualities to the fundamental constituents of matter*

There are two ways of categorising the fundamental constituents of matter. The most natural is to treat them as objects of certain kinds – protons, electrons, quarks, gluons, etc. These objects would have to have a qualitative core. The crudest version of this theory would think of these particles as consisting of little patches of colour, or of sounds, itches etc., with these conceived of as not simply physical qualities but phenomenal or proto-phenomenal. The other option is to follow Russell and Maxwell in regarding these so-called particles as names for groups of pure events. Maxwell thinks that the latter option is the only one that makes sense.

If C-fiber activity is thought of as consisting of threadlike pieces of matter ... waving around and perhaps stroking each other, then any attempt to identify such activity with pain (as felt in all its excruciating immediacy) does become patently absurd. However, if we recognize that C-fiber activity is a complex causal network in which at least some of the events are pure events and that neurophysiology, physics, chemistry etc., provide us *only* with the *causal structure* of the network, the way is left open for the neuropsychologist to theorize that some of the events in the network *just are pains* (in all their qualitative, experiential, mentalistic richness). (1978: 386)

Maxwell does not explain why he thinks that the event ontology is so much more amenable to his theory, but one might imagine the reasons to be as follows. Pains are occurrent events, but C-fibres or complex brain states endure no doubt for a long time. If the pain is identical with the qualitative nature of the constituents of the fibres or cells, which over-whelmingly remain the constituents whether activated or not, why is the sensation not there for just as long? But it is not clear that an event ontology really gets round the problem. A brain process is, from the perspective of the sub-atomic, a massive and complex event. The pain must be a compound from the qualitative natures of the micro events that go up to compose it. But the ontology of particles cannot simply be ignored. Such things according to Russell, who has a basic ontology of events alone, must be compounds of events. The theory is not that it is a *mistake* to say that there are electrons, photons etc., but that such things are constructed from events. If we think of an electron that endures from t^1 to t^n as constituted by events e^1 to e^n, then one might assume that, as the electron remains the same electron, its intrinsic nature does not change. Indeed, one might expect all electrons to have the similar intrinsic natures. In this case there will have to be a consistency in the intrinsic nature of the events that compose it. But given the relatively small number of different kinds of fundamental particles (particle event-kinds) there seem to be, it would seem to be mystery how one could produce so many different kinds of experience by combining so few elements. The alternative appears to be that the qualitative nature of elementary particles – whether or not constructed from events – changes according to the nature of the large-scale causal net into which they are placed, and even though their causal contribution does not (electrons have always the same mass, the same charge, etc.). This would seem to be a very strange top-down phenomenon, as the intrinsic nature of, e.g., electrons (electron events) change according to the complex of which they are parts.

It is difficult to avoid the suspicion, from reading the passage quoted above from Maxwell, that he thinks of the pain event as a primitive, not something constructed from more primitive events ('some of the events in the network *just are pains*').[5] The same is true about Russell's statement that in experience one is perceiving the inside of one's own head, as if the qualitative content of our sense data was what constituted the matter. It is as if the qualitative content entered on the scale of brain parts and processes, not on the scale of the smallest constituents of matter. There is, I suspect, an empiricist impulse to crunch together a phenomenalist and a physical realist conception of the world, without paying enough attention to the fundamental problems with this project. The introduction of the term 'protophenomenal' to characterise the qualitative nature of the elementary

---

[5] Maxwell remarks that perhaps it is 'this "middle sized" realm that provides the relevant context for investigation of mind-brain identities' (1978: 399). Lockwood takes this as suggesting that the neutral monism only applies at a relatively macroscopic level, and shows that such a theory is no different from a standard sort of emergence. (Lockwood 1993: 280–1).

particles seems to be a gesture towards solving this problem, but to succeed only in being a label for it, more than an articulate solution. It amounts to no more than the suggestion that there must be something such that, if you get enough of it, you get a real experience, whilst hiding from the question of whether this involves moving from the non-experiential to the experiential. It is very difficult to form a conception of the consciousness of an earthworm – indeed to decide whether or not one can ascribe consciousness to it at all. What meaningful minimal consciousness-involving content is to be ascribed to a quark, or to one of the events that, as a group, constitute a quark?

(iii)   The problem of the unity of experience

On any type-*F* materialist strategy, the qualities which are supposed, in the end, to explain consciousness, belong to the most elementary particles or events. When they do constitute consciousness they are bound together in unified sense-fields and in total cross-media consciousness. How are we to explain this unity by reference to the phenomenal core of the individual elements? Notice that this is not the so-called grain problem, which is concerned with why a smooth and continuous consciousness should emerge from particles that are spatially distant from each other. The implication of the grain problem is that we should expect consciousness to be 'grainy' – a crude picture full of holes, gaps and blanks. What I have called 'the unity problem' is the problem of explaining why there should be an overall picture at all, of whatever quality. This puzzle is strengthened if one considers what happens in other hunks of matter outside a limited area in brains. The lower brain, the kidney and the table are all made up from matter which has a qualitative core, but no one seems inclined to attribute a unified subjectivity to them. If one followed Russell in treating consciousness as simply a matter of causal consequences, then there would be an answer to this problem, but such an approach to consciousness is no different from reductive functionalism. I quoted Lockwood above as seeming to adopt a reductive view, but in a later article he says 'it is difficult to see how *awareness itself* could be anything other than an emergent phenomenon' (1993: 280). Indeed, the bonding of the phenomena into a unity, though no doubt supervenient on functional organisation, cannot be wholly explained by it, as liquidity is explained by atomic structure, and so must be emergent. But if awareness is emergent, what is achieved by attributing its objects to the matter of the brain? That awareness must be emergent is also attested by the following consideration. The individual elements have, at best, only the dimmest consciousness. Supposing them to be united into one consciousness, why should that not be equally dim? On what principle is the quality of consciousness accumulated?

(iv)   Type F *materialism and intellectual states*

The discussion of neutral monism is usually conducted with reference to the sensory *qualia* of consciousness and most of the original protagonists of the theory were radical empiricists with reductionist accounts of thought. They tended to be imagists, associationists or, later, behaviourists about intellectual activity.[6] More recent proponents of the theory tend not to share this reductionism. Strawson, for example, rejects such reductionism, together with reductionism about sensory experience (1994: 4). The elementary entities, therefore, must possess not just proto-phenomenal qualities, but proto-intellectual content. This problem is easily overlooked because of the historical emphasis on the irreducibility of sensation rather than thought. Because perception gives us a conception of the physical world as being saturated with sensible qualities, it is natural for us to think of matter as essentially characterised by such qualities, and even, with some imaginative-cum-conceptual effort, by more primitive analogues of the same. The idea that minute matter manifests similar proto-intellectual features is harder to grasp. One might just about make a gesture in this direction by conceiving of the electron as possessing a proto-conceiving of its own proto-phenomenal nature. This, however, will not be adequate to build up the distinctive character of thought unless all our thinking is built up logically from the concepts whose contents are restricted to the qualities they directly capture. This would be equivalent to a form of conceptual logical atomism, as found in linguistic phenomenalism. Such a programme is both demonstratively impossible and presumably not what Strawson or the other contemporary Type *F*s intend. One cannot build, without brute emergence, thoughts about Manchester United, the Trinity or even our normal physical world, from self-conceiving proto-phenomenal patches.[7]

7.6   Explicit panpsychism

Galen Strawson (2006, 2007), unlike Russell, Maxwell and Lockwood, opts for the panpsychist solution. He calls his position 'real physicalism',

---

[6] Some empiricists – for example, A. J. Ayer – seem to think that it is possible to be non-reductionist about qualia, but reductionist about our cognition of them. For an argument that this is impossible, see Robinson (1982: 105–7) and Robinson (2010).
[7] This point is made in Robinson (2012a) and in Nagel (2012).

but this label is misleading because 'real' does not qualify 'physicalism', rather the point is that the position is a physicalism that asserts the irreducible *reality of experience*. The use of 'physicalism' is also broad. Any concrete object that occupies space-time is physical, and this includes conscious animals such as ourselves. The bite in calling this 'physicalism' is a commitment to the idea that all the properties of such concrete objects, including the conscious states of those that are conscious, somehow flow from their nature as physical; that is, from the properties of the ultimate parts.

Strawson's argument for panpsychism can be reconstructed as follows.

(1) Reductionism about experience is false.
(2) Physicalism is true.
(3) If reductionism about experience is false, and if physicalism is true, then, if 'physical stuff is, in itself, in its fundamental nature, something wholly and utterly non-experiential', there must be 'brute emergence' of the experiential.

Therefore

(4) If 'physical stuff is ... utterly non-experiential' then there must be brute emergence of the experiential.
(5) Brute emergencies an incoherent idea.

Therefore

(6) Physical stuff is not in its fundamental nature utterly non-experiential.

The argument is valid. Strawson regards (1) as intuitively obvious, but it is also *ex hypothesi* at the current state of the argument in this book. The strategic situation is that, if (5) is true, either matter is essentially experiential or one must abandon physicalism and accept that consciousness is an essentially different nature or substance from matter, as the dualist claims. Why is Strawson so convinced of (5)? There are, I think, two reasons. First, he argues that what are usually cited as cases of emergence – for example, liquidity arising from atoms that are not themselves liquid – are not cases of brute emergence, because the nature and the behaviour of the atoms rationalises and entails the liquid product. Once you understand how the atoms behave you are in a position to see that the macro phenomena could not fail to be liquid: that is, there is no 'explanatory gap'. Second, he thinks that the belief that there could be such a thing as brute emergence derives from an exaggerated conception of what it is for causal relations to be contingent, which itself derives from a misunderstanding of Hume; once one is purged of this error, then one will see that brute emergence is a nonsense.

I cannot here discuss causation in general or the interpretation of Hume, but it is generally accepted that the emergence of consciousness involves an 'explanatory gap' not present in cases such as liquidity. It therefore follows for the physicalist that either the seeds of experience are in matter in the panpsychic sense, or that experience emerges in so unique a way as might be thought to constitute a form of dualism.

Suppose we agree that a physicalist who accepts the irreducible reality of experience is obliged to be a panpsychist. Why should we not regard this as a *reductio* of physicalism rather than an argument for panpsychism? Why, in other words, does Strawson think that it is so plausible to claim that physicalism can absorb the experiential? The answer is that he thinks that, given the topic neutral nature of our scientific conception of matter, physicalism that accommodates irreducible experience is common sense.

Strawson follows Russell in believing that the experiential and the scientific conception of the physical slot easily together and that treating them dualistically pointlessly offends against Ockham's razor. This of itself, of course, does nothing to answer the four problems I raised above for type-F monism, so how does Strawsonian panpsychism fare on these?

The first problem – how one moves from qualitative content to consciousness – does not arise for a theory that is explicitly panpsychist. On the second problem – the mental life of quarks and strings – I see no helpful guidance in Strawson.

This problem is to say what kind of mental life a quark or a proton is supposed to possess. There are two forms of panpsychism and Strawson's physicalism commits him to the less plausible. The more plausible version is holistic, in that it sees the whole of the material universe as somehow pervaded or infused by mind or intelligence. This 'world spirit' is a property of the whole and is not constructed from the mental features of the parts. The other version is atomistic – Strawson calls it 'smallism' – and seeks to attribute to each atom an appropriately minute form of consciousness and to build more sophisticated consciousnesses out of this material. The mentality in the former case, though no doubt mysterious, is at least modelled on mind, spirit and intelligence as we know it. In the latter case, it is utterly obscure what the atomic materials could consist in. When setting out this problem, I said that the consciousness of an earthworm – a massively complex organism by sub-atomic standards – is hard enough to conceive and asked what it might mean to attribute a suitably diminished version of consciousness to an electron. I suggested that it might be impossible to imagine or give theoretical content to such an idea. It is important that it is not just a matter of imagination, in the way that it might be impossible to imagine what it is like to be a dog, even though one is quite confident that there is something that it is like. It is plausible to maintain that being conscious involves a certain complexity of structure: one is taking something in a certain way and responding to it. This is true of a dog and just possibly of an earthworm. 'Responding' need not mean external behaviour: it could be any mental affective or cognitive response. But the occurrence of a single, minimal qualitative content, in association with an undifferentiated external causal response (for example, in the case of electron, unalterably exercising the influence of the mass of 1/1860 of a proton and of a negative charge), cannot constitute any inner consciousness. It seems to me reasonable to think that the existence of any kind of subject presupposes a certain movement of mind and hence the active grasp on more than one content. Strawson says that the experiential is always active, not passive, but the only activities that he can ascribe to the electrons, strings, etc. are the kinds of external, unvarying properties I have cited for the electron; this is not mental activity.

Strawson has more to say about the unity of non-simple consciousnesses, which he calls 'the composition problem'.[8] There are in fact three components to this problem. First, there is the issue of why and how the inner core of separate simples could or should merge into one consciousness. Second is the issue of why and how the very dim and different contents of simples come to make up the kind of conscious experiences we have, given that they can come together at all. Third is the issue of how separate *subjects* can make one subject, especially whilst escaping detection to introspection.

It is not clear to me that Strawson distinguishes the first two problems. On the first problem, Strawson cites William James as having gone from believing that composition was impossible, to believing in a 'not-rigidly-particulate, field-quanta-friendly form of Composition' (Strawson 2006: 248). The rationale is as follows. Provided that one has a field, rather than a particulate, conception of the simples, then the thought that they overlap and 'flow into' each other to form a new unity does not seem so unnatural. Furthermore, this helps with the second problem, because this intermixing might explain how they can produce contents that are significantly different from those of the elements that mix – their fusion is more like something chemical than like mere physical combination. These thoughts seem to be backed up by two general principles. One is the optimistic belief that 'we know it is actual so it must be possible' and the other is that 'unintelligible experiential-from-experiential emergence

---

[8] For discussion of this issue, see Strawson (2006). The discussion by Goff in that volume is very clear and helpful. Strawson's reply is at 248ff.

is not nearly as bad as unintelligible experiential-from-non-experiential emergence' (2006: 250).

We have now moved a long way from the original position, where the role of the qualitative/mental was to provide the monadic intrinsic properties of matter, to which the causal properties discoverable by physical science could belong. The mental atoms have now developed a chemistry of their own which does not seem to follow from the physical laws which were originally conceived to be their only powers. One has disposed of the obligation to make any sense of how or why the mental developments come from their elements. We are much nearer to a holistic idealism than we were at the start of the project. Perhaps one is near to thinking of the whole process as having some mind-serving teleological focus.

The third problem of composition was how many selves can form one. This itself has two sub-problems. One of these, raised by Goff (2006), is how, given the transparency of consciousness, we could fail to notice that we were constituted 'like the eye of a fly'. Strawson's reply to this specific point seems to me to be adequate. He says that transparency of consciousness does not guarantee awareness of all its features. I would put it by saying that we are aware of qualitative content but not metaphysical structure. As an analogy, it could be pointed out that simple introspection does not reveal the correct philosophical ontology of perception, only its qualitative phenomenology. The more serious problem, I think, concerns how one subject can be aware of the logically private contents of another mind. Either what I am aware of is in some fused way *identical* with the contents of all the lower level subjects, or it is a causal product of these. The former option infringes logical privacy; the latter is a case of brute emergence. Strawson prefers conscious to conscious brute emergence, to unconscious to conscious, but this seems to me a pretty desperate position.

On the fourth general problem, – the emergence of thought – the original problem stands, for any version of panpsychism that seeks to have a tight and systematic account of how thought can develop from minimal qualitative consciousness. Whether the allowance of Jamesian flowings and fusings really makes this any better is hard to estimate.

7.7   Conclusion

One might summarise the argument of this chapter as follows.

The knowledge argument shows

(1) there can be no adequate account of the conscious mind in standard physicalist terms.

It follows from this that, unless one accepts a uniquely brute form of
emergence

(2) if mind is to be explained from a materialist perspective at all, there must be
some feature of matter in addition to those contained in a standard physicalist
account which, unlike the standard ones, does provide an explanation of the
generation of the conscious mind.

(3) This further feature must itself be either mental or proto-mental (conscious
or proto-conscious) because

(4) nothing that was purely and simply physical – nothing that was essentially
accessible from a third-person perspective – could conceivably explain the
generation of the subjective and hence the mental.

This last is what Stoljar denies, but I have tried to refute his arguments.

(5) The attribution directly to elementary matter of full-fledged mental properties, the same kind of properties as figure in our experience – colours, sounds
itches, etc. – is totally bizarre. This is even more especially true in the case of
the contents of intellectual conscious states.

Maxwell, we have seen, tried to get round this problem by locating these
qualities (the sensible, not the intellectual, which he does not mention) at
a relatively macro level, but Lockwood shows that this makes his theory a
standard version of emergentism.
    Therefore

(6) The materialist needs proto-mental, or proto-conscious states.

But

(7) no clear sense has been given to the notion of such proto mental or conscious
states that differentiates them from *whatever it is* that adequately explains the
generation of mind. It does not help in understanding what sort of thing
might provide such an explanation, what such a thing might be like, or that
there could be such a thing.

Furthermore

(8) there is no remotely plausible account of how proto elements might combine
to produce full or normal conscious states. One would be forced back to
emergence. This is especially true of intellectual states.

Putting these results with the conclusions of the previous chapter – which
was itself the result of all that had gone before it – we can conclude the
following. The theory-based physicalism of the physicist cannot capture
the qualitative nature of the world and so is condemned, as a total world
view, to be incoherently abstract. This cannot be remedied by any version
or development of neutral monism, which tries to load what is missing in

the physicist's world into a richer conception of matter. If there is a physical world independent of our experience, it cannot provide an explanation of why that experience should exist. There cannot be a materialist, or a materialistically based, monism that is adequate to the phenomena.

8 Conclusion
The real power of the KA – qualia, qualities
and our conception of the physical world

8.1   The initial predicament

We have found that standard forms of physicalism cannot make a plausible answer to the knowledge argument (KA), but I think that even the protagonists of the argument do not appreciate its full or comprehensive force.

The dialectical situation in which the KA for property dualism is usually taken to be located is the following. It is taken as agreed that physicalism gives an adequate account of non-conscious reality, and that this part of reality constitutes almost 100% of the universe. But despite this overwhelming success, however, the physicalist account struggles to accommodate certain features of mental life, namely the 'what it is like' or qualia of certain conscious states. These qualia constitute the qualitative nature of sensations and probably of secondary qualities, but have nothing to do with our robust conception of the physical as it applies to the vast mindless tracts of reality. These awkward entities constitute what Chalmers called 'the hard problem' for physicalism. But the fact that they also constitute such a tiny part of the world is implicitly understood as being a strong prima facie reason for thinking that there must be some way of reconciling their apparent existence with the otherwise triumphant and clearly adequate physicalist account of the world: if it were not for the qualia that occur in a few corners of reality, the adequacy of physicalism would not in any way be in dispute.

I think that this interpretation of the situation constitutes a radical misunderstanding of and understatement of the problem that faces physicalism and the role that the KA plays in bringing out that problem: the dialectic is quite different from the way it is represented in the previous paragraph. To see why and how this is so, one must direct attention at our conception of matter and the physical, rather than at our concept of mind. Science, whether of the macroscopic or the microscopic, is very largely concerned with measurement and quantification and with the expression of its findings in mathematics, as far as is possible. But the resultant abstract – we might call it Platonistic – conception of the physical cannot, we think, wholly capture our concept of the physical, especially as it is conceived in our naïve or common-sensical conception of the world. Taken in this abstract form, the concept of the physical is insufficiently concrete. But what concretises it is the addition of qualities – essentially sensible qualities – that figure so importantly in our naïve or common-sensical conception of the world. These are essential to our ability to 'cash' or 'model' or 'interpret' the abstract, mathematical conception.

Physicalism's real predicament, as has been brought out by the KA, can be represented in two propositions.

(1) Standard physicalism cannot capture the *qualitative* nature or aspect of reality.

(2) The qualitative is an essential feature of any conception of the physical that goes beyond the purely abstract and mathematically expressed.

These two together entail

(3) Standard physicalism cannot capture any conception of the physical that goes beyond the purely abstract or mathematically expressed.

This is, of course, a much stronger conclusion than that which the normal understanding of the 'hard problem' attributes to the KA, namely

(4) Standard physicalism cannot capture the qualitative nature of certain mental states.

On my reinterpretation of the situation, what the KA really shows is (1). I take (2) to be independently plausible, possibly analytically true and probably largely uncontested. (1) and (2) together show that standard physicalism is not merely incomplete, failing to cope with consciousness, but something more like incoherent, because it cannot give a coherent account of the physical itself.

In the next two sections I shall do the following. First, I shall show that the KA, if sound, proves that physicalism cannot capture the qualitative at all: that is, I shall try to prove (1). Second, I will argue that this does not merely strengthen the KA's conclusion, it also undercuts all known attempts to refute the argument, for they all rest on the assumption that the physicalist's conception of the purely physical is itself unproblematic; that is, the physicalist's conception of the physical would not be inadequate if it were not for the need to explain consciousness.

8.2   Extending the scope of the KA

The KA as traditionally stated appears to concern only the nature of mental states. This appearance is founded on two factors. First, the argument concerns 'what it is like' to have certain experiences, and this expression clearly names something subjective. This alone is not enough to confine the topic to the mental world. If one is talking about *what it is like* to feel pain or jealousy, then this might seem to be purely internal, but *what it is like* to see colour or to hear sound is directly connected with our notion of *what colour is like* or *what sound is like*, as those things are, or as we naïvely conceive them to be, in the external world. There is an irony here. It is a feature of the accounts many physicalists present of experience that it is *transparent*. This means that the only feature that characterises the experience *qua* experience is the apparent presence of some objective or external property. So *what it is like* to experience red or C-sharp is no different from *what red is like* or *what C-sharp is like*. This transparency alone is not enough, however, to show that the KA concerns our conception of the external or physical world, because the qualities that are invoked in the argument are secondary qualities, and, at least since Locke, it is standard within the scientific form of physical realism to treat secondary qualities, insofar as they are not just powers or dispositions but monadic qualities, as subjective. This leaves the physical world untouched, for that is characterised wholly by primary qualities.

Once one has reached this point, it ought to be becoming clear why the argument does not concern secondary qualities alone. 'Red' is defined in terms of what it is like to perceive it; 'square' is not. But someone's conception of 'square' is not independent of what it is like for them to perceive (see, touch, or whatever else possible sense) square things, for if it were it would be wholly axiomatic and mathematical. Using Sellars's convenient terminology, our 'manifest image' of the world is a projection of what it is like to perceive it, in respect of both primary and secondary qualities. The secondary qualities are attached to a particular form of experience, the primary are not. But without any experience – in our case, visual or tactile or both – there would be no conception of spatial properties beyond the wholly mathematical.

What the KA really brings out is that only experience of the appropriate kind can reveal the qualitative, as opposed to purely formal and structural, features of the world. What the standard modern physicalist fails to notice is that the kind of thing that Jackson's Mary did not know, generalised from colour vision to all the other sensible qualities, is essential to any contentful conception of the world, and hence that physicalism without it would lack any empirical content. The generalisation of the KA can be expressed as follows.

Take any property, P, which is a quality or has a qualitative aspect, then it will be true of any subject, S, who has no experiential grasp on that qualitative aspect, but otherwise has full knowledge of all matters relating to P, that S lacks knowledge of P's qualitative aspect.

I call this the *generalisation* of the argument, but one might, with equal justice, say that it is the principle underlying the argument. The thought experiment merely makes its truth clear.

It is vital to appreciate that this rationale applies to primary qualities as much as to secondary. The fact that it is easier to describe a thought experiment in which someone has experience like ours except that chromatic colour is missing, than it is to imagine experience like ours without spatial features (if that is possible at all) does not affect the fact that an empirically contentful (as opposed, say, to a purely axiomatic) conception of space depends on visual or tactile or some other experience of a spatial field to give us a conception of what space might be empirically like, and that this is dependent on what it is like to perceive it in some particular way. Strawson (1959) argued that a purely auditory universe would not be enough to generate a conception of space, however the sounds were managed and organised. Whether he was right in thinking hearing alone could not generate a conception of space is not something we need now consider. What matters for present purposes is that, whether or not there could be a purely auditory and genuinely spatial world, we can certainly make prima facie sense of a mind with auditory experience, where the sounds are organised in a way which could not sustain a conception of space, and which lacks any other senses that might be sufficient to contribute a sense of space. The sounds it hears are simply those, say, of verbal discourse. If such a mind could be taught verbally all the proofs of geometry and of relativity theory, it seems clear that its resultant grasp on the nature of empirical space would be no better than Mary's on colour. This mind would have a purely scientific or formal conception, in a way that did not guarantee he would have any conception of what space was, or might be, like in itself or qualitatively. I want to emphasise that any worries one might have about whether there could be such a mind as this are not to the point.[1] The prima facie intelligibility of the suggestion is enough to bring out the point that our conception of primary qualities as more than purely formal is not independent of what it is like to experience

---

[1] In case one is worried by the apparent impossibility of such a case, one might consider the following. Imagine someone who had developed with the normal spatial experience, but then suffered brain damage that destroyed all memory of the spatial features of his experience whilst not harming his general and mathematical intelligence. There was then an attempt to teach him scientifically the properties of space. This would lead to the same situation.

them. So, though the KA is most easily stated in terms of secondary qualities, which are seemingly easily relegated into the dustbin of the mind, the principle of the argument can be carried through for primary qualities that are fundamental for our conception of physical reality. Our conception of these is, at bottom, no more independent of what it is like to perceive them than is our conception of the secondary qualities. I say 'at bottom' because primary qualities are not dependent on any particular form of experience, but this does not mean that we can have an interpreted or modelled conception of them without some form of qualitative content derived from experience. Furthermore, the doctrine of the 'transparency' of perception applies as much to primary as to secondary qualities, so what it is like to see square is only the obverse of what squareness is visually like.

Our own experience in fact bears this out. I suggested above that a mind with no spatial experience could not gain a better-than-abstract conception of space on the basis of learning geometry, relativity theory and the like. But this is not so far from our situation. Insofar as our own grasp on four and above spatial dimensions, or on relativistic or bent space is not purely mathematical, it depends on trying imaginatively to extend the two and three dimensions of which we have actual experience. This attempt is only very limitedly successful; we do not really achieve a grasp on what four and more dimensions, or other spatial exotica that go beyond experience, could actually be *like*. The narrative of *Flatland* (1884/2015) makes plausible the thought that creatures that lived in two dimensions would have a similar difficulty to the one we have with more than three dimensions, in giving imaginative content to three dimensions. In none of these cases is the problem a lack of 'theoretical knowledge'; it is a lack of the kind of experience that could give interpretation to that knowledge.

The correct way of looking at the rationale of the KA is to see it as granting content to the physicalist hypothesis only for purposes of argument. 'Even if we grant', it says, 'that physicalism could cope with the rest of reality, it still cannot cope with what it is like to experience things'. But once one recognises the connection between what it is like to experience the world and what we can conceive the world we experience to be like, one can see that if physicalism cannot capture the former, it cannot capture the latter; one cannot have an adequate conception of the physical which does not include those qualitative components that are the 'transparent' projections of the qualitative nature of experience. Seen in this way, it begins to look as if the KA cannot fail to be right, for if there were not some special kind of content that is revealed only in experience, then we could not have an empirically significant conception of the physical in the first place. So, if you are tempted to think that physicalism might somehow be able to defuse the intuition that Mary learns something substantive and new, you need only direct your attention to the way that any non-formal conception of the physical is dependent upon the qualitative nature of reality as revealed uniquely in experience to see that this could not possibly be true. If, in general, the acquisition of experience did not teach something new, then a purely descriptive account of reality ought not to lack anything essential. In sum, the argument draws our attention to the fact that physicalism that depends on a notion of the physical that is somehow independent of the qualitative nature of experience can only present us with a world that is so formal as to be empirically contentless.

8.3   How all objections to the KA miss the point

A natural response to the argument so far might be as follows. It might be conceded that the KA, *if sound*, has a much stronger conclusion than has previously been thought. This merely emphasises the need to show that it is not sound and increases the incentive to support one of the considerable set of objections that have been made to it.

This response is over-optimistic, however, from the physicalist's perspective. All the responses to KA of which I am aware assume that the physicalist's conception of the material world is or could be adequate for the non-mental realm and then explain how, starting from this basis, Mary's apparently new knowledge can be accommodated. I do not find these responses plausible, even in their own terms. But, not merely does KA challenge the physicalist's assumption that he has an adequate conception of the physical; it does so in a way that it is difficult to see that the physicalist, once the situation is drawn to his attention, can deny.

No-one, I think, would wish to deny the following:

(1) Our naïve, common-sensical or manifest image of the physical world essentially has qualitative features: that is, in addition to formal or mathematical features it has qualitative features which cannot be reduced to the formal ones.

From what has already been argued, it is clear that

(2) These qualitative features derive, via the 'transparency' of perception, from the nature of qualia.

As qualia contribute an essential component in the common-sensical conception of the physical, it would seem that

(3) The nature of qualia cannot be *analysed* as some function of, or on, the operations of the physical, naïvely conceived.

This is relevant to the usual responses to the KA. Two of the most popular responses are the *abilities* response and the *phenomenal concept* response. Both these strategies take for granted the adequacy of a conception of the physical that does not essentially rely on the qualitative nature of experience to give it content, and then try to explain the latter – the qualitative nature of experience – in terms of this autonomous conception of the physical. In the case of the *abilities* account, the explanation of experience is in terms of behavioural abilities of physical organisms. In the case of the *phenomenal concept strategy*, it is in terms of a special form of conceptualisation of certain physical states, non-mentally conceived. But if the qualia in experience are foundational for our notion of the physical, there is no autonomous conception of the physical; so experiential states cannot be conceived in terms of some function on the physical as autonomously conceived.

This consequence might be taken as suggesting that the KA is set up in a way that is unfair to physicalism. It might seem to be unfair because it saddles the physicalist with having a purely descriptive or intellectual account of reality, and surely he is not denied the resource of sense-experience in forming his conception: something must have gone wrong in our understanding of what physicalism or materialism requires.

Nothing, however, has gone awry. Of course, the physicalist is allowed to rely on perception to explain the acquisition of particular information about the physical world. But he is not allowed to draw essentially on the subjective dimension of experience – on what it is like to experience the world – in forming his conception of the physical nature of the world, for his conception is one committed to the availability of a purely objective account of the world. Insofar as the qualitative content of our conception of the world – that part which goes beyond what can be wholly captured descriptively – is a reflection of 'what experience is like', then it is a resource denied to the physicalist. This is the point at which traditional empiricism and physicalist realism as a metaphysical theory diverge. It is a starting point for empiricism that the qualitative components of experience are, or are amongst, the building blocks from which our conception of the physical world is constructed. Physical realists, on the other hand, simply ignore the role of perceptual experience in, not simply giving us information, but in giving our empirical concepts content. Whilst this can be thought of as an oversight, it is also essential to the orthodox physicalist project, for if the physicalist were to allow that *what it is like* to experience features of the world played an essential constitutive role in our conception of *what the world is like in itself*, he would have to abandon his fundamental project of assimilating the mental into, or reducing it to, the physical as autonomously conceived, for there is no such autonomous conception.

The way the argument undermines physicalism can be put even more comprehensively. A standard statement of physicalism is that it is the theory according to which phenomenal (and other mental) states supervene with metaphysical necessity on physical states. Supervenience is an asymmetric dependence relation. It presupposes that the nature of the supervenience base does not essentially depend on that which supervenes on it; one can at least conceive of the base in the absence of the supervenient properties. But the KA shows that the physical cannot be conceived autonomously of elements dependent on the mental.

Now the physicalist might be tempted to argue that this is just a clash of intuitions: the proponent of the KA, as I interpret it, says there is no autonomous conception of the physical, and he, the physicalist, denies this. But I do not think this is true: the physicalist does not deny the role of the qualitative in any more-than-formal conception of the physical; he simply fails to notice the connection between this and the qualitative nature of experience and hence between it and qualia.

It is more or less explicit for the physicalist that

(i) we can have a grasp on the nature of the physical in scientific terms.

What I suspect most physicalists accept but which is not discussed in this context is

(ii) our concept of the physical is not purely mathematical and formal but involves a qualitative component.

Once one recognises (ii), and one considers both or either of the KA as I have re-expressed it, and the apparent transparency of at least some features of our experience, it is difficult to deny

(iii) we can only have a clear grasp on a quality – be able to imagine what it is like – if it is ultimately based on qualia: a quality is a 'transparent' projection of [some aspect of] a quale.

From this it follows

(iv) our conception of the physical is conceptually dependent on the nature of qualia.

From this it follows that

(v) qualia or qualia possessing states cannot be analysed or explicated in terms of some function of or operation on the physical, as independently conceived.

8.4   A direct realist response

A direct or naïve realist might respond to the above in the following way. He might say that, of course, the physicalist requires the qualitative, but that is just part of the physical and it only enters into the experiential as the object of experience. In having the qualitative as a part or component, experience does not precede the mind-independent conception of matter; rather this qualitative aspect of matter is what constitutes the qualitative content of experience.

We have, in fact, already discussed this strategy when discussing Jackson's adoption of representationalism as a way of defusing the KA. Representationalism, at least when combined with transparency, is a form of direct realism, and we saw in the course of Chapter 4 that such direct realism cannot serve the physicalist's purpose, for many reasons.

8.5   Empiricism and physicalism

The case I have been presenting can be put in a more formal manner, as follows. There are three initial assumptions

1. Qualities based on the 'what it is like' (WIL) of experience are essential to our 'common-sense' or 'manifest image' world, and to our conception of the features in it.
2. Our scientific conception of the world is either purely mathematical/formal, or, insofar as it is not just this, is modelled on the basis of the manifest image.
3. A purely mathematical/formal conception of the physical world cannot be complete.

Therefore

4. A complete scientific conception of the physical world must be modelled on the manifest image.

Therefore

5. A complete scientific conception of the physical world requires a qualitative component.
6. Our conception of qualities rests on the qualitative nature of experience – that is on qualia.

Therefore

7. A complete scientific conception of the physical world rests on (among other things) qualia.

Therefore

8. There is no scientific conception of the physical world which is conceptually independent of qualia and in terms of which qualia can be analysed or reduced.

We can also add.

9. WIL concepts depend essentially on the first-person perspective.

Therefore

10. The manifest image is essentially dependent on the first-person perspective.

Therefore

11. The non-formal/mathematical scientific conception of the physical world is essentially dependent on the first-person perspective.
12. (As 3 above) The formal/mathematical conception of the physical world cannot be a complete conception.

Therefore

13. The scientific conception of the world is essentially dependent on the first-person perspective.

There are two interconnected lines of argument here. One aims to show that the qualitative nature of experience (WIL) cannot be adequately accounted for by any scientistic account, the other that the first-person perspective is essential to any view of the world that is more than purely formal: there is no empirically contentful, wholly third-personal scientific picture. These together illustrate the difference between empiricism and scientific realism of the physicalist kind, and demonstrate the superiority of empiricism over physicalistic scientific realism. As the consensus of the last half-century or so has been just the opposite of this, the argument requires close attention.

Premise 1 has been defended above, both in Chapter 1 and in the earlier parts of this chapter. Premises 2 and 3 are also defended earlier in this chapter, 6 has been defended *passim* in this book, 9 should not be controversial, and these are all the premises. The arguments from them seem fairly straightforward.

It has been a standard feature of much contemporary philosophy to classify empiricism with the bogey of Cartesianism. It is correct, of course, to classify them together for these purposes, but it is one of the objectives of this chapter to show how radically implausible it is to reject the fundamental elements of empiricism.

Where might physicalist opponents of traditional empiricism try to object to the argument?

One standard move has been to deploy the slogan 'meaning is use' to disjoin experience from our concepts, and hence, by implication at least, from our understanding of how the world is. If this is correct, our conception of, for example, colour will not be at all dependent on visual qualia – if there are such. I am inclined to think that this ploy is now generally discredited,[2] but even if it is accepted, and the connection between meaning and experience is severed, is it at all plausible to understand this in a way that also implies that our conception of what the world as we experience it is like has nothing to do with the qualitative nature of experience? One standard use of the 'meaning is use' slogan has been to argue that the meaning of e.g. 'red' is independent of how any individual experiences it: if I see red the way you see green; that does not affect what 'red' means. But it will not follow from this that what the world seems to me to be like is no different from what it seems to you to be like.

Based on Wittgenstein's anti-private-language argument, there used to be an attempt to deny the existence of a private and subjective dimension to experience, and this might seem to be a denial that there is any 'what it is like' at all. But, given transparency, someone who believes that everything is public thinks that what it is like is simply determined by the public quality. This is in no way inconsistent with the claim in the first premise that the WIL of experience is what provides the qualitative content to our conception of the world. The denial of an 'inner theatre' makes no difference to the argument as presented here.

Some philosophers might be sceptical of 'formal or modelled on the manifest image' dichotomy, but as far as I can see it ought not to be controversial. When we try to represent theories in more than a mathematical way, we have to picture what, for example atoms or molecules are like, and we end up often literally building models out of ordinary materials and properties – there is nothing else. Of course, we realise that this is not what things are actually like, but it is the best we can do.

Someone might try to argue that the manifest image does not depend on the first-person perspective because it is an intersubjective construct, but intersubjectivity is itself a construct from multiple first-person perspectives.

Much more plausibly, one could deny the argument to the first person (but not the argument that phenomenal qualities and what it is like to

---

[2] In the 1960s my former tutor, J. O. Urmson, recounted the following story. In the late 1940s there was a controversy in *Analysis* about the status of the statement 'a surface cannot be red and green all over'. The worry was that it seems to be a necessary truth, but not strictly analytic, in which case it must be synthetic a priori – a category of truth then very unpopular. Gilbert Ryle asked the legal theorist, Sir Rupert Cross, who had been blind from the age of one, and who was well versed in philosophy, what he would say if told that the wall was red and green all over. Cross thought for a minute then replied 'I think it would look very nice Gilbert.' There can be no doubt of Cross's command of English and its uses. All he lacked was the normal experience. Urmson was no standard empiricist, but was too sensible to believe that understanding and experience were separated in the way the Wittgensteinian 'meaning is use' slogan, as often deployed, implied.

experience them are irreducible) by invoking direct realism, but this has already been shown to be inadequate from a physicalist point of view.

So we can conclude Part I by claiming to have proved that qualia are essential building blocks of our empirical world: they are not embarrassing extras in the corner of our brains. No standard form of physicalism has come to terms with this fundamental empiricist insight.

Part II

Why physicalism entails epiphenomenalism

9 Reductionism and the status of the special sciences

9.1 What is reduction? The nature of the problem

Any physical thing can be described in a variety of ways and at a variety of 'levels'. We might, using the language of ordinary discourse, characterise something as a rose. But one might also describe it in the language of certain of the sciences. The biologist will describe it in one way, a chemist in another and a nuclear physicist in another. Each of these descriptions will have its own vocabulary, invoking entities and properties at least some of which will be missing from the other forms of discourse. But we are happy to accept all the various discourses as capable of being used to say things which are true and we have no doubt that, in some fundamental sense, it is the same thing – the same chunk of physical reality – about which all of them are being used to talk. The core issue of this chapter is how we are to understand the relationship between the different discourses and their ontologies if we are to make sense of the idea that they in some sense have the same subject matter.

The most ambitious claim is that one of these ways of talking is basic – usually this is assumed to be the most fundamental form of physics – and that all the rest (which, putting aside our informal discourse, are termed the special sciences) are somehow *reducible* to this basic science. We shall see that the correct account of reduction is itself very controversial. Philosophers who want to avoid talk of reduction (for reasons that will emerge) often resort to claiming that the higher levels *supervene* on the lower ones. This means that there is no higher-level difference without a lower level one – for example, no biological difference without a chemical difference and no chemical difference without a difference at the level of physics. This supervenience relation is meant to articulate the nature of the dependence of higher on lower levels without a need to deploy any tighter notion of reduction.

Emergence is the opposite of reduction. Properties and behaviour are emergent at higher levels with respect to the lower if they cannot be reduced to the properties and laws manifested by the lower-level objects.

147

Because emergence is the obverse of reduction, however, what counts as emergence depends largely on what account of reduction one accepts. As we shall see, the strongest sense of emergence is associated with the idea that the world is not 'closed under physics' – that is, that what happens at all macro levels cannot be thought of as simply the necessary product of objects at the basic level following the laws uncovered by an ideal fundamental physics; some macroscopic levels manifest behaviours or other phenomena which, in principle, could not have been predicted from physics.

In order to avoid confusion when discussing these topics, it is necessary to distinguish what might be called the analytic from the substantive or ontological issues that might be at stake. Some objects are uncontroversially 'purely physical'. This applies, for example, to any inanimate material object and probably to vegetable life, which is living but mindless.[1] Nevertheless, such things will satisfy physical, chemical and biological descriptions, and the issue of how to understand the relation between these descriptions and their ontologies will arise, even though, on an intuitive level, one takes there to be no substantive ontological issue. Other questions are taken to be more substantive. The issue of whether mental states can be reduced to physical ones, for example, is not usually regarded as a question about how different levels of description are to be harmonised, but about whether mental states differ radically in kind from physical states. So the question 'can the other special sciences in general be reduced to physics?' and the question 'can mental states be reduced to physical states?' are importantly different. The latter is closer to the following: whatever the relation is between the physical special sciences and physics (for we do not think that these raise serious ontological issues), can the relation between mental and physical ascriptions be treated in a similar way, whatever that may be, or is the mental-physical relation seriously different from the others?

9.2   Different theories of reduction

The following line of thought has intuitive appeal. If physicalism is true for a certain domain, then it should be possible, in principle, to give what is, in some sense, a total description of that domain in the vocabulary of a completed physics. To put it in the material, not the formal, mode, all the properties that there *ultimately* are should be those of the basic physical entities. But there are many ways of talking

---

[1] I am assuming, for purposes of illustration, that life does not of itself involve a 'vital force' which is, in some way an immaterial principle.

truly about the world other than that couched in the vocabulary of physics; and there are, in some obvious sense, many properties that the world possesses that are not contained in that physics. These higher-order predicates and properties are expressed in the other – or so called special – sciences, such as chemistry, biology, cytology, epidemiology, geology, meteorology and, if physicalism holds for the mind, psychology and the supposed social sciences, not to mention our ordinary discourse, which often expresses truths that find no place in anything we would naturally call a science. How does the fundamental level of ontology – which we are presupposing to be captured ideally in physics – sustain all these other ontologies and make true these other levels of discourse?

The logical positivists had a simple answer to this question. Any respectable level of discourse was reducible to some level below it and ultimately to physics itself. The kind of reduction of which they were talking has a *strong form* and a *very strong form*. According to the very strong form, all respectable statements in the special sciences and in ordinary discourse could, in principle, be translated into statements in the language of physics. In the end, therefore, all truths could be expressed using the language of physics. This strongest form of reduction can be summarised as:

(1) *'Translation' reductionism*: for the concepts of any special science, there is a specification of definitional necessary and sufficient conditions for their satisfaction, which is expressed in the concepts of some more basic science and, ultimately, in the concepts of physics. Because the concepts of the sciences can be expressed in the terms of physics, so can the laws.

Early Hempel and Carnap exemplified this approach. The former, for example, said of psychology:

All psychological statements which are meaningful, that is to say, which are in principle verifiable, are translatable into statements which do not involve psychological concepts, but only the concepts of physics. The statements of psychology are consequently physicalistic statements. Psychology is an integral part of physics. (1980: 18)

This does not apply to psychology alone, but to all the sciences, natural and social. After listing some of these he says:

Every statement of the above-mentioned disciplines, and, in general, of empirical science as a whole ... is translatable, without change of content, into a statement containing only physicalistic terms, and consequently is a physicalistic statement. (1980: 21)

Carnap tells us what 'physical language' is:

The physical language is characterised by the fact that statements of the simplest form ... express a quantitatively determinate property of a definite position at a definite time. (1934: 52)

In other words, physicalistic statements ultimately attribute measurable quantities to spatio-temporal locations. He concludes:

On the basis of [this account] our thesis makes the extended assertion that the physical language is a universal language, i.e. that every statement can be translated into it. (1934: 55)

Such a reduction to physics would not be possible, for most sciences, in one step. In the case of biology, for example, the hope would be to provide a translation of biological statements using only the language of chemistry, and chemistry would itself have been given a translation into 'physicsese', thus completing the process for biology.

This form of reduction was soon perceived to be hopelessly implausible. The idea that a statement in economics, for example, means the same as a statement about the behaviour of particles or even about the behaviour of macroscopic bodies is impossible to believe.[2] In the case of a human science like economics, this problem might be thought to stem from the *substantive* irreducibility of human consciousness and, hence, of psychology. But it is hard to see how a statement in genetics, for example, could be said to mean the same as something cast in the language of physics. The motivation for this theory is clear, however, for if statements in a special science are just shorthand for statements in the idiom of physics, it is clear how they could be about the same subject-matter and involve no inflation of ontology.

Because of the obvious implausibility of the *very strong* translation form of reductionism, a merely *strong* form was adopted. This is the version of reductionism most often cited and it asserts that there has only to be scientific laws (called 'bridging laws'), not sameness of meaning, connecting the concepts and laws in a higher-order science with those in the next lower, and ultimately to physics. So the concepts and laws of psychology would be nomically connected to those of some biological science, and these, in turn, with chemistry, and chemistry would be nomically reducible to physics.

---

[2] There is always something of an ambiguity in the idea of 'reduction to physics', between reduction to statements that mention only entities of the most atomic kind, and physical laws that govern bodies of all sizes. Newton's laws of motion, for example, apply at least as paradigmatically to planets as to atoms.

(2) *'Nomological' reductionism*: this consists in the provision of non-definitional nomological necessary and sufficient conditions for being *F* in terms of some lower-level discourse, ultimately physics.

So 'reducible to' in this sense, meant that the entities and properties invoked in the non-basic discourse were *type identical with* certain basic structures. For example, our ordinary concept *water* is reducible to the chemical type H_2O, and this chemical molecule always consists of the same atomic arrangements. This pattern makes it easy to understand intuitively how the existence of water and the truths of sentences referring to water need involve nothing more than the existence of things in the ontology of physics. With the help of these bridging laws, the theory or science to be reduced can be derived from the theory or science to which it is to be reduced. Nagel (1961) is the classical source for such a theory:

When the laws of the secondary science ... contain some term 'A' that is absent from the theoretical assumptions of the primary science ... [a]ssumptions of some kind must be introduced which postulate suitable relations between whatever is signified by 'A' and traits represented by theoretical terms already present in the primary science ... With the help of these additional assumptions, all the laws of the secondary science, including those containing the term 'A', must be logically derivable from the theoretical premises and their associated coordinating definitions in the primary discipline. (1961: 353–4)

Despite the fact that Nagel here calls these bridging assumptions 'coordinating *definitions*', he does not think them to be normally analytic; they are essentially empirical.

The assumptions ... are empirical hypotheses, asserting that the occurrence of a state of affairs signified by a certain theoretical expression 'B' in the primary science is a sufficient (or necessary and sufficient) condition for the state of affairs designated by 'A'. It will be evident that in this case independent evidence must in principle be obtainable for the occurrence of each of the two states of affairs, so that the expressions designating the two states of affairs must have identifiably different meanings. (1961: 354–5)

But not all concepts in the special sciences, let alone ordinary discourse and the social sciences, can be fitted into this pattern. Not every *hurricane* that might be invoked in meteorology, or every *tectonic shift* that might be mentioned in geology, will have the same chemical or physical constitution. Indeed, it is barely conceivable that any two would be similar in this way. Nor will every *infectious disease*, or every *cancerous growth* – not to mention every *devaluation of the currency* or every *coup d'etat* – share similar structures in depth. Jerry Fodor, in his important article 'Special Sciences', (1974), correctly claims that the version of reductionism expressed in (2) requires that all our scientifically legitimate concepts be *natural kind* concepts and – like *water* – carry their similarities down to the foundations, and that this is not plausible for most of our useful explanatory concepts. It is particularly not plausible for the concepts of psychological science, understood in functionalist terms (that is, even without bringing in dualism), nor for the concepts in our lay mentalistic vocabulary. All these concepts are *multiply realisable*, which means that different instances of the same kind of thing can be quite different at lower levels – in their 'hardware' – and that it is only by applying the concepts from the special science that the different cases can be seen as saliently similar at all. Whereas you could eliminate the word 'water' and speak always of H_2O with no loss of communicative power, you could not do this for ''living animal', 'thought of the Eiffel Tower', 'continental drift', etc.

Supposing the failure of type-reductionism, even for non-controversially physical objects or domains, where does that leave us in the task of articulating how the different scientific descriptions apply to the same piece of physical reality? Fodor's answer is that though thoughts of the Eiffel Tower will not be type-identical with any neural state, let alone any atomic configuration, each such thought will be token-identical to some neural and atomic state. The same will apply to hurricanes, cases of an infectious disease, and anything else from the ontology of a special science. Token identity is what maintains the sameness of ontology.

We have so far been discussing the type-type reductions of Carnap (1955) and Nagel (1961) as expressed in (2), and treating them as definitive of reduction in the philosophy of science. This, too, is Fodor's assumption. He considers that his own theory of token, not type, identity is a non-reductive theory. Indeed, many philosophers who boast that they are non-reductive physicalists in the philosophy of mind have the nomological model of reduction in mind when they reject the label. Davidson is a prime example of such, as we saw in some detail in Chapter 6. Token identity, on this account, sustains something which is not reduction. But the definitions of 'reduction' provided by Kemeny and Oppenheim (1956) and Oppenheim and Putnam (1958) seem to be wholly consistent with the token identity that Fodor advocates. The requirements for reduction provided are:

Given two theories T1 and T2, T2 is said to be *reduced* to T1 if and only if:

(1) The vocabulary of T2 contains terms not in the vocabulary of T1.
(2) Any observational data explained by T2 are explained by T1.
(3) T1 is at least as well systematised as T2.

These criteria are satisfied without type reduction. All that this definition requires is that a particular explanatory task performed by T2 – namely the explanation of observable data – be performed also by T1. Suppose that every observable physical state of affairs were explicable by reference to basic physics *in principle*, then all other physical sciences would be reducible to physics, irrespective of the availability of bridging laws or type reductions. It is important to notice that Kemeny, Oppenheim and Putnam do not require that every kind of explanatory task performed by T2 be performed by T1, but only that all the observational data be explained. It is not required that the point or purpose of the reduced science be equally well served by physics. So the token identity propounded by Fodor as a form of non-reductionism and what Kemeny, Oppenheim and Putnam call reduction are quite compatible.

There is a relation between base and special sciences that satisfies what Fodor, Putnam, Kemeny and Oppenheim all require, and that is that the base should be a priori and conceptually sufficient for all that supervenes on it.

That there is such a strong sufficiency of the base for the higher levels in the case of physics and the special sciences is intuitively plausible. Let us suppose that meteorology is a nomically irreducible science. There is no logically possible world which, at the level of physics, is just like one in which a hurricane is destroying a village, but in which there is not a hurricane destroying a village: the physics base is a priori sufficient. There is no need to invoke some elusive conception of supervenience here: in the broadest sense of 'logically possible', there is no possible world with the same physical base as the given one and no hurricane; the relation is one of entailment in the strongest sense. The same would apply to any special science in a realm in which there were no occult or immaterial features. If, for example, some version of functionalism were correct about the mind, having the atoms arranged just as they are on earth would be logically sufficient – though not necessary, for there might be other ways of making minds – for the existence of conscious beings.

The version of reductionism just developed might be described as *the a priori sufficiency of the base*: that is

(3) *'A priori sufficiency of the base' reductionism*: the next level down, and, ultimately, the world as characterised by physics, is conceptually and a priori sufficient, but not necessary, for the higher-level states. This is the situation between physics and all the special physical sciences that are not reducible in senses (1) or (2).

The reductionism defined in (3) is equivalent to what David Chalmers (1996) calls 'logical supervenience'. Logical supervenience occurs when there is no logically possible world in which higher-level facts vary whilst lower-level facts remain constant. This contrasts with *natural supervenience*, which is typified by a causal, and therefore contingent, dependence of one level on another, and which allows logically, but not naturally or nomically, possible worlds in which the supervenience does not hold. Stating the point in terms of the a priori sufficiency of the base explains *why* there is this logical supervenience – why there is no logically possible world in which the higher level varies without the lower – namely that there is a clear entailment between the two.

One must be careful about what it means to say that there is an a priori sufficiency of the base, for some philosophers have understood it as meaning or entailing that someone could work out a priori that, for example, H_2O is water. (See, for example, Block and Stalnaker (1999).) This misses the force of 'sufficiency' in this context, which might be less misleadingly rendered 'adequacy'. The point is not that one can go a priori from facts about H_2O to facts about water, but that one can see a priori that the relevant facts about H_2O provide an adequate account of ordinary water facts. The science of XYZ on Putnam's Twin Earth would also do the same. What you can tell a priori are two conditionals: if the chemistry of which the H_2O facts are part were the case, this would constitute an adequate account of water phenomena; and if the chemistry of which the XYZ facts are part obtained, that would constitute an adequate account of water phenomena. You cannot tell a priori whether either of the sciences are the actual explanation of water phenomena on our earth, only that either would constitute an adequate account. This contrasts with what is claimed by dualists who accept the knowledge argument or the conceivability of zombies, who deny that there is an a priori sufficiency of the base, or any logical supervenience, in the relation between matter and consciousness.

9.3   Non-reductive conceptions

Because reduction is mainly associated in philosophers' minds with versions (1) and (2), which make the base both sufficient *and necessary* for the special sciences, the theory that it is only sufficient is often treated in terms of the concept of supervenience. 'Supervenience' is defined as the impossibility of variance at the higher level without difference at the lower. Put simply in this way, there is no explanation of *why* independent variation should be impossible and supervenience to obtain, in a given case, for that they cannot vary independently is stated as a bare fact – albeit sometimes as a 'metaphysically necessary' one. The definition provided in (3) explains why supervenience holds, namely that there is a priori or conceptual sufficiency for the higher truths in the base.

Getting clear about the a priori or conceptual sufficiency of the base is important for avoiding confusion about the various senses in which the concepts of the special sciences can be deemed 'irreducible' or 'emergent'. We can distinguish between things that are *merely explanatorily* irreducible, and things that are *substantively* irreducible.

(4) *(Mere) explanatory irreducibility.* This is the situation for all discourse with causal explanatory force, which is not nomically reducible to the base, but for which the base is conceptually – a priori – sufficient.

A hurricane is strictly constituted by the things physics describes, and that is why there is no problem about our ordinarily attributing causal power to hurricanes. A hurricane is *nothing but* the action of physical particles, though talk about hurricanes is not nomically reducible to physics. This is the situation for all the physical special sciences. This kind of weak explanatory irreducibility is the natural concomitant of (3). (3) talks in general about the relation between two ontological levels, (4) specifically about explanation. If we focus on properties, we have

(5) *Weak property emergence.* This is the position of a property in a special science with independent explanatory value, but conceptually sufficient conditions in the physical base.

A nominalist or conceptualist approach to such properties is prima facie plausible, because it is plausible to see them as just different, higher order *ways of describing* the base subject-matter. This contrasts with

(6) *Real property emergence.* This is the status of a property with no conceptually sufficient conditions in the base for its exemplification.

This is the status allowed to emergent properties by those who believed in emergent evolution. It is also the status allowed to psychological properties by anyone who allows the conceptual possibility of zombies. It involves the rejection of reduction as in (3) above, and the acceptance of the 'explanatory gap' between brain and mind. In the philosophy of mind, it is a realist version of a dual aspect theory of mind.

In fact, most of the debate about supervenience and 'soft' materialism in the philosophy of mind has concerned an attempt to create a weak version of (6):

(6w) *Real but supervenient property emergence.* This is the status of a property with no conceptually sufficient conditions in the base for its occurrence, but with some stronger dependence on that base than the merely causal and contingent.

This is the relation that most people who describe themselves as 'non-reductive physicalists' in the philosophy of mind seem to favour. This is not the place to discuss this issue, but the annexation of the term *reduction* to (1) and (2), and the consequent failure to notice (3) has led to much confusion about what 'non-reductive' physicalism amounts to. (See Robinson (2001) and the discussion of Davidson in Chapter 6 above.)

9.4   The limitations of type (3) reduction and the opening to dualism

I hope that I have given a plausible account of the different senses of 'reduction', shown why my sense (3) is the only credible one, and explained how the notions of supervenience and emergence orbit around one's notion of reduction. I now want to investigate some limitations of reductionism (3) and see what their consequences might be.

Fodor thinks that the weak reductionism that I express in (3) – and which he denies is a form of reduction – is no threat to physicalism, because each instance of a higher-order concept will be identical with some structure describable in terms of basic physics, and nothing more. This token reductionism is all that physicalism and the unity of the sciences require; type reduction is unnecessary. I shall now try to explain why, contrary to appearances, this may be wrong.

Fodor is quite right to think that the very same subject matter can be described in irreducibly different ways and it still be just that subject matter. What, in my view, he fails to do is to explain how this is possible. Now this might seem a strange request: why should it be deemed at all problematic that one portion of the world can be characterised in various ways? Why one might think that there is an issue here can be brought out by contrasting Fodor's view with the more traditional forms of reduction. What they would make possible is a 'bottom-up' explanation of how the more macroscopic features arise and why they are just a function of the base ontology. Insofar as the special sciences merely translate statements in physics, as in reductionism (1), or express the same natural kind or essence, as in (2), they add nothing real to the base. But in (3) there seems to be something further which cannot be deemed simply identical with base level. There seem to be two options. One is that there are new and real properties at each new level. But given closure under physics, there seems to be a clear sense in which these are epiphenomenal – they do no extra work in addition to what is effected by the entities and properties at the base level. This would presumably apply to the psychological level as much as to the other special sciences, hence the fear that physicalism about the mind does not avoid epiphenomenalism. The other option is even worse for the physicalist. The special sciences look like a 'top-down' conceptual interpretation of the base. This seems to suggest an interpreter or conceptualiser who views the world from his own perspective. They are more like a perspective from outside on the same subject matter. The rest of this part of the book is an investigation of these options, defending in the end the second option. As a preliminary for, or a taste of, this here are a few exploratory remarks about the 'interpretation' or 'perspective' approach.

The outline of the perspectivalist position is as follows. On a realist construal, the completed physics cuts physical reality up at its ultimate joints; any special science which is nomically strictly reducible to physics also, in virtue of this reduction, it could be argued, cuts reality at its joints, but not at its minutest ones. By contrast, a science which is not nomically reducible to physics does not take its legitimation from the underlying reality in this direct way; rather it is formed from the collaboration between, on the one hand, objective similarities in the world and, on the other, perspectives and interests of those that devise the science. If scientific realism is true, a completed physics will tell one how the world is, independently of any special interest or concern: it is just *how the world is*. Plate tectonics, however, tells you how it is from the perspective of an interest in the development of continents, and talks about hurricanes and cold fronts from the perspective of an interest in the weather.

But what is the solid content of calling the special sciences a 'perspective from outside'? The special sciences tend to be marked by three features. (i) They are selective; their subject-matter is only part of the world. So that, whilst everything physical consists of the basic entities of physics, only some of the world consists of the entities that concern chemistry, less is living and hence biological, cytology concerns only cells and so forth. (ii) Many, if not all, the special sciences are teleological or interest-driven. This is clearly true for certain special sciences, such as meteorology, which exists only because of a practical concern with the weather, but it is more generally true. The flow of physical events has no natural beginnings and ends between the Big Bang and the Apocalypse, if there is such, but we are interested in marking things off as the beginnings and ends of processes that concern us. All processes that we mark off as the beginnings and ends of non-atomic entities come into this category, so the whole of biology and, hence, the medical sciences are like this. (iii) Many of the entities involved are *Gestalt*-like phenomena. What I mean by this is that there is no exact similarity between them physically, but they are *seen as* similar from a certain perspective or for a certain purpose. Entities in physics are analogous to a perfectly circular object, which needs no interpretation to be taken as a circle; those in irreducible special sciences are like a series of discontinuous dots or marks arranged roughly in a circle which one sees as circular. Two hurricanes, for example, are not perfectly similar and would present themselves as a kind only to someone with an interest in weather: plate tectonics exists only given an interest in the habitability of the earth. This is not, of course, to say that these entities are invented. There are, in Dennett's phrase, 'real patterns' out there, but, like *Gestalten*, they are reified as being of a certain kind by an interpretative act.

These three features – selection, the reading-in of a teleology and the reification of certain patterns to create the ontology of the special sciences – suggest that Fodor's 'non-reductive' theory – what I have called reductionism (3) – presupposes a perspective on the subject matter, which is the viewpoint from which these interpretative acts take place. The stronger forms of reductionism enable one to understand the special sciences in the light of physics without the addition of such interpretative perspectives; that is why I called them 'bottom-up' theories. But the perspectival approach, involving a view from outside the subject matter, seems to give the interpreting mind an irreducible role in the creation of these sciences. Perhaps the clearest case from within science of the role of interpretation and imposition by our interests is the importance of function in the biological sciences. That functional explanation is absent from the foundations of science has been a dogma of physics since the seventeenth century. Its absence from the evolutionary explanation of the emergence of species is also fundamental; random mutation and selection do the job instead. But within biology, what an organ or other system does and how it contributes to the survival and even flourishing of the creature are essential features of the science. None of this is *irreducible* function, in the sense that there must be an account of how the mechanism with the function operates or is realised that is simply efficient causal, and there must be an evolutionary explanation of how this mechanism 'randomly' came about. That is, in conformity with (3) above, there is an adequacy of the mechanistic base to explain the existence and mode of operation of the biological feature. But to understand it within biology you need to know what it is *for*. You need to know both what *role* the liver plays and *how* it does it. The latter question would not even arise if former matter were not at issue. So, if the physical world is closed under physics, the functional explanation does not reveal the physical forces that are responsible for how matter is distributed and how this distribution will develop, but it does satisfy our desire to explain how it contributes to things in which we are interested.

So Fodor's theory appears to be essentially dualistic. It seems that the same portion of the physical world is being viewed from outside in a variety of ways for a variety of purposes.

One might be tempted to take this last claim metaphorically, and as simply pointing out that it involves a contrast between the subject-matter and its interpretation. But it is more than metaphorically dualistic. It can avoid a literal dualism of mind and body only if the interpretative perspective and our interests can be treated as part of the physical realm which is being interpreted. This concerns the ontological status of the mental acts that constitute such interpretation. These are amongst those psychological states which are described by propositional attitude psychology. But propositional attitude psychology is one of those special sciences which is, at best, reducible only in a Fodorian way; it meets no more than the standards of type (3), with no translational or nomic reduction. Indeed, it was with this science in mind that Fodor introduced his theory. The science of psychology is, therefore, itself something that emerges as an interaction of real patterns in the physical world and interpretation: the external perspective cannot be eliminated, on pain of regress, and it would appear that the interpreter must transcend the physical world that he is interpreting. This will be defended in more detail when we discuss Dennett in Chapter 13.

10 Vagueness, realism, language and thought

10.1 Introduction

In Chapter 9 I tried to show how a proper understanding of reductionism between scientific theories tends to undermine physicalism, either by making all the entities of the special sciences epiphenomenal or by placing the mind outside the physical system and so leading directly to dualism. I also gave some preliminary arguments in favour of this second option.

In this chapter I shall be arguing from the nature of ordinary language (or, more accurately, from language in general, scientific or not) for the second of these options. The starting point for, and foundation of, this argument is the problem of vagueness.

10.2 The problem of vagueness

To say that a predicate is vague is to say that there are objects to which it is unclear whether that predicate applies. 'Is bald' is a vague predicate, because, whilst there are many people, such as Yul Bryner, C. D. Broad and Michel Foucault to whom, in their hey-day, it clearly applies, and many people, such as Samson and Bertrand Russell, to whom it clearly does not, there are also many people whose state of hairiness is modestly compromised, of whom it is not clear whether or not they are bald. Similarly, there are many mounds of earth which clearly are not mountains but only hills – such as anything in the Cotswolds – and things, for example, in the Himalayas, which clearly are mountains; but it is unclear whether Snowdon is a mountain or only a hill.

The philosophically more interesting concept of identity is also infected by vagueness, especially under certain counterfactual circumstances. No one would deny that the table at which I am sitting would have been the same table if it had been placed six inches to the left of its actual position; and few would deny that it would have been (or *there* would have been) a different table if one had been produced in solid gold. But would it have been the same table if it had been made with 10, 15 of or 20% different wood? There hardly seems to be a fact of the matter.

So what? Why should these common-place indeterminacies worry us? They worry us because platitude appears to be at war with logic. Classical logic says that something either is the case or it is not: P or not P. So, given Smith's existence, either he is bald or not, Snowdon either is a mountain or not, and this would have been the same table if created with 20% different matter or it would have not. Timothy Williamson (1994) presents this as a formal argument which shows that denying bivalence actually leads to contradiction.

The principle of bivalence (B) is stated as

(1) If u says that P, then either u is true or u is false.

Then he expresses a simple Aristotle-Tarski definition of truth

(2) If u says that P, then u is true if and only if P.
(3) If u says that P, then u is false if and only if not P.

Taking some supposed counterexample to (B) as a substitution for P, he makes the preliminary assumption

(4) u says that P

If it is to be a counterexample, the consequent of (1) must be falsified

(5) Not: either u is true or u is false.

With (4) we detach the consequences of (2) and (3)

(6) u is true if and only if P
(7) u is false if and only if not P.

Substituting the equivalences of (6) and (7) in (5), we get

(8) Not: either P or not P

and by De Morgan's law

(9) Not P and not not P

which is a contradiction.

The crisis is made worse by sorites paradoxes. What I have just said suggests that vagueness challenges classical logic: the sorites problem suggests that vague predicates are incoherent, by the following pattern of argument:

(1) n grains constitute a heap.
(2) When something is a heap, the removal of one grain does not render it not a heap; i.e. if n grains is a heap, so is $n - 1$.
(3) Applying this recursively, 0 grains constitutes a heap, which is absurd.

Any vague predicate will be vulnerable to such an argument as this, for vagueness is equivalent to the holding of some principle of the same general form as (2); the loss of one hair does not make the hirsute bald, the gaining of one inch never makes a hill into a mountain; if it did, the concepts would not be vague, for there would be exact boundaries.

This looks like a typical philosophical problem, for it is typical of such problems that something quite ordinary – like the fact that things often look other than they really are, or that it is not a logical truth that the future must resemble the past – suddenly seems to have threatening consequences. In the case of vagueness, some concepts which we have no difficulty using coherently both threaten our logic and seem primed to self-destruct.

10.3   Possible solutions

There are three main ways of dealing with vagueness in the current literature. One way is to abandon classical logic, in the form of the principle of bivalence, so that not every proposition is either true or false, and developing 'deviant' logics. All these sophisticated logics have serious technical difficulties but they are also of dubious use against the sorites problem. This is because vagueness reiterates itself at higher levels, so that if one allows three truth values, True, False and Indefinite, it will still be vague whether certain cases are true or indefinite, and, for others, whether they are false or indefinite. The deviant logics do not seem able to cope with this 'higher-order vagueness'.

Another way out of the problem is 'supervaluationism', which pre-serves classical logic by operating in terms of all the ways in which a vague predicate could be made precise. This, though an interesting approach, faces serious problems with higher-order vagueness and with the disquotational features of truth, and I shall not attempt to do it justice in this essay.[1] It is from the third way that I wish to begin to explain my approach.

This third way is to claim that vagueness is always an epistemic phe-nomenon: there is always an exact answer to the question of whether something is a heap or whether someone is bald or something a mountain, we are just incapable of finding out what it is. So, even though it may always remain unknown to us (for nothing would count as a method for determining it), there is a fact such that for a particular man there is a precise number N such that if he has $N + 1$ hairs on his head he is not bald,

---

[1] Interesting discussions of this approach can be found in Williamson (1994: 142–64) and Sainsbury (1988: 31–40).

but if he has only N hairs he is bald. This apparently bizarre position is adopted to avoid the contradiction demonstrated above. In Williamson's words:

Classical logic and semantics are vastly superior to the alternatives in simplicity, power, past success and integration with theories in other domains. In these circumstances it would be sensible to adopt the epistemic view in order to retain classical logic and semantics [even if strongly counter-intuitive]. (1992: 162)

The striking difficulty for the epistemic theory is to imagine what could constitute the fact that – or make it be a fact that – 27 grains of sand (say) not 26 nor 28 are the minimum number that constitute a heap. It would appear to be the case that there are very many optional precisifications of our concept, consistent with our current usage, and it is difficult to see what could constitute one of them being correct, rather than another. In fact, Williamson denies that there are a variety of precisifications that are consistent with our usage. He maintains both that our usage determines a precise sense and that it is impossible for us ever to find out what this is and how it does it. He says:

To know what a word means is to be completely inducted into a practice *that does in fact determine* a meaning. (1994: 211, my italics)

and:

Although meaning may supervene on use, there is no algorithm for calculating the former from the latter. (1994: 206)

I must admit that, like Priest (2003) and many others, I am completely at a loss to see in what way or by what non-algorithmic mechanism (or non-mechanism) use can determine exact meaning when this exactness is not merely never exemplified in use, nor deducible from the most exact examination of language, but every reflective speaker would positively deny that reflection on his own competence or on the performance of others gives one any penetration into the area of indefiniteness. This latter fact may not *prove* that there is no precise border, but it does mean that the epistemic theory rests a bizarre conclusion on an appeal to mystery. It would be nice to do better.[2]

---

[2] Even if one were persuaded by epistemicism, it is not clear that this would undermine the principal moral of this chapter, which is that much of our discourse is to be taken in a conceptualist, not a realist fashion. Dummett equated realism with classical logic, but realism, as I explain it in Section 11.2, rests on the independence of 'real' things from our forms of conceptualisation. According to Williamson, however, it is use that determines the boundaries of concepts. This gives rise to many problems, for example, whose use of 'bald' determines the meaning when I use it? Is it English through the ages, Mancunian use

There appears to be a choice between deviant logic and the epistemic approach, and neither is attractive. I shall argue that the belief that theories such as these are the only major options rests on a false and over formal philosophy of language that shows a failure properly to understand the way we relate the ontologies implicit in our language to the world itself. The source of the problem is hinted at when Williamson says:

> [The need to make sense of sorites paradoxes] is felt by philosophers who take an ordinary language as a model of what is to be understood but a logically perfect one as a model of what it is to understand. (1994: 72)

In part, at least, the sentiment expressed in this quotation is easily understandable. One wants to understand ordinary language and not to follow Frege and Russell in discarding it for supposedly being unable to bear the weight of logic. Whatever natural language is, it is not something that merely fails to meet proper standards of logicality, a kind of *defective* formal system, for if it were it would simply generate nonsense. Therefore it is correct to say that in trying to understand how natural language works, the normal standards of logicality must be applied to inferences that are made using it. There is a sense, therefore, in which a proper logicality must be built into our understanding of ordinary language. But need this respect for logic commit us to taking a 'logically perfect' language as the model for understanding? Need the commitment to finding rationality in natural language itself, oblige one to treat it as, or as mappable onto, a perfect formal language, as Williamson implies? Furthermore, if this is to be the model of *understanding* – not merely the model for natural language we understand – it seems to imply that thought itself is carried out in something like a Fodorian *language of thought*, and calling this language 'logically perfect' implies that its structure can be represented in a purely formal – that is, syntactic – way. Ordinary semantics, we can presume, is merely added, as an interpretation, to this formal syntax. I want to present an alternative picture of language and our understanding of it, and one in which what the language is about – its semantics – plays an essential role in how it is put together: the unity of the language cannot be expressed in formal and syntactic

---

in the 1950s or Robinson idiolect? But more directly relevant is that this is a form of conceptualism – our use determines the nature of the property. The only way around this is if all the possible boundaries that all the possible uses might determine represent real properties out there, and various uses merely select from these. This is a self-destructive move from a realist perspective, because it abolishes the distinction between the vague property and separate exact ones. 'Bald' will become equivalent to having 1,000 hairs or less, having 999 hairs or less, having 998 hairs or less . . . and will no longer be a property in its own right. The same will go for 'mountain' and certain exact heights. The vague words will select from other properties which are already there.

terms alone. I want to try to develop such an alternative model and see where it leaves the problems of vagueness and sorites.

10.4   The alternative picture of language

The view of language which I am attributing to Williamson can be expressed as what I will call the *Logical Unity of Language*, and it has two component conditions: (i) *Consistency condition*; that all true propositions expressed in a natural language be consistent with each other; and (ii) *formality condition*; that the relations between all propositions be definitively expressible in some formal canonical way; for example, in classical logic, or in some more elaborate, but also formal, system.

The requirement is that natural language be a formal – or formalisable – system without paradox. The formality of the system means that every sentence in the language has definite entailment relations to other sentences, thus, in a sense, defining all concepts in terms of such relations. One could replace all concepts by variables and have a determinate, semantically uninterpreted, syntactic structure.[3] As we have seen, Williamson presents arguments for wanting it to be classical logic which provides the syntax, not some more sophisticated development. The motivation for the requirement is that it is supposed to be the only way to meet the intuitive demand for consistency and rationality in our natural language practices: this is what linguistic rationality consists in. Vagueness offends against condition (ii), for there appears to be no acceptable canonical way of representing the logic of vague predicates; and sorites offends against the first condition, as would any paradox, by allowing in inconsistency. The two are interconnected to the extent that what constitutes inconsistency is, as we shall see, crucially affected by the requirement that the parts of language be related in a strictly formal sense.

The strategy of this chapter is to argue that the intuitive demand for consistency and rationality in natural language can be satisfied by something weaker than the *Logical Unity* principle, and that this weaker conception of the way natural language works and hangs together provides a way of avoiding both sorites and the need for exotic logics, whilst presenting a quite different model of language.

This alternative conception replaces the *logical unity* principle with a combination of three other principles.

---

[3] One might wonder where the semantic paradoxes have gone, on this conception of natural language. It seems, however, to be a general truth that, since Davidson's dismissal of this problem (1984: 28–9) little notice of it has been taken in this context.

(1) *The logical unity of the basic ontology*; that *at the level of one's fundamental ontology* there must be a characterisation of what there is which is free of inconsistency and which can be regimented according to some canonical form.

Thus the logical unity principle is applied, not to the whole body of truth expressed in natural language, but to one's picture of how the world fundamentally is. That it should apply to one's basic ontology I take to be part of what one means by taking that ontology realistically. The fact that the rest of our discourse, with its non-basic ontology, does not possess such a tight logical unity does not, of course, mean that it possesses no kind of systematic relatedness. It will be constrained by two principles.

(2) *The competence of logic*; that all deductively valid inferences can be captured in a formalisable logic: one might hope that this can be a classical two-valued logic.

(3) *The harmonisation requirement*; that all ontologically non-basic ways of characterising the world can be related to the basic (or to some more basic and ultimately to the basic) ontology in a way which makes it intuitively clear that and how the basic ontology legitimises and sustains the others.[4] This, I assume, will be along the lines of the third type of reduction discussed in Chapter 9, the logical sufficiency or adequacy of the base. This involves no particular conceptual connections between the levels.

My claim is that different ways of talking about the same ultimate material can be intuitively harmonised in a way that falls short of formal consistency, and that, though a formalisable logic describes deductively valid inferences, moves from one ontological level to another are based on intuitive semantic considerations that are generally not a matter of formal, syntactic validity. As I agree that formal consistency is a condition for a strict realism, this means that most of one's non-basic ontologies are taken in less than a strictly realist sense: if they were strictly part of the same reality as the basic one, they would have to be formally consistent with it. It is clear that justification of this approach depends principally on making sense of the harmonisation requirement. I shall try to do this with the help of two rather different illustrations.

(a) One form that harmonisation can take is illustrated by the connection between the quantum and the Newtonian ontologies. Assuming that quantum theory is the fundamentally true ontology, then Newtonianism,

---

[4] This, I assume, will often be along the lines of the third type of reduction discussed in Chapter 9, the logical sufficiency or adequacy of the base. This involves no particular conceptual connections between the levels. But the examples I am about to give show that it need follow the discipline according to which all the discourses are strictly true, as with the special sciences, or that Everest is a mountain.

though approximating to the truth for most purposes is, in all circumstances, strictly false: objects are not the way Newtonianism pictures them, as cohesive, solid atoms, and their properties, such as Newtonian mass, are not possessed by real objects. But the world can be read as Newtonian, the Newtonian ontology can be superimposed on the quantum one, for almost all purposes; it is an interpretation that reality will support, and in a way it will not support certain other 'false' theories. But the two cannot be made formally consistent, for they are not. The two levels of discourse are not one scheme with its concepts defined by the entailment relations between them; there are such relations within each theory, but not across. We can see intuitively, however, how one can be made to bear the other and we can think of ourselves as talking about the same world using either. Roughly, this is because the objects in both occupy almost exactly the same location, in a literal sense, in a speaker's map of the world, and the corresponding properties, such as Newtonian and quantum mass, occupy analogous locations in the frameworks of explanation, in a somewhat more metaphorical sense of 'location', so they map onto each other. There is a referential isomophism, ultimately of a demonstrative nature, without a conceptual isomorphism. But the referential isomorphism carries with it a causal parallelism that enables one to match the properties, at least approximately.[5]

It seems to me that something like this kind of relation holds, not just between different scientific theories or 'levels', but quite generally, between different discourses with their respective ontologies which are held to be generally true. Language contains many different descriptive fragments.

(b) The Quantum–Newtonian analogy provided one case where there are some entailments running between the frameworks, but not enough to constitute definitions giving a unified scheme. An importantly different analogy would be with the relation between a photograph and a sketch of the same scene. Some lines on the sketch would correspond to specific lines on the photograph, but of others it would make little sense to ask to which of various details in the photograph they corresponded: there is no way of synthesising a sketch and a photograph into one representation that preserves all the features of both and presents a totally coherent picture. What this analogy suggests is that a relatively coarse representation is related to a relatively detailed one by a referential mapping – we can say they are both *of* the same scene – that does not require harmonisation of detail. The way one avoids outright inconsistency is to say that there is a

---

[5] Of course, these remarks hardly constitute a thorough discussion of the relation between Newtonian and quantum concepts, but I believe they indicate the right direction.

sense in which one is not to be taken as realistically as the other; there is an important sense in which the sketch is not to be considered realistically, compared to the photograph. That area of reality can be *seen in* the way it is represented in the sketch, but this is a view, an appearance, a kind of secondary quality of the underlying reality.[6] One ontologically sketchy way of seeing the world is to see it as containing hills and mountains; another is to see it as containing bald and non-bald things. Relatively more basic ontologies – and, therefore, more general ones (in the sense of applying to a greater area of reality) – will deal with feet above sea level, and with hairs and their exact location on heads. These different ontologies are not unifiable into one wholly consistent picture, except in the sense that one can abandon the less basic one and take the relatively more basic one as definitive of what there is. 'Feet above sea-level' talk has no need, and, strictly, no room for hills and mountains; and an exact science of hairs and heads would not need the category of baldness.

The harmonisation requirement operates between what we might call different *representational ontologies*:

Representational Ontology: any descriptive discourse that represents the world as containing certain kinds of objects and/or properties.[7]

A *representational ontology* is, therefore, a conceptual picture of the world. Sometimes it will be a detailed or in principle complete picture, as with the quantum and Newtonian theories, but sometimes it will be a mere sketch, as with the vague ontologies.

A special case of a representational ontology is

A Basic Ontology: any account of what kinds of things and properties are the basic constituents of the world, not constituted by anything else.

The notion of basic ontology can be taken either extensionally or intentionally; that is, one can either think of it as signifying whatever in

---

[6] One could call them 'descriptive games' provided that one remembers that they are all descriptive, whereas the purpose of Wittgenstein's expression 'language games' is to emphasise something called 'use' at the expense of description and reference. I am agreeing with Wittgenstein that language contains semi-autonomous fragments, but see them as distinguished by their ontologies, meaning by that, by the kinds of descriptive properties they ascribe to things, and, sometimes, by the kinds of things to which they refer. Whilst they are distinguished by their ontological differences, they are also related by the way they can be seen as relating to the same ultimate subject matter.

[7] It is necessary to stress that properties may be all that is at stake. The use of the word 'ontology' is naturally taken as implying things, but this natural interpretation will not always be the applicable one. Thus the choice between grains and heaps, or between Newtonian or quantum atoms, is a choice between things, but in other cases it is only a matter of different grains of classification. This is most plainly the case in application to Wang's Paradox, where the different classificatory systems are, on the one hand, numbers and, on the other, large and small numbers, which it is not natural to describe as different ontologies. The looseness of the term 'ontology' makes no difference, as the proposed solutions work for both cases.

fact constitutes the ultimate nature of reality, or as a set of representations purporting to capture what there ultimately is. Both the Newtonian and quantum representational systems are basic representational ontologies, though at most one of them could be the actual basic ontology.

The following general principle seems to me to be true. For any two levels of descriptive discourse, one of which is ontologically more basic relative to the other, they cannot both be taken in a fully realist sense unless the less basic one is, at its level, isomorphic with the more basic one. For example, if there is a precise 'natural kind' mapping between physics and chemistry, so that every chemical boundary corresponds to a physical boundary, then they can both be equally real. Quantum reality, on the other hand, can only be *seen as* Newtonian for certain purposes. The Newtonian world is a determinate one, so it could be treated as fully real – there is a possible world in which it is fully real, but this is not the case in the actual world. Supervenient vague discourses, however, seem essentially to be both non-basic and not isomorphic with basic ontologies. The world can only ever be *seen as* possessing hills and mountains, or bald and hirsute heads; it never does in a fully realist sense. But, if I am right, these ontological categories are not meant in a fully realist sense, but only in a kind of projectivist one. We often aspire to capture the world as it exactly is, and then we intend our representation in a fully realist manner; but if we attempt a sketch, then we do not mean what we do in a fully realist manner, but only as an appropriate approximate way of seeing it.

As a final sketch of a definition we can talk of –

Taking a Representational Ontology Realistically: a representational ontology is taken realistically when it is taken either as a basic ontology or as isomorphic with a basic ontology in a given world or domain.

It should now be clear that belief in the logical unity of language as a whole is simply a limiting case of the harmonisation requirement. It follows if one thinks that the only logically proper harmonisation between the different representative ontologies is where all the different discourses are strictly interderivable. If interderivability is the only proper form harmonisation can take, then language as a whole must be a logical unity. Such an approach is associated with positivism and is a strong version of the 'unity of science', applied to all ways of describing the world. Approaching natural language with a 'logically perfect one as a model of what it is to understand' seems to me to be a hangover from this kind of positivism.

We are now ready to apply these thoughts about language to the problems.

10.5   Vagueness

The problem with vagueness is supposed to be that, whilst it is desirable that propositions be either true or false, with vague predicates there seem to be many statements employing them which are neither. The reason that it is desirable that propositions be either true or false is that basic logic is intuitively clear when it has this two truth valued structure.

The response to this problem should be clear from the account of language just given. There is a sense in which no representative ontology is vague in itself, but only by contrast with one that is more fine-grained. An ontology is designed only for use in those cases where it is not vague. By using it, one is pretending that it is not a vague discourse, rather in a way analogous to what one does in idealisation in science: one is ignoring or thinking away the rough edges in reality that do not conform with the categories of that ontology. The solution to the vague cases is not a deviant logic to apply to the problematic discourse, but retreat to another way of speaking. The comparison between logic and arithmetic is illuminating. The fact that there in some sense are fuzzy or indefinite objects does not lead most philosophers to think that there ought to be a fuzzy or deviant arithmetic which can be used to count them; we think instead that if one is to do some counting one ought to precisify what it is one is counting before one starts. If you want to know how many waves there are in a particular area of sea, or how many recessions there have been in European economies since the second world war, you first decide how, for whatever purposes you want to know these things, it would be most useful to individuate waves or recessions; you do not struggle to invent a deviant arithmetic that reflects the initial indefiniteness of your subject-matter. Why is it different for logic from the way it is for arithmetic? Logic – that is, patterns of inference – works no differently with 'is bald' substituted in a predicate place than it does with 'is a man'. If it is not clear whether 'Fred is bald' is true, then, if you want to do some arguing, you had better find some more exact description – for example, 'Fred is less hirsute than he was two years ago' – which will suit the purposes for which you are trying to construct an argument. This is in fact the way discourse works. If someone tries to draw conclusions by cashing in on vagueness – for example by arguing that Fred is bald therefore Fred has absolutely no hair, when it is clear Fred has some hair left – then one will insist that he employs a predicate exact enough for the kind of inference he is interested in drawing. Otherwise he is doing something equivalent to cashing in on ambiguity.

Those who think that vagueness constitutes a problem for logic, in the way that it does not for arithmetic, assume that, when it is asserted that Fred is bald, with a clear reference for 'Fred', then what is produced is something which, if two-valued logic is to be preserved, must be either true or false. This picture does not, I think, do justice to how we operate with language.

When we employ predicates that are in fact vague, we treat them as if they were not, until the vagueness becomes salient; then we either contrivedly precisify them for the present purpose, or move on to another discourse that is not vague under the relevant circumstances. Logic applies to the discourse whilst its vagueness is not in play, just as counting works whilst one has a clear idea of what it is that one is counting. When the vagueness intervenes, the discourse is either modified or suspended, so that normal logic can once again be deployed.

Why should it not be the case that logic only applies at the point at which one has made the assertions specific enough for it, as applies in the case of counting? The reason seems to be that philosophers of logic and language require, not merely that *logic* be two valued, but that 'the logical structure of language' also be two valued. This means that every contentful statement be either true of false, for the purposes of exhibiting its meaning, relations to other statements. This is the thesis of the *logical unity of language* that I rejected above. This, I suggest, is no better than asserting that it must be built into our language that it follows from any description how many objects are referred to in that description. In fact this can only be determined once one has decided what are to count as individual objects for one's purposes. The relations between the multiplicity of representational ontologies that constitute natural language is not of the kind represented by the logical unity thesis, but is of the referentially driven sort illustrated above. Vagueness, therefore, presents no threat to classical logic in its role as the science of valid argument, any more than it presents a threat to arithmetic as the science of numbers or counting; it is incompatible only with mistakenly casting logic in the role of providing the sole unifying structure of natural language.

It is natural to respond to this argument by pointing out that language and *logic* are intimately connected in a way that language and *arithmetic* are not. Although this is true, it does not follow that the logical grammar that gives natural language its coherence is the same as the logic that determines validity in argument, nor that it is a grammar alone that gives language its coherence. In particular, if what I have said about the harmonisation requirement is correct, the failure of tight formal relations between all areas of discourse does not threaten the coherence of language, for that depends, in part, on the non-syntactic component in our understanding.

How do these remarks affect the formal argument presented at the outset to show that denial of bivalence leads, via the denial of excluded middle, to contradiction; for, if that argument remains untouched, general considerations about the nature of language will be irrelevant to solving the problem? I am denying the first premise of the argument, that all propositions are true or false. But does not this denial of bivalence involve accepting a three-valued logic, whereas my supposed position is to accept classical logic? No, because, though logic proper is two valued, natural language is not, just in the sense that some propositions lack truth-value. This does not represent the need for a deviant, three-valued, formal logic, but is an indication of where formal logic and syntactic criteria cease to apply. In the analogy with vagueness and arithmetic, there is a distinction between, for example, 'not ten' in 'it is not the case that there are ten objects in the room', where it means there is some other exact number, and the external negation which allows the possibility that, as things stand, it makes no sense to assign a number to the objects in the room because it is not specified what is to count as an object. The judgement about how to proceed – what entities to choose for some assessment – is essentially informal. The best place to see this as affecting the argument is at the last move, the application of De Morgan's Law. If neither P nor not P is true, because P has ceased to be an appropriate characterisation, then one is not asserting *both* P and not P; one is asserting neither, and in the relevant non-formal sense, that is not the same as asserting the negation of both. One is simply withdrawing that way of speaking as inappropriate.

Nevertheless, everything that I have said about vagueness will be useless unless an adequate response can be made to the sorites argument. It is sorites that appears to bring together logic proper and the logico-grammatical features of language. It does this by appearing to show, by elementary logic, that predicates that do not enshrine strict logical principles lead to paradox. This appears to justify the view that language as a whole must possess a strict *logical unity*. I must, therefore, try to show how my weaker account of the unity of language can deal with these paradoxes.[8]

---

[8] Barry Smith and Michael Martin both expressed worries that it was unclear, on my theory, whether vague statements did or did not express propositions. The problem posed about propositions was, I think, the following.

Take as a case of vagueness 'Snowdon is a mountain' (S). It was being suggested that I faced a dilemma.

Either (S) expresses a proposition or it does not. If it does not, then there will be a problem about what does and what does not express a proposition – the line will not be clear, because the line between vague and non-vague is unclear. This is embarrassing. If it

10.6 Sorites

Some paradoxes at least strike one as if they revealed something myster-ious about their subject matter. Some of Zeno's, or others connected with space and time, for example, suggest there is something deeply myster-ious in the continuous nature of these phenomena. This feeling may or may not be right, but sorites paradoxes give one no feeling there is some-thing mysterious about baldness and hairs or hills and mountains, only that there is something annoyingly inadequate about our attempts to articulate the way these bits of language work. The phenomena that are mysterious are the linguistic phenomena, not the objects of reference. We shall see, however, that sorites does reveal something surprising about language, or, more generally, about our ontological thought. What sorites paradoxes show is that you get in a mess if you try to relate systematically certain vague concepts to the relatively more exact reality on which they, in some sense, supervene. Perhaps the obvious conclusion to draw is that one is not supposed to relate them systematically. What would be involved in not so relating them?

The sorites argument as stated above presupposes that talk of heaps and grains are to be regarded equally realistically. If what goes above is

does express a proposition, then, as it is neither true nor false, I am saddled with 3 (or more) values, which I had denied.

I think that there is more than one way to answer this, but I prefer the following.

S does express a proposition because (i) 'Snowdon' unambiguously refers; (ii) 'is a mountain' is a perfectly good predicate, defined by paradigm cases; (iii) the overall import – that Snowdon falls in the same class as Everest and Mont Blanc, not with Cumnor Hill and Box Hill – seems a clear enough claim.

I am quite happy with notion that there are 'many values', and deny only that one needs 'many valued' logics. In fact I think that in natural language there is a rich, messy plurality of the ways and degrees in which statements do or do not capture how the world is. We are often concerned about how accurate a statement is, or whether it is 'accurate enough'. There is often no useful answer to the question of whether a statement or estimate that is 'not quite accurate enough for our purposes' is true or false. My only claim is that issues such as these need to be sorted out (or shown not to matter) before deploying such statements in arguments – as with the need to decide what you will count as an object before starting counting.

Contrary to what I say above, however, I think it is possible to live with the notion that it is vague whether something is a proposition. You can say that only when something is definitely a non-vague case does a sentence express a proposition, provided that you do not assimilate cases like S to cases like straightforward reference failure of demonstratives or logically proper names, or the use of meaningless, nonsense predicates. In those cases, one cannot tell what the speaker is trying to say but this is not true of S. On this view, there is a sort of continuum between a mere meaningful sentence, like 'he is bald' with absolutely no reference for 'he', and an absolutely clear proposition. This fits in, I think, with my view above that linguistic representation of the world is usefully messy.

correct, this is not true. The premise that asserts that heaps are constituted by grains should be interpreted as meaning

(1a) *n* grains can properly be *seen or conceptualised as* a heap

It might seem that this requires that the second premise be reconstructed as

(2a) When something can properly be *seen or conceptualised as* a heap, then the removal of one grain cannot render it not seen or conceptualised as a heap.

If (2a) were true, then we would end up conceptualising zero grains as a heap. But is (2a) true? It is at least ambiguous between

(2b) When something can properly be *seen or conceptualised as* a heap, then the removal of one grain cannot render it obligatory to see or conceptualise it as a non-heap.

and

(2c) When something can properly be *seen or conceptualised as* a heap, then the removal of one grain cannot render one any less inclined to see or conceptualise it as a heap.

(2b) is simply a statement of the vagueness of 'heap'. It is, therefore, true, but it is not strong enough to carry through the sorites argument. That argument requires not merely that one change will not take you from heap to non-heap, but that one change cannot make one less inclined to apply the ontological classification 'heap'. When that is put into the 'seen as' jargon, it becomes (2c).

But (2c) is false, because it is a psychological matter whether making some small change affects a subject's inclination to classify an object in a certain way. What will presumably happen is that the subject will become progressively less confident in calling the object a heap as grain removals make perceptible differences. There will be a 'last straw' phenomenon. This will be true even if the individual changes are too small to be noticed. It is at this point that the less realist view of non-basic ontologies makes a difference. Thus, if 'heap' is understood in a fully realist sense, then the question of whether it *really is* a heap can be raised at any point, but if non-basic ontologies that are not isomorphic with basic ones are thought of as ways of seeing the world, then this kind of matter of fact does not arise. There may be no objective point at which, conceived realistically, something moves from being definitely a heap to its being indefinite whether it is or not, but it does not follow that there can be no point, in any given case, at which someone in fact comes to feel less certain about whether to classify it as a heap or not: that is, whether or not to continue to apply this particular form of non-basic discourse to it.

10.7   The resultant nature of language

Natural language is far from being one united formal syntax with an interpretation or model. At most, some ontologically basic or privileged description of the world can be treated in this way. Perhaps Frege and Russell, with their idealised languages can be thought of as concentrating on this, and treating the rest of language as irrelevant to their purposes. Much of natural language is bound together *both* by entailments of a formal kind, that alone are not sufficient, *and* by the speaker's ability to grasp the co-referentiality of different kinds of linguistic sketch. The kind of thinking that enables us to interchange from one representational ontology – one conceptual sketch – to another will have more in common with the kind of ability that enables us to recognise different kinds of picture as being of the same sort of subject matter than it will be like syntactical rule-governed activity on a conceptual level. The unity of natural language can only be understood via the semantics or representational content of its component discourses.

I have been asked whether I am not an eliminativist about vague and non-basic properties, claiming that, in the end, there is no such thing as baldness or being a mountain. My view is better expressed by saying that one should treat non-basic predicates in a conceptualist, rather than a realist, manner. Only basic predicates, and those reducible to basic predicates should be treated in a strictly realist way. But this is not an unusual view for a realist about universals to take. David Armstrong, for example, argues that only scientifically fundamental universals are genuinely present *in rebus*, other properties are merely *predicates*. According to some interpreters, at least, Plato's position is similar, in that he thinks only metaphysically fundamental properties are truly forms. A mixture of conceptualism and realism is not, therefore, an unusual position for someone who is fundamentally a realist; the properties that are to be understood realistically ground the conceptualism which applies to the rest. Those predicates understood in the conceptualist way can be deployed or dropped as is convenient.

I think that this approach to language illuminates and alleviates many of the problems that have concerned contemporary ontologists. For example, the problem of constitution *versus* identity for the clay and the statue disappears if one thinks of the clay as being *seen as* and *conceived of as* a statue. Similarly, disputes between universalists, moderates and nihilists in mereology lose their force if non-basic predicates are treated conceptualistically. The role of realism and conceptualism in the issues confronted in this part of the book will be raised more explicitly in the next chapter. And the contrast between the Newtonian and the modern views of the physical world will emerge as powerfully relevant.

There are, also, I believe, more dramatic metaphysical conclusions when one applies the theory to vagueness in identity, for I believe one can then show that there are no truly realistic physical individuals. I shall deal with that matter in Chapter 12.

11 Composite objects, the special sciences, conceptualism and realism

11.1 Introduction

In this chapter I will try to draw together and apply the results from Chapters 9 and 10 to the ontology of the natural world in general. Initially, I am concerned with the ontology of composite physical objects. I shall be assuming the by-no-means-uncontested proposition that there is a fundamental physical level, which I shall designate, for convenience, as 'basic physics'. The issue is what, given the reality of the entities in basic physics (which I will usually call 'atoms' for convenience) and their arrangement in space-time, is the ontological status of objects composed of the atoms. I shall also be assuming that the purely physical realm is 'closed under physics', that is there are no emergent laws: atoms do not behave in a way that they should not do, according to basic physics, when they enter into certain combinations. So the issue concerns the ontological status – the reality – of, e.g., molecules, living cells and plants, mountains or tables. The status of possibly immaterial things, such as minds, is not part of the initial problem, though it will become relevant in the discussion of some of the solutions, as we shall see, and as was anticipated in Chapters 9 and 10.

There seem to me to be three different positions on this issue which I wish to consider, and which can be expressed in four propositions. The first two propositions constitute one of the positions:

1. A composite object is no more than the things that compose it.

This is put together with

2. It follows from 1 that the composite does not exist in a realist sense, but only in a conceptualist one.

I shall explain this below.

One might simply deny 1, in the following way.

3. A composite object is more than the things that compose it *because it has its own identity conditions.*

Finally there is a no-nonsense, no-problem view.

4. A composite being no more than the things that make it up means that it is just as real as those things. If you make a house of bricks, and the bricks are real, so is the house.

The view that I want to advocate is that 1 and 2 together are the best that a physical realist can do. This view has a costly consequence, because, as I have argued in Chapter 9 and implied in Chapter 10, it entails mind-body dualism. Before explaining further why I believe it has this consequence, I shall say something about the distinction between the conceptualist and realist senses of the claim that *there are F*s, or *F*s *exist*.

11.2   Conceptualist and realist existence claims

I think the question 'are there *F*s?' can properly be interpreted in either of two ways, depending on the '*F*' in question. One I call the conceptualist interpretation (CI), and it can be read roughly as follows:

(CI) We have the concept '*F*'. Is the world so organised that it satisfies this concept in the way that is necessary for the standard or paradigm uses of that concept?

If the answer to this is affirmative, then there are *F*s, in the conceptualist sense. The other interpretation is realist (RI), and goes roughly as follows.

(RI) Forget about us and our concepts. If there were no conceptualisers around (putting God or Divine minds aside) would there be *F*s?

If the answer to this is affirmative, then there are *F*s in the realist sense. Conceptualism about '*F*' is the view that it satisfies CI but *not* RI: realism is the view that it satisfies RI. Conceptualism and realism, as represented in CI and RI, are not meant to be rival theories about the nature of universals as a class, as is the case in the more usual use of these terms. The suggestion is rather than CI alone may be correct for some universals and RI for others.

Common sense does not make this distinction, but I do not think that it finds it rebarbative. Why I think this will, I hope, become clear in what follows. Nominalists will find RI objectionable because they will not find the realist view of properties and universals entailed by it acceptable. I will not be concerned here to engage with nominalism of this sort, for I think that, if there is a world, it must be thus and so, and, therefore, it must be characterised by some properties independently of our conceptual practices. The nearest I can come to nominalism is (v) below.

There are the following positions one might take on adopting the conceptualist and realist positions.

(i) Realism for all standard concepts, including those for natural objects and those for artefacts.

(ii) Realism applying to natural objects, but not to artefacts, which are treated conceptually.

(iii) Realism for objects at the fundamental level and for a sub-class of standard objects, e.g. organisms (not stones or planets or chemicals), and everything else is treated conceptually.

(iv) Realism for objects at the fundamental level but conceptualism for the rest.

(v) Conceptualism for everything we know and possibly for everything we are ever likely to know, or even are capable of knowing. How the world is in itself will always evade our grasp: we can only approximate to its actual properties.

Most discussion of these issues in modern analytic metaphysics is in what one might describe as a 'mad dog realist' spirit, as in (i), and is only interested in RI. To say with Peter van Inwagen (1990: 109), for example, that there are no tables, but only table-shaped arrangements of simples is to ignore CI as a candidate for answering the 'are there any Fs?' question. Van Inwagen's position assumes that the only interpretation of this question is the strict realist one. If one took CI seriously, then it is clear that, in that sense, there are tables, for the world is clearly so constructed as to make the application of this concept fruitful.[1]

As the above options show, the CI–RI distinction allows for a more nuanced divide than I initially set out: the choice is not necessarily between 'only atoms are real' and 'everything is real'. Nevertheless, this gives a neat schematism.

Why does adopting 1 and 2 entail dualism? Because, if all physical composites are artefacts of conceptualisation, and if the human being, brain, mind etc. are physical composites (and they are certainly not physical simples), then they are products of conceptualisation. What is it that does this conceptualising? Not something that only exists conceptually, on pain of a regress, as I argue in Robinson (2010), in Chapter 9 above and Chapter 13 below.

The alternatives to the 1 and 2 combination are 3 and 4. 3, I think, is often appealed to. For example, in the case of clay and statue, the fact that the clay and the statue have different identity conditions is taken as showing that there are two things present. But if the [atoms composing the] clay are real and the statue only conceptual, one is not forced to treat non-basic levels realistically. Identity conditions go with concepts and

---

[1] It is not obvious that van Inwagen either need or would object to my way of characterising the situation.

this does not force one to take the entities covered by those concepts in a realist sense. That issue must be decided independently. So 3 has no independent force: one must decide whether to take '*F*' realistically before knowing what weight to give *F*'s identity conditions. This brings (ii) and (iii) into consideration. (iii) is represented by van Inwagen and by some of the 'new hylomorphists', such as Jaworski. We will return to this.

11.3   How to decide the issue

The issue is as follows. Assuming that the fundamental physical level is to be taken in a realist sense, how is one to decide how to take the other levels – and, indeed, how can one decide what is at stake in the issue? One might picture it in the following way. We all agree that there are certain atoms arranged in a certain pattern, exercising certain causal influences on each other. How are we to understand the question of whether there is *realistically* a further object that consists of the atoms taken together, or whether it is just a matter of the usefulness of the application of a further concept? What exactly are two people, one of whom says that there are just the atoms so arranged and someone who says that they constitute an object, disagreeing about, given that they agree about all the causal influences? Is it more than a verbal dispute?

These issues have been much discussed in contemporary metaphysics, a classic source being *Metametaphysics*, edited by David Chalmers (2009). How does my approach in this book relate to this literature?

First, I intend my discussion to be self-standing: the considerations I bring in the discussion of reduction and vagueness, and in most of this chapter, are independent of the arguments in the bulk of the literature (which is not to say that there is no overlap in the kinds of considerations brought to bear).

Second, there is in the literature a distinction made between assertions made 'inside the "ontology room"' and those made outside it (Chalmers 2009: 81). This distinction is between contexts where a serious ontological question of a philosophical sort is being raised, and those in which a discourse is being accepted and some issue raised within that discourse. Thus a question like 'is there a highest prime number?' raised in a mathematical discussion does not concern the ontological status of a particular kind of number. A fictionalist about numbers, who denies that numbers really exist, could still agree that there are prime numbers but that there is no highest, whilst talking within mathematics. The distinction between inside and outside the ontology room is similar to Hume's distinction between what he thinks in his study and what he allows himself to think outside. This distinction stands in an ambiguous relation to my distinction between RI and mere CI. On the one hand, any normal discourse which can be made to make what are generally accepted as true statements can be given CI, so mere CI is similar to statements made outside the ontology room. On the other hand, CI is a *philosophical* theory about how certain concepts work, so it is a judgement made whilst in the study, not just a practice outside of it. And it is not simply equivalent to saying that 'really' the entities in question do not exist, but is an account of how certain concepts are properly understood to work.

Third, there is a tendency in the contemporary debate to see the issue in formal and semantic terms, raising questions such as whether the quantifier is ambiguous between serious ontological contexts and 'ordinary' ones. This would apply to my distinction as the question of whether it is ambiguous between CI and RI. This seems to me to be a fundamental question only if you think that the formal apparatus is philosophically foundational, and not merely an aid to clarifying philosophical statements and arguments. The issues of how to understand reductionism and the relation of physics to the special sciences, or the operations of vague predicates, or whether certain predicates should be treated realistically or conceptualistically are not, I believe, helpfully treated as formal questions; substantive philosophical questions rarely are.

The arguments in Chapters 9 and 10 began my approach to this problem. I argue in the former that the relationship of the special sciences to physics requires a kind of perspectivalism, which has two consequences. One is conceptualism about the special sciences, for their properties are a matter of interpretation. The other is that it seems to require dualism, if we are to find a place for the interpreter. Chapter 10 backs this up by arguing that vagueness, which applies to large areas of discourse, should be treated conceptualistically.

I want now to look at two further considerations favouring a conceptualist approach to most or all non-fundamental physical ontologies. The first is the causal inefficacy of the non-fundamental levels, if the physical realm is closed under physics. The second concerns the significance of the strict falsehood of Newtonian science, given the close alliance between such science and most of the properties we attribute to the world when not doing fundamental physics.

11.4   Causal efficacy and existence: (a) defending 'common sense'

We here obviously have two questions. First is the question of whether, if the physical realm is closed under physics, it follows that the entities and properties special to the other sciences are causally inefficacious – epiphenomenal. Second is the question of whether, if they are inefficacious, this is a good reason to deny them existence, in a realist sense.

These two issues are naturally considered together and relate to options 3 and 4 above, namely:

3. A composite object is more than the things that compose it *because it has its own identity conditions.*
4. A composite being no more than the things that make it up means that it is just as real as those things. If you make a house of bricks, and the bricks are real, so is the house.

It is appropriate to begin with 4 because if simple common sense can be made to hold philosophically, then no further discussion is needed.

4 sounds like common sense and is defended by Kim. The truth makers for higher-level explanations are just as real as those for physics. If bricks are real, then so is a house made of bricks. And if bricks have causal powers, so does the house, in virtue of the bricks' powers. So if atoms have real force, combinations of atoms can constitute a real object which has real causal efficacy compounded from the real forces of the atoms of which it is made. This seems to be common sense. Kim states the common-sensical nature of this position emphatically.

The errant baseball didn't after all break the window, and the earthquake did not cause the buildings to collapse! This strikes us as intolerable. (1998: 81)

Kim was talking about causal efficacy rather than mere existence, but if the macro is causally efficacious, it must exist! Kim's insistence on common sense is not wrong, but the impression that it assists the realist is an illusion, for these truths are neutral between conceptualist and realist interpretations. The baseball broke the window, but both 'baseball' and 'window' are to be understood in the conceptualist sense. So if one adopts CI as appropriate for such concepts, there are baseballs etc., but in the conceptualist sense. Similarly for the earthquake and the buildings. Only an extreme realist would feel that common sense was threatened by this reading. Kim's earthquake and van Inwagen's table both exist, but on the CI of what that means.

This is liable to prompt the following thought: what is the difference between saying 'there are atoms arranged table-wise' and 'there is a table'; is there a real ontological issue here? In the context of a slightly different discussion, namely the ontology of universals, David Armstrong (2010) characterises conjunctive universals as 'an ontological free lunch'. Perhaps composite objects are also 'ontological free lunches'. But this expression ought to prompt suspicion, for it seems to suggest that a composite both is and isn't something extra. In what sense can it be 'free' except in the sense that it adds nothing extra to one's ontological total, but in what sense is it a lunch unless one is getting something more? But there is a more substantial objection to 4 based on the role of identity conditions. If there really is a table there and not just atoms arranged table-wise, it could, at some time have been constituted by at least a few different atoms from the one's that actually constituted it. This shows that there is a real difference and that the lunch is not entirely free; something grounds the identity condition difference. The conceptualist has a non-mysterious account of this: it is grounded in the nature of the concept 'table'. For the realist to respond 'well, it is a table, isn't it' does not seem to be explanatory.

The comparison with the case of universals is in fact more than a parallel. Many if not most modern realists about universals follow Armstrong in supporting a sparse theory, according to which only certain instantiated predicates correspond to universals. Usually this follows basic science which may or may not mean physics only. It is plain that one cannot combine a sparse theory of universals with a rich theory of objects. If there is no tablehood, there are no instances of it, and so there are, in the realist sense, no tables. The rationale behind sparsity is, usually, that one does not need or want causally redundant universals, and if the physical world is closed under physics, then no more than the universals needed by physics are needed to account for the distribution of matter.

11.5   Causal efficacy and existence: (b) the reality and power of structures

There are philosophers who think that macroscopic objects are real because of the fundamental nature of *structure* and the causal properties that they say go along with this. The individuation of structures also carries along with it the identity conditions of objects.

Often flying under the label *hylomorphism* is the idea that *structure* or *organisation* is ontologically basic.[2] The term *hylomorphism* of course originates from Aristotle, but the modern theory is simply taking macro organisation at face value and so treating it as being as real and efficacious as the microscopic. Nothing exclusively Aristotelian or scholastic need be invoked.

This idea is very clearly articulated in Jaworski (2011)

---

[2] For a wider discussion of hylomorphism, see Robinson (2014b).

Hylomorphism claims ... [t]hat structure is a basic ontological and explanatory principle. (269)

Structure is also a basic explanatory principle in the sense that it explains why members of this or that kind are able to engage in the behaviors they do. It is because humans are organized as they are, for instance, that they are able to speak, to learn, and to engage in the range of activities that distinguish them from other living things and from non-living ones.

Hylomorphism implies ... that there are two distinct kinds of properties: properties due to something's structure and properties things possess independently of a broader structure. (272)

The properties of these structures are not idle.

Emergent properties are not epiphenomenal ... but make a distinctive causal or explanatory contribution to a system's behavior.

To emphasise this point.

Emergent [hylomorphic] properties are not logical constructions out of lower-level properties; they do not represent abstract ways of describing lower-level occurrences or processes. (274)

There follows what might seem to be a direct denial of the causal exclusion principle.

Hylomorphists endorse **causal pluralism**. They claim that there are causal properties and relations that do not fit the mold set by physics ... [this] view is compatible with all forces operating at a fundamental physical level [i.e., none at other levels] and is therefore immune to the empirical objections raised against emergentism. (290–1)

This last quotation is particularly important. In subscribing to causal pluralism, the hylomorphist appears to be denying Kim's causal exclusion principle. But notice that the avowal of causal pluralism is immediately followed by the assertion that 'all *forces* are operating at a fundamental physical level' [italics added]. What one has, in fact, is an *explanatory* pluralism, with causation adopted into the domain of explanation; the wholly external, mind-free element is *force* and this is exclusively micro. Causal exclusion has been replaced by force exclusion, and explanatory pluralism is now characterised as, or as including, plural causal explanation. But no one thought that explanations, of all levels, excluded an appeal to causation. Jaworski is really only claiming that, once one realises that most explanations are causal explanations, explanatory pluralism is pluralism enough to constitute or ground a full realism about all levels. This sits well with Kim's belief that different ontological levels are not in competition with each other, but it shows that this requires only an explanatory pluralism, and this is compatible with CI for non-basic levels.

What is at stake is whether the human perspective has a certain role in reifying what is in fact the micro world in the way we do. There is a sense in which any mereological combination of atoms could be treated as an entity and so could the combined sum of their forces. Which are chosen are a matter of human interest and perspective – not arbitrary, of course, but well-groundedness of conceptual practice does not entail a strict realism. Talk of 'human interests' might make it seem too intellectual. One of the most important things is the grain of human perception – what is salient to us and how it manifests itself to our senses. If we can see the independent constituents of an entity we are less likely to think of that entity as basic. We can see the elements in a crowd, in a swarm of bees or in a weather system and so are less likely to think of these things as fundamental, even if they seem to have a dynamic of their own. We are generally happy to make a CI of them. But for most organisms, we see them only whole, for such parts as we do see are essentially parts of the thing – branches, leaves, limbs, teeth etc. – not independent parts. If we saw a plant as a swirling mass of particles passing in and out of an organisational vortex, like a rioting crowd, then, once we came to believe that the organisation was a product of the interaction of the particles following only the laws of physics and not an extraneous imposition, we would probably find it natural to make a CI of plants. As it is, the nature of our perception seems to endow them with a greater degree of natural integrity than they would seem to possess from a more microscopic viewpoint.

Both as entities and as causal agents, macroscopic objects seem to be by-products of their micro constituents. What does it mean to call the higher-order processes 'by-products'? It rests on the premise that everything that happens happens because of the micro-dynamics. Apparent higher laws, though useful generalisations from our standpoint, do not give the real reason why anything happened. It is like the case of the plant 'turning towards the light'. Common experience leads us to say that it does so in order to gain more light, because it needs light to survive and replicate. But science tells us that this turning happens because of the chemical reactions involved, without any fundamental teleology. But were not these chemical processes 'selected' because they allowed the plant to get the light and thus teleology is restored at the level of biology? Yes, in a sense, but only in the sense that certain micro-processes, from their own dynamics, repeat themselves in a certain way. The micro-processes do not get repeated *because* they lead to the replication of the organism; their repeating themselves *is* the replication. Dawkins's expression 'the blind watchmaker' as a label for nature is illuminating. The 'blindness' in question is not primarily cognitive; it is volitional. Nature does not intend to produce watches – or eyes or organisms in general – the developing of the quantum field, which is 'blind to' its by-products, merely produces things which can be usefully so classified from the perspective of a macroscopic rational animal.

Davidson (1993) rejects Kim's exclusion principle, but, rather ironically, we can draw on a legitimate point of Davidson's in its support. Davidson claims, very plausibly, that it is only at the fundamental level that there are what he calls *strict laws*. Laws at other levels involve *ceteris paribus* clauses and a certain degree of approximation. This strongly suggests that, though they are useful explanatory tools formulated on the basis of more exact processes that underlie them, the laws of the special sciences are not entities in their own right. It would be natural to argue the same way for the entities to which those laws attach. Davidson's reason for rejecting the exclusion principle rests on some very controversial features of his position. He claims that causal relations are entirely extensional and so events are not efficacious *in virtue of* any of the properties involved in them, so you cannot claim that some of them are active and others idle. The motive behind this is some kind of nominalism, which wishes to treat properties as simply 'descriptions' under which events fall, and, as such, not agents in the world. At the same time he wants to treat the mental as 'purely conceptual' and the basic physical as, in some sense, more real. For further discussion of Davidson's confusions, see Chapter 6 above and Robinson (2001).

11.6   Causal efficacy and existence: (c) explanatory force and realism

Barry Loewer defends a version of what might be called 'realism light'. This view arises from his dispute with Jerry Fodor over what realism involves.

In his (1974) Fodor argued that physicalism does not require reductionism. An important part of this claim is that non-reductionism does not in any way cast doubts on the reality of those physical entities that cannot be reduced; they are not in any way 'secondary quality-like', in being dependent for their reification on human categorisation or response. He even calls the properties found in the special sciences 'natural kinds'. This is a very different sense from that deployed following Putnam, according to which natural kinds are those kinds of stuff categorised by reference to the sameness of their hidden real essence. They are the opposite of multiply realisable properties, which are the ones in which Fodor is interested in in psychology, and the reason why he rejects reductionism. For Fodor, 'natural kinds' in the special sciences are simply properties found in nature – not, in some way, dependent on us. To emphasise their naturalness, he even seems to go to the extreme of denying that they supervene necessarily on their base. Taking psychology as a case of a special science, he says:

> Only God gets to decide whether there is anything, and likewise only God gets to decide whether there are laws about pains; or whether, if there are, the pains that the laws are about are MR ['Metaphysically Real']. (1997: 161)

Fodor here seems to be denying the standard physicalist maxim that once God had created all the facts of physics, he had nothing more to do, and this does place him in a bizarre situation. In challenging Fodor's extreme realism, Barry Loewer distinguishes between what he calls *Non-Reductive Physicalism, Metaphysical* (*NRPM*) and *Non-Reductive Physicalism, Light* (*NRPL*). The former is Fodor's position and the latter Loewer's alternative.

> *NRPM* and *NRPL* agree that the special sciences are conceptually, epistemologically, and methodologically autonomous/irreducible to physics but disagree about what autonomy/irreducibility consists in and how it is to be explained. *NRPM* says that the autonomy/irreducibility is metaphysical and seeks to explain the conceptual and epistemological autonomy in terms of the existence of metaphysically basic special science kinds and laws. (2009: 222)

Loewer then raises the question of what the difference would be between a world, W1, in which *NRPL* held and one, W2, in which *NRPM* obtained. Given closure under physics, everything would behave in exactly the same way, so the addition of the further entities and their concomitant laws appears to be vacuous.

One might argue that Fodor does not need to go over the top in this way. The realist about the special sciences might simply deny that W1 is possible, on the grounds that, once the microphysical reality has been created, the higher-order entities and concomitant laws are, *eo ipso*, present too. It is a case of what has been called an 'ontological free lunch'. So God need only create the world of physics, but it does not follow from this that the more macroscopic objects and properties of the special sciences do not exist in their own right.

Nevertheless, the phrase 'ontological free lunch' might still leave one puzzled over what the difference between the 'light' and the 'metaphysical' consists in. Asserting that it means that a further set of entities exist, without any consequences, makes the assertion look suspiciously empty. The expression 'ontological free lunch' itself suggests something very dubious, namely that there both is, and is not, something more. Only the 'human perspective' account of the non-basic can provide us with a coherent explanation of the ontology of the special sciences. Let us look more closely at the 'light' (*L*) and the 'metaphysical' (*M*) versions of non-reductive physicalism.

Loewer says of *L* that it

> attempts to account for the conceptual/methodological irreducibility of the special sciences in terms of facts and laws of microphysics and our epistemological situation in the world.

This seems to involve the human perspective – 'our epistemological situation' – in the constitution of the *L* view, but there are different possible interpretations of this. One might think that the difference can be stated as follows.

(A) *M* says that the ontologies of the special sciences are *basic* and *L* says that they are *derivative.*

But this is ambiguous between

(B) *M* says they are basic, but *L* says they are derivative *but perfectly real in their own right,* that is, no reference to human activity or perspective is involved in what it is for them to exist.

On this interpretation, the role of 'our epistemological situation' is to decide what we pick out of what is anyway there. This contrasts with

(C) *M* says that the ontologies of the special sciences are basic, in the sense that they exist independently of our sensibilities etc., but *L* denies this, giving our perspectives or concerns a role in their reification.[3]

One might characterise (B) as the *Selective Realist* conception of the special science ontologies, and (C), recalling what was said above about the reification of patterns, the *Gestalt Constructivist* conception. If we look at Loewer (2009), we can see that the conception of a 'genuine property' (G-property) is neutral as between (B) and (C).

> In addition to the fundamental properties [of physics] any property that corresponds to a kind term in any science is a G-property. Kind terms are predicates or concepts involved in the appropriate way in laws. By 'law' I mean a simple true generalization or equation that is counterfactual supporting and projectable. This includes fundamental laws of physics and also *ceteris paribus* laws of the special sciences. (Loewer 2009: 245)

---

[3] Loewer kindly leant me a draft of his paper which I quoted in my (2013), in which he said that *L* was to be accounted for 'in terms of facts and laws of microphysics and *our conceptual scheme* and epistemological situation in the world' [italics added]. When I quoted this I did not realise that the italicised phrase was later excised. This suggests that Loewer was torn between (B) and (C), for if our conceptualisation is needed for their existence, then what is real is merely the grounding for our practices.

This account simply deems anything to be a property that has a certain role in science and does not make a distinction between (B) and (C). I do not think that Loewer in any of his (2007), (2008) or (2009) distinguishes between these options. I think that the dialectic between him and Fodor, however, shows that he should come down in favour of (C), for the following reason.

In Loewer's words, Fodor

finds it '*molto mysterioso*' that the motions of particles to-ing and fro-ing in accordance with F=ma ... lawfully end up converging on special science laws ... How do particles that constitute an economy 'know' that their trajectory is required (*ceteris paribus*) to enforce Gresham's Law? [i.e. the law that 'bad money drives out good money']

[Fodor] grants that every special science system is micro-physically constituted and that the dynamical laws of physics are complete but he claims that the laws of physics are *explanatorily* and *modally* incomplete. He adds that there are explanations and counterfactuals expressible in the language of the special sciences that are not necessitated by the laws and facts of fundamental physics. On his view special science counterfactuals and explanations require for their truth irreducible special science laws. So while a regularity expressed by a special science law is not independent of physics (i.e. it is implied by micro-physics laws and facts) its status as a law is independent of physics. (2008: 152)

Loewer believes that his argument cited above that W2 adds nothing to W1 shows this to be false, but whether this is so depends on what one means by 'its status as a law'. The physical facts determine that events will follow the pattern that make the special science laws applicable, but unless one brings the special science laws to bear, one will not have the explanations that those laws make possible. You could not say 'if such and such had not happened then *reproduction would not have taken place*' or '*bad money would not have driven out good*'. So without the laws you cannot provide certain kinds of explanation, but explanation – as opposed to making it the case that matter is where and how it is – is a human activity. What is missing without the special sciences is essentially anthropocentric.

The macroscopic world is the world of the manifest image – manifest, that is, to us and to creatures sufficiently like us. Concepts that fit our manifest world may – perhaps, in a sense, must – apply in a realist way to the contents of our sense experience, subjectively conceived, but it seems impossible that they should so apply to the world itself, if non-Newtonian science is fundamental. This is what I shall now argue.

11.7   Human perspectives, Newtonian science and conceptualism

The role of the human perspective came up in our discussion of reductionism. But it seems to me that there is what may be a knock-down argument for conceptualism, and, therefore, the human perspective. It runs as follows. Let us assume

(1) That either or both of quantum theory and relativity are broadly correct.
(2) The Newtonian picture of the world is strictly false, though workable because it approximates to the quantum/relativistic facts on everything but the very small and very large scale.
(3) All the properties ascribed in the special (physical) sciences are an essential part of the Newtonian, as opposed to quantum or relativistic pictures.

Therefore

(4) None of the properties ascribed to objects in the special sciences are strictly true of the world.
(5) Concepts that are workable but do not correspond to properties that exist in the full realist sense (as defined in RI) fit the definition of the merely conceptual.

Therefore

(6) The concepts of the special sciences are to be understood conceptually, not realistically.

I think that the only premise that might reasonably be contested here is (3). The universal quantifier at the beginning of (3) may be an overstatement, but any concept involving space (or time?) which does not directly build in relativity is bound to suffer a trivial oversimplification, which cannot be corrected without moving to the more basic science; similarly, many concepts approximate to the behaviours of selected parts of the quantum field.

The only alternative is to say that the properties of the special sciences are the wholly real features of *macro* reality, though not of micro. But how can this be so if the properties of the base show them to be ever so slightly inaccurate and, perhaps, false in their fundamental nature of the objects in question (for example, things we must conceive of as solid are really fields which necessarily instantiate essentially different kinds of property)?

11.8   General advantages of CI

There are a variety of stock problems that adopting CI can help solve. In Chapter 10, I argued that it can solve the problems associated with vagueness, and in Section 11.2 of this chapter I outlined how it dissolves constitution problems, such as that raised by the clay and statue. I think it can also help with the 'many *F*s' problem.

The 'many *F*s' problem has two versions: one essentially involving vagueness, one not. The vagueness version – in which the '*F*' in question is typically 'cloud' – concerns objects with indeterminate borders. Peter Unger (1980) argues that, in these cases, one can draw the border in many different places, thus individuating many overlapping objects. The non-vagueness-involving case goes as follows. Suppose that a complex physical object – a table, an oak tree or a cat – is made of a million atomic parts. There are almost indefinitely many sub-groups of those atoms which would be – or are – sufficient to constitute an object of the relevant kind. So, in the case of the table, imagine all its atoms minus two which are presently integral to the table – they still constitute a table. If pursued, this line of thought leads to the idea that there are a vast number of actual tables contained within this one table, though they massively overlap. Or imagine the tree minus a branch. That would still be an oak tree. But that tree-minus-the-branch is present within the actual tree. Similarly for the cat without one of its paws – or simply without a few hairs or the odd atom. There are a tremendous number of proper part combinations sufficient to be an *F* within the actual *F*, and, as each of these is sufficient to be an *F*, all those *F*s are there and real.

The realist has to struggle with the fact that there are many well qualified candidates for being an *F* of the kind in question. Now I am not entirely convinced that a realist cannot cope with the non-vague cases, but the conceptualist has an easy route. He can simply say that this is not the way we deploy this concept: we deem there to be only one *F* whenever there is an *F* present and the only practical way of treating it is as a single object. This 'deeming' is not a conscious choice. Given our perceptual system, the table presents itself as unitary and we interact with it as one thing. For example, even if there are an indefinite number of tables present, you cannot do an indefinite number of different things with them – have dinner off one of them whilst playing table tennis on another. So our conceptualisation is practical as well as – or, perhaps, rather than – intellectual. It is a matter of how we interact with the object.

11.9   Conceptualism and the mind

CI might be adequate for objects that are more or less organised 'masses of matter', but will it do for organisms – oak trees, cats and, worse, human 'beings? Surely these are not entities brought into existence by conceptualisation, but are real in their own right.

Even if what I have said so far is satisfactory for vegetable organisms, surely it will not work for animals, like cats, that are normally thought of as conscious, and human beings? The answer to this will depend to a great extent on whether one is a physicalist. Considered as a non-conscious organism, an animal would be in the same category as a plant, namely a vortex of changing atoms formed entirely in accord with the laws of microphysics. Seeing this as an entity which is more than a highly organised cloud of particles would depend on our finding ourselves conceptualising it as such, as with the oak tree. But isn't the cat's consciousness real in a way that is independent of our conceptualisation? The correct answer is, I think, 'yes', but it is difficult to see how this could be the case if the cat's subjectivity were not something over and above the organisation of elementary particles in its brain. It is not my purpose in this chapter to engage deeply with the philosophy of mind, but I shall briefly give reasons for this claim. If it is right that, in general, organic life is to be interpreted conceptually, as our way of making sense of certain patterns which are a by-product of development at the micro level – say in the quantum field – as presented through our senses, then the same will apply to subsystems within organic life. Thus it applies to neural processes, especially as functionally understood. This leads us to the self-undermining position that I said above Armstrong is committed. The very engine that is responsible for conceptualisation – the human mind – is itself a unit only within the light of conceptual activity. This is the same problem as faces Dennett's interpretationalist stance, and I have argued against it elsewhere (Robinson 1993b: 6 and, in more detail, 2010), as have others (Hornsby 1997: 181–2); it will be the topic of Chapter 13. So here I shall simply assume that conscious states are fundamental in at least a property dualist sense. These mental states will be 'out there' in a fully realist sense, in the same way as whatever constitutes the fundamental level of matter. But will the cat's mind, considered as a complex entity, also be real or will it depend on our reifying it by one of our concepts? Is there, for example, a 'many minds' problem corresponding to the 'many bodies' problem, if one tries to be realist about minds? Remember that the 'many Fs' problem has two forms. One of them depends on the vagueness of the boundaries of most bodies. It is plausible to deny that minds are vague in this sense. If M is a mental state, then there must be some mind to which it belongs. This will not be true for a pure Humean, for on that theory an impression can exist independently, detached from any mind and, therefore, presumably, in an indeterminate relation to a given mind – half attached, like a hair that is falling out or a water droplet at the margins of a cloud. I shall simply assume that this cannot be true of mental states. One may be only vaguely aware of some states, but, in so far as it counts as mental, it belongs to some particular mind. This still leaves the non-vague version of the 'many *F*s' problem. After all, if you take all the cat's mental states and think away one sensation, you still have a feline mind, so are there not many cat-minds present? I said when introducing this problem in Section 11.2 that I was not certain that there might not be a realist solution to it. In the case of minds, I think there certainly is. Insofar as it is determinate whether a certain mental state belongs to a given mind, then one can insist on a maximal criterion for the identity of a mind: it consists of all the mental states that are co-conscious. That very mind *could have* contained one mental state less, but it *does* contain all the actually co-conscious ones. (See Kovacs (2010) for an argument that this is inconsistent with the supervenience of the mental on the physical.)

So the answer is that the mind as a whole will be real and unitary provided that the co-consciousness relation and its scope are real independently of our conceptualisation. The cat will then have only one body *not* – or *not primarily* – because of the way we conceptualise it, but because the one consciousness of the cat acts upon it as a single object. The cat does not have to manoeuvre a set of bodies, as if it were herding cats. So the cat's agency does for it something parallel to what our intelligent interaction with the world does for us. The same line of argument as applies to cats applies to humans. And the individuality or uniqueness of one's body is the result of the fact that one thinks of it and acts upon it as a unity.

11.10   Conclusion

It seems to me that the case is very strong for the claim that non-basic levels are to be understood conceptually and not realistically. In the next chapter, I shall argue that this applies even to the fundamental objects (as opposed to states or properties) in the physical world. In the final chapter of Part II I shall argue that the human perspective is ineliminable and so give support to the claim that conceptualism requires that we place the mind outside the physical realm.

12 Why there are (probably) no physical individuals

12.1 Vagueness and individuality

The argument for the seemingly very improbable conclusion contained in the title of this chapter divides into two parts. The first part is that there is a sense in which there are no physical individuals. This is because a full-fledged individual can sustain a range of counterfactuals, and, I claim, physical objects cannot sustain a sub-category of these, namely certain counterfactuals of origin. One could express my conclusion by saying that counterpart theory is true for physical objects, but this is an inexact way of putting it. The situation is not that if some feature of a world had been different, then, strictly, all the objects would have been different, as is claimed in counterpart theory; rather it is that assertions of individual identity add nothing to assertions couched in entirely general, existentially quantified terms. So that questions of the form 'would this F have been the same F if p?', where p is counterfactual, are asking about nothing beyond whether there would have been an F with certain properties if p. Judgements of identity and difference in these contexts are not part of the strictly realist picture. The second element in my conclusion is that, contrary to first impressions, no substantial part of our common sense view of the world is lost with the demotion of counterfactual-sustaining identity for bodies to the realm of the purely conceptual.

The argument for the first of these propositions is closely connected with the account of vagueness presented in Chapter 10.

(1) Vagueness cannot be eliminated in the predication of identity for bodies in counterfactual situations.
(2) Reality cannot be vague.
(3) A predicate the content of which ineliminably possesses features not possessed by reality cannot figure in a fundamental characterisation of reality.

Therefore

(4) Counterfactual identity for bodies cannot figure in a fundamental characterisation of reality.

12.2 The ineliminability of vagueness in counterfactual identity: the prima facie case

It is nowadays respectable to maintain that individuals have essential properties, though it is somewhat less generally agreed that they have essences. The essential properties I am interested in concern the origin or original composition of the object. Kripke's (1972) claim that a particular wooden table could not have been made of ice seems to be widely accepted, so there is at least one necessary condition for the existence of that individual table: but whether there are necessary and sufficient conditions – i.e. an essence – as well as merely necessary conditions for it being the object it is, is more controversial. Even granted that the table has some essential properties, it is doubtful whether it has an essence.[1] We can scale sentences as follows:

(i) This table might have been made of ice.
(ii) This table might have been made of a different sort of wood.
(iii) This table might have been made of 95% of the wood it was made of and 5% of some other wood.

There will come a point along the spectrum illustrated by (i) and (iii) and towards (iii) where the question of whether the hypothesised table would be the same as the one that actually exists have no obvious answer. It seems that the question of whether it 'really' is the same one has no clear meaning: it is of, say, 75% the same matter and of 25% different matter; these are the only genuine facts in the case; the question of numerical identity can be decided in any convenient fashion, or left unresolved. There will thus be a penumbra of counterfactual cases where the question of whether two things would be the same is not a matter of fact.

Applying the point to the elementary physical objects and assuming that somewhere or at some time matter is created in the universe, can we decide whether in some different possible world from ours the same particles were created? For example, suppose that in the stead of a present electron E there had sprung another, E' at a slightly different place; how near would the points of origin of E and E' have had to be for them to count as the same particle? If we assume that matter exists eternally, we can imagine a world with a counterpart to E which does not quite follow E's path, though very nearly. Would that be the same particle as E? If indefiniteness can be introduced at this level, it can, in principle, be extended to those things composed of the particles, insofar as their identity depends to some degree on the sameness of matter.

---

[1] Essentialism is generally – and correctly – thought of as an Aristotelian doctrine, but Aristotle is interested in the essences of *kinds*; individuals do not seem to come into his discussion.

I argued in Chapter 10 that vague predicates – especially those that generate sorites regresses – cannot be treated as basic, but as belonging to some interpretative *representational ontology*, which should be understood in a merely conceptualist way. The point of this chapter is to argue that the predicate 'would have been the same *x* as', when applied to physical objects, falls into this category. We are used to the idea that there is no real fact of the matter for certain identity statements. For example, to the question 'was England *the same country* after its political transformation following 1066?' we do not think there is a simple affirmative or negative answer. Once you know the facts concerning what remained the same and what changed, you know all the facts; there is no further 'but was it really the same?' question. My claim is that the same applies to counterfactuals of origin, as applied to physical objects. These predications do not, therefore, belong to the basic, realist level. I shall be arguing in Chapter 15 that the same cannot be said of minds, and that counterfactuals of origin in their case cannot be vague and their individuality must be foundational.

12.3   Is vagueness in identity possible?

There is, however, a powerful argument designed to prove that vagueness in identity is impossible. Salmon states it as follows:

> In so far as I understand the idea that identity is sometimes vague, it is provably mistaken. For suppose that there is a pair of entities x and y . . . such as it is vague . . . whether they are one and the same thing. Then this pair (x,y) is quite definitely not the same pair as (x,x) since it is determinately true that x is determinately one and the same thing as itself. It follows that x and y must be distinct. But then it is not vague whether they are identical or distinct. (2005: 243)

This simple argument may be persuasive against the view that there can be genuine identity relations which are vague. The apparent cases of vague identity, therefore, present us with a problem, which could be dealt with by showing that the supposed cases of vague identity either are not really vague or are not really cases of identity, but of some weaker relation. The empiricist treatment of identity through time, for example, is intended to show that such 'identity' is not identity, but some form of continuity. The analogue of continuity for counterfactual identity is the replacement of referring to individuals by quantified descriptions that do not raise the issue of identity: this is a sort of modified counterpart relation. Salmon's argument misses the point if it is directed against those who talk of vague identity only as a preliminary to replacing it: in fact the philosophers he cites as vulnerable to his argument, namely Parfit and Kripke, are in fact reductionists and thus avoid it. Parfit represents the empiricists approach to identity through time referred to above, and Kripke says that vague counterfactual cases should be treated as counterparts. If one wishes to retain identity by showing that the controversial cases are not really vague, one can take any one of four essentially different strategies. These are (1) follow Wiggins in denying that counterfactual identity is vague because it is stipulative; (2) accept some kind of *haecceitas* that goes beyond other, more empirical, criteria and fixes identity; (3) claim that the identities are in fact, if one looks closely, actually quite determinate; (4) accept what I shall call the Lockean solution, of exactness for atoms and elimination for macroscopic objects. I shall now show that none of these works.

12.4   Denials of vagueness: Wiggins's treatment of vagueness in identities

Wiggins rejects the problem of the counterfactual identity of individuals because he does not believe in strict individual essences (1974 and 2001: 105ff). The simplest way of rejecting such essences is to accept counterpart theory, for then the question of whether a certain object would have been the same object if the world had differed in some respect does not arise. This is not Wiggins's way for he does believe in 'transworld individuals', that is, in counterfactual sustaining individuals. He wishes to combine a belief in such individuals with the claim that there are no necessary and sufficient conditions for being a particular individual – nothing that makes something the individual it is. He says:

We do not have to find something *in virtue of which* the object of speculation is Julius Caesar. Let me go one step to meet Kripke, however. Perhaps the speculation has to be able to *rebut* the charge that he has actually lost the subject of discourse if he changes its parents or origin. But I ask: can he not rebut the charge by claiming to speculate about how *the man whom* Brutus murdered in 44 B.C. would have fared if (say) Marius had been his father? (1974: 335)

This suggestion seems to confuse, not help, the matter. If 'the man whom Brutus murdered' is a rigid designator, then the question is equivalent to 'how would Caesar have fared if Marius had been his father?' This question either (a) presupposes that the very same man would have existed under those conditions or (b) is asking whether he would have. On the latter interpretation we have merely re-posed the sort of question we are trying to answer. If we take the former interpretation, then the presumption is that Caesar need not have had the same father. But if there are no individual necessities attaching to Caesar that is no necessities other than his being of the natural kind 'man' with all that that entails what would be wrong with the suggestion that Caesar might have been born of Hitler's parents, with Hitler's genetic make-up, etc.? If this suggestion is sound (which I cannot imagine Wiggins would wish), then what is the content of the hypothesis that pseudo Hitler is really Caesar?

A Cartesian might be able to make sense of this by saying that *the soul that in fact went into Caesar's body might have gone into Hitler's*, but for a non-Cartesian the supposition is meaningless. If we do not take 'the man whom Brutus murdered' as a rigid designator, then it is equivalent to 'whomsoever Brutus murdered'; this will cover an indefinite range of different people in different worlds and does not in any sense guarantee our grasp on Caesar.

The only middle position between individual essences (of which the Cartesian theory is an unusual case) and counterpart theory is that enough of the statements true in fact of Caesar should be true of anyone who is Caesar in a different world. But this takes us back to the Fregean approach to names which Kripke's apparatus of rigid designation and the necessity of identities was designed to replace. Even so, the Fregean approach leaves one with the vagueness in identity of difficulty cases of the sort I have described.

In brief, the objection to Wiggins is as follows. If one says that the identity of individuals 'across worlds' is not a matter which is determined by some necessary and sufficient conditions, but by the stipulation by which the world is set up – that is, by our deciding what and who is in it – then there is the problem of deciding what are the intelligible limits of stipulation. Most parties seem to agree that Caesar could not have been other than human, but if we are to allow that he could not have been just any human we need to go further and move from the species essences that identify him as human to things which fix him as *that* human. If this cannot be done – as the arguments of the previous section suggest they cannot – then transworld or counterfactual identity is indefinite.

12.5   Denials of vagueness: Salmon and *haecceitas*

The rationale of Salmon's theory is that there always is an answer to questions of identity, even though one might not be able to tell what it is when all the other facts are in. The criteria underdetermine the facts about identity, showing that there are special facts about the 'thisness' (*haecceitas*) of objects.[2]

---

[2] Salmon's account is to be found in Appendix I of his 1981/2005, which runs from 219 to 252. The crux of his position is 239ff.

Salmon treats vagueness in the following way. Imagine a boat made of a hundred planks, which we will name '1', '2', '3' ... '100'. Call this boat a and the world in which it is supposed to exist '$W1$'. Suppose that we are sure that there could be a world, $W2$, in which a was made with planks 1–98 plus two new ones, 101 and 102 (and equally for any other world involving a with 98 of the original planks). Equally we are sure that if there had been a four-plank difference – e.g. a boat made from 1–96, 101–4 (call this $W3$) – then the boat in that world would not have been a but some other, which we will call b. However, we may be uncertain as to whether a could have been made with three-plank difference, e.g. 1–97, 101–3. Certainly there could have been a boat made with those planks, but would it have been a?

Salmon says that there is a world, $W4$, in which a is constructed from 1–97, 101–3, but that what is not clear is whether that world is accessible or possible from $W1$. The notion of worlds being accessible and possible *from* others, rather than possible *simpliciter*, is reached as follows. The example we give shows that a two-plank difference is permissible. If, contrary to fact, the boat a had been made two planks different from the way it actually was in $W1$, and we had instead $W2$, it would in these circumstances have been possible that it might have been made with a further two planks difference ($W5$). This would have given a boat just like that in $W3$ and, indeed, a world just like $W3$. But it would not be $W3$ because, *ex hypothesi*, the boat in $W5$ is the same as that in $W1$ whereas the boat in $W3$ is different from that in $W1$. Now $W5$ is accessible or possible from $W2$, but not from $W1$; for if $W1$ had been actual then any boat made with four planks different (as is that in $W5$) could not have been a, but the boat in $W5$ is a.

Similarly, because it is uncertain whether a three-plank difference is permitted, it is uncertain whether $W4$ defined as a world containing a, three-plank difference from a in $W1$ is possible directly from $W1$. There is a world with a in it possessing the three-plank difference from a in $W1$ because if a had been as it is in $W2$ it could have been made as in $W4$. So $W4$ is possible from $W2$.

The difficulty with this approach to the problem of vagueness is that it means that two worlds might differ in nothing other than the *haecceitas* of the objects in them. That is, all the objects in two worlds might be made of exactly identical (numerically, not just qualitatively identical) matter, with all the same details of origin etc., yet the objects be deemed to be barely different. This is the relation of $W3$ and $W5$. They contain boats made from exactly the same matter etc. but one has boat a and the other boat b. The identity of these boats is completely emergent with respect to all material facts.

This conclusion may seem strange, but not unacceptable, if the alternative is to do away with counterfactual identity altogether. However, it is a good deal more unacceptable than it might seem at first sight, for it entails that there are almost indefinite numbers of different possible worlds which are absolutely identical materially, both in type and in the numerical identity of their components. These are different worlds solely because the objects in them have different *haecceitas*. *W3* and *W5* are not the only possible worlds in this situation. If boat *b* had been made with two planks different we could have a world just like *W2* (call it *W6* except that the boat in it was *b* not *a*). And if *b* had been so made, it could have been two planks further different which could give a world exactly like *W1* (*W7*) except that it contained *b* not *a*. Indeed, we can see that by extension in this way we can derive fantastic conclusions. I suppose that there are almost an unlimited number of different combinations of different planks of wood from which a boat of the relevant design could have been made at that time. Every possible boat, *a, b* ... *n*, is made from each of these possible combinations in some world, though only a few are directly accessible from any given world. Incredible conclusions can be derived even if we restrict ourselves to worlds which are directly accessible, for the boat will not be the only object in the world whose identity depends on something beyond its matter. Suppose we apply the same standard of counterfactual identity, namely the necessity for 98% of the original matter to bodies. Just as the same material construction could constitute either of two boats (as in *W2* and *W6*) for every other complex object, the same material structure will be found in two different worlds with two different identities. A boat made *as in W2* might be either *a* or *b* and the world could be either *W2* or *W6*. Suppose that it is *W2* and that *W2* has *n* objects in it, all subject to similar standards of identity as those applying to boats. Each object in *W2* will have an exact counterpart in another world (and by 'counterpart' here is meant an object composed of exactly the same matter and exactly the same origin). There will be 2^n different worlds of exactly the same material constitution, for there are 2^n different series of the objects in different combinations, that is, combining first or second counterparts for each object. If we consider a modest world containing a million million objects, then there will be $2^{10^{12}}$ worlds which are like that world, differing from each other only in the distribution of *haecceitas*. Remember, too, that these are only the worlds which are directly accessible to each other. If we go further afield there will be indefinitely more than two possible identities for each material structure, and this will be the number which must be raised to the power *n*.

It might be argued that this ontological profligacy is harmless, like the generation of infinities of numbers, propositions or other abstract entitles.

It is true that possible worlds take up no space, but that is not the point. The point is that *haecceitas* itself must be thought of as something real and emergent (not supervenient, for it reflects no material difference) with regard to a material basis. It is not some harmless reflection of the logic of identity, but a substantive piece of ontology necessary to give sense to a particular application of the concept of identity. Worlds differing only in *haecceitas* would differ ontologically just as much as worlds with different material components.

To make matters worse, we could never know which of the enormous number of worlds similar to our own was the actual world, the one we are actually in. Suppose we live in a world with a boat constructed as the boats in *W2* and *W6* are constructed. Are we living in *W2* or *W6*? To answer this we have to answer the question: is the boat in our world the one which, if it had originally been made as in *W1* could have been made as in *W2*, or is it one which, if it had originally been made as in *W3* could have been made as in *W6*? (Once again I have restricted myself to directly accessible possibilities.) These questions plainly lack empirical content as they ought, for they are unsuccessful attempts to ask more informatively whether the boat in our world has the *haecceitas* of *a* or *b*, when this supervenes in no actual empirical difference. This does not merely have the consequence that we do not know which possible world we inhabit (this might seem harmless, given the abstract nature of possible worlds) but that we do not know the identity of any of the objects in our world, even though we know all the facts about their actual material composition and origin.

Salmon's system is massively counter-intuitive, and, I suspect, for reasons I cannot pursue here, it may even be incoherent. It is plainly an option not worth pursuing.

12.6   Denials of vagueness: fixed leeway and no leeway

If Salmon's attempt to employ *haecceitas* to solve the problem of vagueness fails, it does not follow that one must resort to counterpart theory. It is possible to deny that there is vagueness in counterfactual identity either by insisting that the leeway for counterfactual changes in matter is fixed, not vague, or by denying that any difference in original matter is consistent with sameness. Either of these ploys may be thought to be less costly for intuition than counterpart theory.

These options are not acceptable. Let us first consider the suggestion that there is some leeway for difference in origin, but that what this amounts to is fixed, not vague. What fixes it? It would be difficult to argue plausibly that it was built into our concept of, for example, a boat, that it allowed, say, exactly 2% variation in original matter. Is it the same for all objects? Can the percentage be discovered by conceptual analysis? The most plausible claim would be that we are committed to fixing some exact limit or other, if the issue arises, though it is not fixed what. A difficulty here is that, practically speaking, the issue never does arise, for all the cases we are considering are stipulated to be counterfactual. So it can only be a necessity designed to force philosophers to stipulate some limit, for philosophical purposes, in a vacuum.

Even if we ignore this problem, the suggestion that we stipulate some exact leeway has already been implicitly shown to be inadequate by our argument against Salmon. Salmon's theory was intended as a reply to the so-called four worlds problem. That problem (stated in terms of the example above) is that the variation permitted allows *a* from *W1* and *b* from *W3* to be, materially, the same if it is allowed that each might have had a difference of two planks. Thus we have something apparently identical to both *a* and *b*, though *a* is not identical to *b*. This is what leads Salmon to distinguish *W2* from *W6* on the basis of *haecceitas* alone (hence the 'four worlds', in this case *W1*, *W2*, *W3* and *W6*) and we have shown that no such distinction is plausible. The 'four world problem' remains for any theory which allows strict or 'real' identity with leeway, irrespective of whether that leeway is exact or not. There is no reason to think that there is any solution to the problem other than that provided by the counterpart theory. If a boat had been built from planks 1–98, 101–2, then there would have been a boat of the relevant type or form with that matter. The question of which boat it would have been, in some trans-world sense, appears to have no definite meaning.

The alternative suggestion to solve the problem of vagueness, namely that no variation in matter at origin be allowed, is more difficult to refute. It is counter-intuitive, but perhaps these intuitions only reflect our sloppy common sense. And it is less implausible to suggest that the necessity for exact sameness can be proved by conceptual analysis than it is that some exact degree of leeway can be so proved.

Problems for this hypothesis are best stated with reference to the physical atoms of the world. They lack material parts, so such parts cannot enter into their identity. The strict approach to them must be to say that identity depends on an absolutely exact time and place of origin.

Suppose that all or some of the matter in the world were infinitely old, that is, had no origin. It would still, presumably, have been logically possible for that matter to have behaved somewhat differently from the way it in fact did, at some point in its history. No difference could be a difference in origin, so it would all be a difference in midlife history. How much of such difference is permitted? If one tries to be rigorist and allows none, then different matter will exist in any world in which it behaves differently and it will lead to a different identity for any composite object in whose origin that matter participates. In effect, if the world's atoms had all, in the course of their infinite life to date, followed any difference of path, then all present objects would have been different. This would give us, in effect, a counterpart theory. If, on the other hand, one avoids such rigorism, how much variation in path is allowed before difference of identity is revealed? All the original problems of leeway and vagueness arise again at this point.

This argument could be taken as showing that no particular atom could be without an origin. On the other hand, one might think it shows that there is something essentially arbitrary in taking origin – or anything else – as somehow determining 'real' or absolute identity.

If we suppose instead that matter was created and that space is relative, not absolute, then we face a further counter-intuitive conclusion. Suppose that whereas in the actual world, *W1*, an atom, *A*, had come into existence at *p1*, instead, in *W2*, an atom had sprung into existence at the neighbouring point *p2*. That would be a different atom by the criteria we are at present applying. But, of course, if space is relative this suggestion does not differ from the suggestion that *A* had come into existence at *p1* and everything else had some into existence at a slightly altered position. In the second world described in this way, *A* existed, but nothing else from *W1* existed. The preference for one spatial frame of reference over another is a matter of convenience, not fact, so imagining any differences in the origin of any atoms destroys the factuality of the identity of any. The rigorist view, therefore, requires that *everything* should have originated just where it in fact did if anything is to retain its identity.

The proviso that my last argument requires a relational, not absolute, view of space is revealing. If space were absolute, then an alteration in the initial state of the world by the replacement of one atom by another in a slightly different place would not affect the location and hence identity of the rest. It is not surprising that a naïve rigorist realism about the identity of atoms, but not about other objects, should be conceptually tied to the absolute or 'container' view of space. Both ideas are parts of an appealing, but unsustainable simple Newtonian atomism. If the absolutist theory of space has to be abandoned, then so does the simple rigorous realism about its elementary occupants. Arguments against the rigorist view are not as decisive as those against theories of counterfactual identity which allow leeway. But they do show that the rigor has ramifications far beyond what at first appears.

12.7   'Lockean' common sense: rigour for atoms, convention for complexes

There is one intuitively appealing option that I have not so far discussed explicitly. A certain sort of scientifically influenced 'Lockean' common sense suggests that the identity of complex objects is a matter of convention or degree or 'counterpart with material overlap', but that the identity of atoms is not. To sustain such a view in the light of preceding arguments it will be necessary to endow atoms with the sort of absolute identity which only *haecceitas* can give. But it is perhaps possible that this sort of strict identity can be granted for atoms without the absurdities following which we saw followed from Salmon's attempt to do the same for complex objects? The nonsense which followed from his treatment of the boat seemed essentially bound up with its material complexity.

Although atoms have, by definition, no material parts, the way of treating them here suggested does face similar problems to those which arose for complex objects. Problems arise in both cases from the difficulty of relating *haecceitas* or absolute identity to the normal empirical marks of identity. Material composition is not one of those marks for atoms, but time and place of origin are. There are the features which I have already exploited in preceding arguments which purported to show that neither vagueness, nor leeway nor rigorism is plausible in the identity conditions of atoms. If none of these is plausible then *haecceitas* would have to carry the burden of identity without support from other criteria; that is, without supervening on any empirical facts. So the very same atom might have been placed at a totally different location in the universe, and perhaps at a totally different time.

Is this conception of the identity of atoms coherent? What does it mean to say that a particular atom, *A*, could have appeared *ex nihilo* at the other side of the universe from that place at which it in fact occurred? How would that differ from a different but exactly similar atom's having appeared at that place instead?

In other words, what on earth is an entirely non-supervenient *haecceitas*? I can make no further progress with this suggestion, but we will find in Chapter 15 that minds are the only objects for which the notion of *haecceitas* is empirically interpretable.

The Lockean common sense which suggests that it is the identity of atoms which is absolute is not originally conceived of as depending on anything as superstitious as *haecceitas*. It is meant to follow from a hard-nosed scientific attitude which recognises atoms as the only 'ultimately' real physical entities and which is prepared to take a rigorist attitude towards identity. But we have seen in the previous section that a rigorist treatment of the identity of atoms depends on absolute space. It is not surprising that this Lockean picture should depend on the 'container' theory of space, for the atomism and the theory of space are indeed historically part of the same general theory. It is the abandonment of absolute space which forces the atomist to reintroduce the superstition of *haecceitas*, contrary to his natural instincts.

12.8   Conclusion

The argument as presented in the examples used – imagining differences in the origins of objects themselves – leads to the conclusion that there is no fact of the matter about whether these would have been the same objects, and then, through the conclusions we formed concerning vague predicates in Chapter 10, that the predicate 'would have been the same *x* as' has no fundamental, realist application to physical objects. This seems to be a very radical conclusion. It implies that, on a realist, as opposed to a conceptualist, level, there is no fact of the matter about whether the Earth would have been the same object if it had contained slightly different matter, but also that there is no realist fact of the matter whether it would have been the same object if I had had, counter to actual fact, sausages for breakfast yesterday – or even if something in another galaxy had done so. Causal influence is not the point, as might be imagined from the case of altering the object itself; the predicate itself cannot belong to the fundamental level. The physical base can only include general features at locations, which are naturally conceptualised by us in terms of individual objects. This, of course raises the question of the source or nature of the identity of the locations. I shall sidestep that question here; this is not a work about the nature of space-time. I shall be arguing in in Chapter 15 that minds are truly individuals, and it follows, given the conclusions here, that they are the only true (non-abstract) individuals. I shall argue in the final chapter that the individuality of mind is what makes possible the understanding of other things in individualised terms. This picture paves the way for idealism, though that will be the topic for another work. I have placed a note of reserve in the title of this chapter because I believe that one can accept everything else I say in this book whilst having reservations about the argument here – one can, that is, try to be more solidly dualist, and I do not want to discourage or discredit that option in this context by associating it with a more radical version of the truth. Nevertheless, the position I am defending about the ontology of the physical world is not that unusual amongst empiricist philosophers, for the view that it is events, not substances, that are fundamental is to be found in Russell (e.g. Russell 1931). And counterfactual identity for events is more generally recognised to be a matter of interest and convention than is the case for substances. The arguments in this chapter can, therefore, be seen as reinforcing this view.

Finally I want to present two lines of thought that might seem to support a more common-sensical conclusion than my own. The first is due to David Wiggins.

My approach can, once again, be contrasted with David Wiggins's more common-sensical approach. It might worry a reader that Wiggins accepts three propositions that I regard as inconsistent. Regarding them as consistent seems to be essential to accepting a common-sense picture of the identity of individuals, and regarding them as inconsistent is essential to my position. The three propositions are:

(i) That counterpart theory is false and that there are counterfactual sustaining or transworld physical individuals.
(ii) That there are no necessary and sufficient conditions for transworld identity, especially in relation to origin.
(iii) That there is no such thing as a mysterious *haecceitas* and hence one is not to invoke it to solve problems arising from vagueness subsequent on (ii).

Proposition (i) is of the essence of the common-sense view, (ii) follows naturally from a little reflection on certain counterfactual teasers, and (iii) is common sense rejecting mystery mongering.

Unfortunately, Wiggins shows little sign of recognising that there may be real tension between these propositions, but in this he is optimistic. If the transworld identity of an individual does not supervene on certain conditions, then either it is just an unanalysable, primitive fact, or there is no such thing. There seem to be no other alternatives. To say it is a primitive unanalysable fact is to say that every object has an unanalysable *haecceitas* of its own. To say that there is no such thing as transworld identity is to adopt counterpart theory. So (ii), the rejection of necessary and sufficient conditions forces one to choose between (i) and (iii). The only *tertium quid* would be to accept that identity might be indeterminate, but we have already seen in Section 12.4 that that cannot apply to strict or genuine identity (as opposed, for example, to some empiricist surrogate) and Wiggins certainly wants to apply genuine identity to objects. I have already discussed and rejected the dialectical or pragmatic way Wiggins tries to defuse the vagueness consequent on (ii). He says: 'Perhaps the speculator has to be able to *rebut* the charge that he has lost his subject of discourse if he changes its parents or origin'. If the identity is real, then relativising it to change and reply seems to be a mere evasion. And we saw in Section 12.3, this still leaves us with all the same problems when one discusses the charge.

Wiggins could perhaps try the following escape. He regards the identity or persistence conditions for a particular type of object as discoverable a posteriori. So could it be that the vagueness of (ii) is just a function of our ignorance? A brief look at the examples we have been discussing shows plainly that this is not the source of our problem. It is not ignorance about the real essences of tables, boats or spermatozoa which gave rise to the indefinite counterfactuals. Wiggins's difficulties enforce our analysis, for if (i)–(iii) are an inconsistent triad (which does seem plain) then if *haecceitas* for physical objects is unacceptable (as Section 12.5 surely shows) and vagueness in criteria is not avoidable (as I have argued in Sections 12.6 and 12.7), we must adopt my form of counterpart theory for bodies.

The final reservation that common sense might provoke is that, by now, one might have begun to doubt whether 'would have been the same body as' is a vague expression of the same sort as 'bald' and 'mountain'. This doubt boils down to doubting whether counterfactual identity supervenes on other conditions in the sort of way baldness supervenes on the distribution of hairs. It is plausible to maintain that reference to hairs enters into the definition of 'bald', thus guaranteeing the analyticity of the connection. But identity is not to be defined in terms of the criteria for identity of any particular class of objects. The meaning of the term 'identity' is not, therefore, to be reduced to the criteria on which a particular use of it may supervene, as might seem to be the case for normal vague terms. This applies also to its use in counterfactual contexts. What is said by statements involving identity cannot, therefore, be reduced to what could be said by statements involving instead the criteria for the identity of a particular class of things.

I am not convinced by this response. It is true that there is not the same strong meaning connection between identity and its varied criteria as there is between baldness and hair or mountains and height. It does not follow from this that what an identity sentence says – in the sense of what information it communicates – cannot be expressed in terms of the criteria for the identity in question. Let us assume that the identity of a physical object does not rest on some mysterious *haecceitas*. It follows that the criteria which are sufficient for that identity achieve that sufficiency by being simply what the identity in question amounts to or consists in. If this were not so, then they would be sufficient only by being the outward and visible sign of something extra beyond themselves. What could this be but some mysterious *haecceitas*? So, without the mystery, the criteria are all there is to the identity. Thus elements in 'the meaning of "identity"' over and above the criteria relevant to the particular case do not affect what information about the world is communicated by a particular putative identity statement. And what is said by using the term 'identity' in that particular context supervenes analytically on the criteria for its use there. No a posteriori knowledge is required to discover the supervenience. (A posteriori knowledge may be involved in discovering what the persistence conditions are for a particular natural kind (for example, it has to be discovered that a tadpole and a frog are the same creature); but what sameness of identity is for an object of that kind follows directly and analytically from those conditions: no knowledge is required to move from the persistence condition to identity.) It is the case, therefore, that in counterfactual identity statements concerning physical objects we have a class of statements which supervene analytically and vaguely on a more basic set of facts. The more basic set of facts express more exactly all that there is to be said. In the case of world-relative identities these facts may consist in various forms of continuity (though we have not discussed this) so that everything true about physical identity through time can be expressed in terms of continuity. Similarly, for counterfactual cases, vagueness shows that the criteria consist only in certain forms of correspondence or counterparts, and these constitute the whole of the fact of the matter.

So I conclude – to my own satisfaction at least – that the radical conclusion of this chapter is sound.

But is it so radical, anyway? The idea that, at the fundamental level, reality consists of a series of events in space-time, not of enduring objects, has been common amongst radical empiricists. Of course, these events must be so organised that our object-concepts can apply to them at macroscopic levels, but this is not the fundamental structure. In Russell's words 'I think [that] the universe is all spots and jumps, without coherence or orderliness ... it consists of events – short, small, haphazard. Order, unity, and continuity are human inventions just as truly as are catalogues and encyclopedias' (Russell 1931: 98 and 131). This is very close to my position, with a conceptualist interpretation of our ordinary object-concepts. Furthermore, recent controversy in quantum theory supports this position. Some philosophers of physics have asserted that *haecceitas* must be attributed to certain sub-atomic particles – bosons, for example – if they are to be regarded as proper individuals.[3] But it is agreed that quantum theory itself does not require quantal entities to be individuals – indeed, it makes as much sense, if not more, if they are treated as something less than individuals. It is not possible here to enter into a debate about how best to interpret quantum theory, though it seems to me that those who wish to endow bosons with *haecceitas* do so only because they believe that this is necessary to endow

---

[3] For a lucid account of these issues, see French (2006).

them with the degree of individuality possessed by more ordinary physical objects. As I am sceptical about the status of all physical objects as full individuals, this motive gains no hold and quantum theory itself seems to support the view that what there are at the foundations are types of entity, not individuals.

13 Dennett and the human perspective

13.1 Introduction

I have been arguing in Part II of this book that the ontologies of the physical world, other than the most basic one, must be understood in a conceptualist, as opposed to a realist, sense, and that this leads to a dualism within the physical realist framework, for conceptualism of this sort presupposes a human perspective on to the physical world from outside of it. One might describe this view as the *irreducibility of the Cartesian perspective*: it forces us to see the thinking subject as something different from, and in addition to, the realm of physical objects.

This line of argument interestingly parallels Dennett's argument for the ineliminability of the intentional stance – but Dennett, of course, thinks that this is entirely compatible with a naturalistic and even behaviourist view of the mind. I want, in this chapter, to look at what, from my point of view, is Dennett's important concession that the intentional stance, and, therefore, the Cartesian perspective, is ineliminable, and at his attempts to reclaim this stance for naturalism.

13.2 Why the human perspective is unavoidable

Dennett recounts the following story from Nozick.

Suppose ... some beings of vastly superior intelligence – from Mars, let us say – were to descend upon us, and suppose that we were to them as simple thermostats are to clever engineers. Suppose, that is, that they did not *need* the intentional stance [ie our ordinary 'folk psychology'] ... to predict our behavior in all its detail. They can be supposed to be Laplacean super-physicists, capable of comprehending the behavior on Wall Street, for instance, at the microphysical level ... They can predict the individual behaviors of all the various moving bodies they observe without treating any of them as intentional systems. Would we then be right to say that from *their* point of view we were not believers at all (any more than a simple thermostat is)? (1987b: 25)

The apparent consequence of Nozick's tale is that, if physicalism (together with closure under physics – the absence of emergent laws) is true, then normal psychological explanations are mere heuristics which can be legitimately ignored if the heuristic is not needed. Although the story is told with respect only to the intentional stance, the implications of the Martian's micro-physically based method might reasonably be taken to be more general: higher-order ontologies – the subject matters of the special sciences, including not only psychology but chemistry biology and the rest – are similarly not needed by the Martian. We have indeed here a case of what Kim calls the exclusion principle. We will return to this generalised point later, for it helps to undermine Dennett's response. That response is as follows.

Our imagined Martians might be able to predict the future of the human race by Laplacean methods, but if they did not also see us as intentional systems they would be missing something perfectly objective: the *patterns* in human behavior that are describable from the intentional stance, and only from that stance, and that support generalizations and predictions. (25)

Dennett illustrates the value of the intentional stance with a further story.

Suppose . . . that one of the Martians were to engage in a predicting contest with an Earthling. The Earthling and the Martian observe (and observe each other observing) a particular bit of local physical transaction. From the Earthling's point of view, this is what is observed. The telephone rings in Mrs Gardner's kitchen. She answers, and this is what she says: 'Oh, hello dear. You're coming home early? Within the hour? And bringing the boss to dinner? Pick up a bottle of wine on the way home then, and drive carefully.' On the basis of this observation, our Earthling predicts that a large metallic vehicle with rubber tires will come to a stop on the drive within one hour, disgorging two human beings, one of whom will be holding a paper bag containing a bottle containing alcoholic fluid . . . The Martian makes the same prediction, but has to avail himself of much more information about an extraordinary number of interactions of which, so far as he can tell, the Earthling is entirely ignorant. For instance, the deceleration of the vehicle at intersection *A*, five miles from the house, without which there would have been a collision with another vehicle – whose collision course had been laboriously calculated over some hundreds of meters by the Martian. The Earthling's performance would look like magic! How did the Earthling know that the being who got out of the car and got the bottle in the shop would get back in? The coming true of all the Earthling's predictions, after all the vagaries, intersections and branches in the paths charted by the Martian, would seem to anyone bereft of the intentional strategy [to be] marvelous and inexplicable . . . (26–7)

Dennett then draws our attention to a serious flaw in this latter story, namely that:

The Martian is presumed to treat his Earthling opponent as an intelligent being like himself ... against whom one can compete ... a being with beliefs ... and desires. So if the Martian sees the pattern in one Earthling, how can he fail to see it in others? (27)

Dennett concludes

the moral to be drawn: namely, *the unavoidability of the intentional stance with regard to oneself and one's fellow intelligent beings.* (27)

He explains this as follows.

This unavoidability is itself interest relative; it is perfectly possible to adopt a physical stance, for instance, with regard to an intelligent being, oneself included, but not to the exclusion of maintaining at the same time an intentional stance with regard to oneself at a minimum, and one's fellows *if* one intends, for instance, to learn what they know ... We can perhaps suppose our super-intelligent Martians fail to recognize *us* as intentional systems, but we cannot suppose them to lack the requisite concepts. If they observe, theorize, predict, communicate, they view *themselves* as intentional systems. Where there are intelligent beings, the patterns must be there to be described, whether or not we care to see them. (27–8)

So, though one could avoid treating others as intentional systems, Dennett, by contrast, believes in the inevitability of taking oneself to be a thinking being, or, as I shall put it, *taking the Cartesian perspective* on oneself, for one cannot avoid the thought '*cogito*, I think, I am a thinking thing'. I have been arguing in the preceding chapters that we take a similar stance – that is to say, an interpretative stance – to the physical world and that that forces a dualism on us. How does Dennett hope to naturalise this human – or Cartesian – perspective?

13.3   Dennett's instrumentalism

Dennett says:

I suggest that folk psychology might best be viewed as a rationalistic calculus of interpretation and prediction – an idealizing, abstract, instrumentalistic interpretation method that has evolved because it works and works because we have evolved. We approach each other as *intentional systems* ..., that is, as entities whose behaviour can be predicted by attributing beliefs, desires and rational acumen ... (1987b, 48–9)

This is the strategy that neither we nor the Martian can avoid. Dennett deemed it 'instrumentalistic' because no physical system can actually possess intrinsic intentionality – that would be magic. All 'intelligent' physical systems are syntactic, not semantic engines; that is, they are driven by the physical properties of the symbols they manipulate, not their meanings. So the meaning and intentionality must be put into them by the way they are understood. This immediately prompts the query 'if nothing is intrinsically intentional, what is there to do the interpreting?' I can interpret marks on a page as having meaning, though they are mere marks, because I have an intrinsic capacity for thought, which a printed page does not, but if I did not, I could not interpret the marks on the page.

So the rationale for instrumentalism (or interpretationalism) and then the reason for thinking it viciously regressive can be given as follows.

Argument for Dennett's position.

(1) All actual intentional systems are purely physical. (Ass. of physicalism)
(2) Nothing physical is intrinsically intentional – there are no physical semantic engines. (Ass.)

Therefore

(3) No actual intentional system is intrinsically intentional. (1, 2, HS)
(4) Actual people (etc.) are intentional systems in some sense. (Ass.)

Therefore

(5) There are actual intentional systems. (4, Inst.)
(6) Actual intentional systems are not intrinsically intentional. (3, 5, MP)
(7) The only options are intrinsic intentionality and intentionality instrumentally, i.e. by interpretation. (Ass.)

Therefore

(8) Actual intentional systems – people etc. – are intentional instrumentally i.e. by interpretation. (6, 7, DS)

Reductio of Dennett's position.

(9) Something can interpret x as an intentional system only if that something has the capacity to so interpret. (Ass.)
(10) Something cannot have the capacity so to interpret solely in virtue of being itself interpreted by something else. (Ass.)

Therefore

(11) Something cannot interpret x as an intentional system solely in virtue of its being interpreted by something else. (9, 10, HS)

Therefore

(12) An interpreter must have the capacity to interpret intrinsically or in its own right. (7, 11, DS)
(13) Something having this capacity intrinsically is an intentional system in its own right. (Def.)

Therefore

(14) If there are any interpreters, there are intrinsic intentional systems.
     (12, 13, HS)
(15) There are interpreters. (Ass.)

Therefore

(16) There are intrinsic intentional systems. (14, 15, MP)
(17) 8 contradicts 16.

Therefore at least one of the assumptions must be false. Some are not controversial.

(9) is a platitude – one cannot do something (systematically, at least, and we are considering a systematic ability) unless one has the appropriate capacity. (7) is justified if being imputed by interpretation and having intrinsically are the exhaustive options, which seems right. (13) seems to be a correct definition. The serious options are, therefore: either to deny (1) and affirm that some intentional systems are not physical; or deny (2) and say some physical things are intrinsically intentional; or deny (10) and affirm that the capacity to interpret can itself be endowed by interpretation.

(1) is controversial, because it is the assertion of physicalism, but is the victim of the *reductio* only if (2) and (10) can be supported. As my purpose is to refute the physicalist account of thought, I need to show that (2) and (10) are true.

Denial of (10) is the assertion of Dennettian physicalism, although, as we shall see later, it can be argued that all physicalists are committed to some version of interpretationalism. Denial of (2), on its most natural interpretation, is the claim that reductive physicalism saves the realism of the mental.

13.4   Discussion of (10)

(10) is the anti-Dennett crux. It seems intuitively obvious: simply having a certain attitude to something cannot endow it with powers it does not otherwise possess. If an object cannot think 'in its own right', then understanding it in a certain way will not give it this ability. This intuition is, I think, sound, but diversionary tactics are possible.

It might be argued that the picture of individuals endowing others with semantic capacities, like a particular person reading a text or using a computer, is too individualistic. The interpretation is a mutual and social operation. Many social properties, including ones that endow people with powers and capacities, are endowed or imputed by what one might broadly characterise as the attitudes of others. This is the way one is endowed with legal powers. Even the power of leadership, considered as relatively brute rather than merely legal, comes from the response of others as well as from natural capacity. In some way, if Dennett is right, we must be similarly endowed with the capacity to be a semantic engine. The natural response to this is to make a distinction between *natural powers* and *socially imputed powers*, and to claim that the power of thought belongs in the former category. This claim could be buttressed by arguing that a general power of thought is presupposed by the socially imputed powers – it is because we are intentional systems that we can construct legal systems, endow each other with powers, rights etc.

The interpretationalist might try to deny that the distinction between natural and social powers is a precise one – from a physicalist perspective, after all, social powers must be natural powers, for there is no other kind, so they must just be very complex and sophisticated ones. This response is problematic for a Dennettian, however, because it appears to be at the heart of this position that semantic properties are imputed rather than real. Nevertheless, it might be argued that, though semantic properties have no place in the 'basic' physicalist ontology, they can be thought of as emergent when physical behaviour develops 'real patterns' of the right kind.

The question is what one means by 'emergent' here. The issue is how semantic facts are grounded in physical ones: or perhaps it would be more accurate to say that it is about how semantic concepts get a grip on physical reality; are they an interpretation of that reality made for certain purposes, or do those facts emerge at a certain level of complexity, in a way analogous to that in which biological facts might be thought to emerge?

It might seem that realistic emergence is inconsistent with the inter-pretationalist approach, as I suggested above. But perhaps it is not that simple. One might defend a collective realism, according to which there is a society with a certain 'form of life' in which individuals really exhibit intentional states, but only in virtue of the responses that other individuals in the society have to them. The web of mutual interpretation is a real, natural phenomenon, but it is constructed by mutual interpretation; it does not emerge as a power of people taken individually.

This approach seems to me to be mere 'hand waving'. The problem concerns how more and more sophisticated patterns of behaviour come to *constitute* acts of interpretation. One needs to distinguish between:

(a) The capacity to interpret others can only *develop* or be actualised in the context of appropriate complex behaviours which we dub 'social practices'.

and

(b) The capacity to interpret others is a *logical product* of certain behaviours, such that once the patterns of behaviour reach a certain point they constitute mutual interpretation.

The former is not controversial but tells us nothing about the analysis of semantic capacities, only about a causally necessary condition for our acquiring them.

The latter fails to explain how physical behaviours transmute themselves into interpretative acts. Of course, once behaviour reaches a certain complexity, it can be *interpreted* as semantic and intentional, but this just takes us back to the start: what we want to know is how certain physical movements can simply *be what it is to interpret*.

When interpretationalism has reached this point, it is not clearly different from realist reductionism, except that the reduction base is social, rather than individual, behaviour. We will return to discussing this in Section 13.6.

13.5   Realism and 'real patterns'

Dennett came to dislike the label 'instrumentalist' and to declare that he was a 'moderate realist'. He expressed this by saying that the intentional states and systems whose value he had originally described as *instrumental* were, or were grounded on, *real patterns* in the physical world. Two issues arise. One is whether this move really escapes from the vicious regress of interpretationalism exposed above; and in so far as it does, or might, how does talk of patterns relate to the realism to which I have driven the interpretationalist in the previous section?

Dennett characterises patterns as

something perfectly objective: the *patterns* in human behavior that are describable from the intentional stance, and only from that stance . . . (1987b: 25)

The claim that the patterns are 'objective' suggests that they are there in their own right *as* patterns irrespective of anything dependent on the subject. But Dennett concedes, in the quotation I have just given, that it is only from the intentional stance that these things are discriminable as patterns, so the idea that these are simply physical patterns – more or less similar physical shapes or movements – which we are picking up on is already abandoned. This becomes clearer. Dennett cites the following as a case of a pattern:

Take a particular instance in which the Martians observe a stockbroker deciding to place an order for 500 shares of General Motors. They predict the exact motions of his fingers as he dials the phone and the exact vibrations of his vocal cords as he intones his order. But if the Martians do not see that indefinitely many different patterns of finger motions and vocal cord vibrations ... could have substituted for the actual particulars without perturbing the subsequent operations of the market, then they have failed to see a real pattern in the world they are observing. (26)

The reference to finger movements leaves open the possibility that we are talking about straightforward physical similarities, but in fact quite different movements could constitute buying these shares. Activities on a computer, where the movements would have no physical similarity to bidding actions in an auction room, could achieve the same objective. So the sense of 'patterns' cannot be taken in a literal physical sense. Of course, the foundations of these judgements of similarity – the movements of bodies through space – are entirely real, but their reification as patterns – as seen as unities of a certain sort – involves the action of mind. So the invocation of patterns as mind-independent physical realities, in the kinds of case Dennett has in mind, is mistaken.

In fact I think this is true of the term 'pattern' in general, even where there is genuine physical similarity. If there are a collection of dots arranged in what we would see as a circle, a visually more sophisticated mind might see it as a polygon with the appropriate number of sides. Patterns are reified by the action of the mind. Otherwise – in the case of the dots – there are just dots in certain physical places. In the case of share-dealing behaviours, there are just bodily movements. These are made sense of from the Cartesian perspective – in the sense that there must be a subject to whom are attributed standard folk-psychological characteristics who appreciates them – but this requires that the Cartesian perspective be retained as a primitive component in our idea of what there is.

The current discussion concerns whether instrumentalism/interpretationalism involves a vicious regress. The regress reputedly consists in the fact that this theory presupposes an intrinsically intentional system to carry out the interpreting required by both; it cannot, therefore, constitute an explanation of what it is for something to be an intentional system or a semantic engine. Dennett's account of real patterns does not seem to me to touch this accusation. In order to meet the challenge he would have to show that a pattern, on its own and without the aid of some act of interpretation, constituted an intentional state. One can make a distinction between the view that patterns are *per se real* and that they are *grounded*. On the latter account, a pattern is a kind of *Gestalt*, because it is a matter of a certain structure being seen as a whole in a certain way. The figure created by a continuous line moving equidistant from a central point just *is* a circle. A series of dots placed on the same outline as the circle will also be seen as forming a circle, but they are just dots in certain positions: they could be seen – if they were seen as forming anything other than a collection of dots in certain places – as forming a polygon. The pure circle is not a pattern, it is a self-sufficient shape. The dots form a pattern which requires a mind – an interpreter – to complete it, and it could be completed in more than one way, though one particular way may be the easiest or most natural.

William Seager, in an illuminating discussion of Dennett on real patterns almost gets this right, but not quite and this lets Dennett off the hook. Seager explains the status of patterns as follows.

Inhabiting a curious zone midway between, as it were, objectivity and subjectivity, patterns are *there* to be seen, but have *no function* if they are not seen. By the former I mean that patterns are not just in the eye of the beholder; they are really in the world and provide us with an indispensable and powerful explanatory and predictive grip on the world. By the latter I mean that the *only* role they have in the world is to help organize the experience of those conscious beings who invent them and then think in terms of them. (2000: 117)

It generally looks as if Seager is saying that patterns are really there, but are physically epiphenomenal, because all the causal clout comes from

the fundamental features of the world [that is, its most 'minute parts'] that organize the world into all the patterns it exemplifies, and they do all this by themselves, with no help from 'top-down' causation. (117)

Seager seems to think that patterns are not wholly epiphenomenal because they are picked out by and hence influence minds, and that, for this reason, 'Mind cannot be "just another" pattern' (121).

Dennett has a two-fold reply (2000: 355). First, he rejects the view that patterns are physically idle: ("All those simpler, thermostat-like minds are responsive to patterns …"). This, in a sense, is a verbal dispute, for Dennett is not denying that the world is 'closed under physics' and that, therefore, higher order entities *add nothing* to the causal clout of the minute parts. Nevertheless, Dennett is right that this latter fact does not seem to make it wrong to attribute causal force to non-fundamental entities: it is still the stone that broke the window, even if this supervenes on the action of the atoms. Second, and more crucial, he rejects Seager's main conclusion:

In Seager's opinion, 'Mind cannot be "just another" pattern' Why not? Perhaps I have missed his point. (355)

Dennett has missed the point but only because Seager has not stated it quite correctly, or not clearly so. If patterns are real and are of the same ontological status as higher order, non-fundamental objects in general, and if it is appropriate to ascribe causal roles to such non-fundamental things, even though these supervene on the atomic, then why should not the mind be efficacious, as the stone is, and just a pattern? Seager's mistake is to characterise patterns as real but inefficacious, except upon the mind.

In fact he is ambiguous about the reality of patterns. In one of the passages quoted above he talks of patterns as *invented by* conscious beings. Seager needs to make explicit what he perhaps intends, namely a distinction like that I make above between the *groundedness* of patterns in reality, together with the need for mental activity to reify them on the basis of those grounds. This explains why the mind cannot be just a pattern: it is presupposed by patterns as their co-inventor, together with the grounding. If the mind itself is just a pattern, then there would be the kind of regress with which we started our discussion, for it would not be reified unless it were *seen as* a pattern, and so on.

13.6 Social realism

So Dennett's doctrine of real patterns does not enable him to escape from the regress. But we ended Section 13.4 with a form of social realism-cum-interpretationalism still in play, and must return to the discussion of that theory. In fact, the problems that we found for the real patterns theory also apply here. We saw that Seager, in his rejection of 'top-down' causation was implicitly classifying all non-foundational entities as similar to patterns; that is, he did not demote patterns because they were patterns per se, but because they were higher-order entities and higher-order entities had no independent causal clout, because all such clout is 'bottom-up', not 'top-down'. This assimilation of all non-fundamental entities to patterns is, I believe, essentially correct. In Chapter 9 I presented an account which can briefly be summarised as follows.

There are two forms of strictly 'bottom-up' reductionism. One is the 'translation' reductionism of Carnap (1934) and other logical positivists, according to which all true statements in the special sciences and common-sense ontology can be translated into statements about fundamental physics. The other is the 'nomological reductionism' associated with Nagel's (1961) classical account, according to which higher-order properties and laws are type identical with something in physics. In both these cases the conceptual or explanatory content of higher-order descriptions adds nothing to what can, in principle, be acquired from a proper account in terms of physics. Unfortunately, neither of these forms of reduction actually applies to the relationship between physics and most, if not all, higher-order descriptions. Even if and where the world is 'closed under physics', the relation between that fundamental physical base and the rest is only a form of a priori sufficiency of the base; there is not also the necessity of the base that either translation or nomic reduction requires. By 'a priori sufficiency of the base' I mean the following: given what is happening at the fundamental level, it follows necessarily what is happening at the higher-order levels. For example, though there is no nomological reductive account of 'hurricane', given that the atoms are behaving in a certain way, then necessarily there is a hurricane; there is no possible world atomically just like ours at the time of Katrina in which there was not a hurricane. This is so even though the conceptual frameworks of the higher explanations, such as meteorology, cytology, etc. 'float free' of the conceptual framework of physics. I argued that this shows that the special sciences are best understood as different perspectives on the physical base, usually with certain interests in mind. They are essentially in the same category as patterns, because, though the concepts they involve are well grounded by the basis physical reality, they do not reflect any reality additional to fundamental physical base, except the interests and other perspectives of the humans who employ them. These perspectives do not differ significantly from modes of interpretation of the patterns available at the lower level. In other words, given the failure of tough-minded forms of reductionism, the relation between the base and other levels of explanation, is 'top-down', and this is a form of interpretationalism, which presupposes a mind picking out the *fundamenta* that make the higher-order explanations possible.

If the above argument is correct, all physicalists are interpretationalists, not just about mental states, but about all, or, at least, most of the special sciences (that is, those not reducible in one of the strong senses). Premise (2) of the original argument – the denial of straight realism about the mental, from a physicalist perspective – is correct. Interpretationalism, whether overtly instrumentalist or would-be moderate realist, cannot avoid assigning an irreducible role to the mind in the creation of the non-basic physical levels, and, hence, mind itself cannot be one of those non-basic levels.

Part III

Arguments for mental substance

14 Some current arguments for substance dualism

14.1 E. J. Lowe's argument for non-Cartesian substance dualism

E. J. Lowe defends a form of substance dualism, though a distinctly non-Cartesian one. He holds that a normal human being involves two substances: one a body and the other a person. The latter is not, however, a purely mental substance that can be defined in terms of thought or consciousness alone, as Descartes claimed. But persons and their bodies have different identity conditions and are both substances, so there are two substances essentially involved in a human being; hence this is a form of substances dualism. Lowe (1996) claims that his theory is close to P. F. Strawson's (1959), whilst admitting that Strawson would not have called it substance dualism.

Lowe's argument can, I think, be reconstructed in the following form.

(1) Persons have different identity conditions from any body, or bodily substance.

Therefore

(2) A person is not a body or bodily substance.

Therefore

(3) A person is either a non-bodily substance, or not a substance.
(4) Suppose a person is not a substance.
(5) If a person is not a substance, it must be an interconnected system of mental events in a neo-Lockean manner.
(6) If neo-Lockeanism were true, then it should be possible to identify mental events independently of, or prior to, identifying the person they belong to.
(7) It is not possible to identify mental events in this way.

Therefore

(8) A person is not a neo-Lockean system of mental events.

Therefore

(9) A person is a substance.

Therefore

(10) A person is a non-bodily substance – that is, in fact, a psychological substance.

In Lowe (1996), the argument for (2) is not only (1). He also argues that the bodily substance theory

threatens either to promote what is (to my mind) an ethically dubious anthropomorphic 'speciesism' or to play havoc with zoological taxonomies. (1996: 15)

Lowe's reasoning is that it is 'speciesism' if personhood is confined to human bodies, but if persons could be radically non-human physical creatures then one would have a species – namely persons – that straddled genera, which is not allowed. However, he also argues that 'Persons are substances, as are their bodies. But they are not identical substances: for they have different persistence conditions' (16).

Lowe takes his conclusion further by arguing that mental substances must be simple, for, he says, if they were not simple they would have to have parts, and the only kinds of parts they could have would be physical parts, which would entail, by mereological principles, that the substance was itself physical.

This conclusion – that the mind is a simple non-physical substance, is, at first sight, orthodoxly Cartesian. Before looking at how Lowe makes his conclusion non-Cartesian – and only, in my view, semi-dualist – let us examine the argument so far.

I considered the rationale behind (1) – namely that different identity conditions entail the presence of different real things – in Section 11.4. I argued that the difference of these conditions was consistent with taking the terms merely conceptually, not realistically. But I also argued, in Section 11.9 and Chapter 13, that this could not be applied to the mind because it is needed to be the originator of the merely conceptual. So, applied to the case of the mind, I believe the argument is sound up to (3). The issue then becomes Lowe's arguments against the neo-Lockean or bundle theory. He argues as follows.

What is wrong with the neo-Lockean theory is that, in purporting to supply an account of the individuation and identity of persons it presupposes, untenably, that an account of the identity conditions of psychological modes can be provided which need not rely on reference to persons. But it emerges that the identity of any psychological mode turns on the identity of the person that possesses it. What this implies is that psychological modes are essentially modes of persons, and correspondingly that persons have to be conceived of as *substances*. (1996: 25)

I think that this response is over simple. I cannot now involve myself in all the issues concerning the nature of substance, but will assume that the bundle theory of mind cannot be summarily dismissed on grounds that a bundle cannot be a substance, for that substances are just bundles of properties is one of the theories of substance. So the fact – if it is a fact – that mental states must belong to persons does not, of itself, rule out the possibility that persons are just interconnected mental states. Given that this swift dismissal is not possible, the issue becomes (i) can a mental state exist alone, as Hume thought? (ii) If it cannot, does it make sense to claim that mental states can exist only as part of a bundle, or does the bundle ontology entail the possibility of (i)? Unfortunately, a proper answer to these questions would require a book-length treatment, as would a proper discussion of substance, and, even after such a treatment, the answer is certain to be controversial.[1] On the matter of the substance theory of the person or mind, I shall suspend discussion until the rather different form of argument I shall put forward in Chapter 15. Lowe's positive theory – his non-Cartesian substance dualism – is something we cannot defer.

Lowe rejects straightforward Cartesianism in the following words.

The trouble with this view is that, to the extent that it goes beyond a mere rejection of material substantivalism, it rests on pure speculation without *a priori* sanction or, seemingly, any hope of empirical confirmation. From the fact that I am not identical with my body, it by no means follows that I am wholly distinct and separable from it, much less that I am endowed with no physical characteristics whatsoever. (1996: 8)

He then compares his position to P. F. Strawson's whilst admitting that Strawson would not acknowledge the label 'substance dualism'. I think Lowe's position can be characterised as follows.

(a) A person involves a living body associated with both physical and mental properties. This is the 'Strawsonian' element.
(b) The identity conditions for persons differ from those for bodies.

For this reason:

(c) Persons are different substances from bodies.
(d) Persons are simple – they have no parts, especially bodily parts.

There seems to me to be a tension, if not a contradiction, between (a) and (d). If physical characteristics are what Lowe calls, following Locke, 'modes', then they belong to a substance. It seems natural to say that this must be a physical substance, but then persons would have physical parts, which Lowe denies. But if these physical characteristics are some-how to be attributed simply to non-physical persons, then some of our

---

[1] I have said what I have to say on the nature of substance in the entry on substance in *The Stanford Encyclopedia of Philosophy*, Robinson (2014c).

physical characteristics belong to our body and some to the non-physical person. I doubt if this could be coherently worked out.

I do not think, therefore, that Lowe's non-Cartesian substance dualism works.

14.2   Swinburne's substance dualism

Richard Swinburne defends substance dualism as follows.

My initial argument in its support has two stages. I argue first that knowledge of what happens to bodies and their parts, and knowledge of the mental events which occur in connection with them will not suffice to give you knowledge of what happens to those persons who are (currently) men. Talk about persons is not analysable in terms of talk about bodies and their connected mental life. And more generally, it is logically possible that persons continue to exist when their bodies are destroyed. Secondly, I argue that the most natural way of making sense of this fact is talking of persons as consisting of two parts, body and soul – the soul being the essential part, whose continuing alone makes for the continuing of the person. (1986: 147)

The main argument for the first stage is that

[i]t is, I suggest, a factual matter whether a person survives an operation or not. There is a truth here that some later person is or is not the same as some pre-operation person, but it is, I shall suggest, a truth of which we can be ignorant however much we know about human bodies and the fate of their organs. (147)

He illustrates this with Bernard Williams's 'mad surgeon' story.

Suppose that a mad surgeon captures you and announces that he is going to transplant your left cerebral hemisphere into one body, and your right one into another. He is going to torture one of the resulting persons and free the other with a gift of a million pounds. You can choose which person is to be tortured and which to be rewarded, and the surgeon promises to do as you choose. You believe his promise. But how are you to choose? You wish to choose that you are rewarded, but you do not know which resultant person will be you. You may have studied neurophysiology deeply and think that you have detected some all-important difference between the hemispheres which indicates which is the vehicle of personal identity; but, all too obviously, you could be mistaken. Whichever way you choose, the choice would, in Williams's telling word about his similar story, be a 'risk' – which shows that there is something other to the continuity of the person, than any continuity of parts of brain or body. (149)

The brunt of this conclusion is that the uncertainty about which you will be, even though you know exactly what will happen to the brain and what mental states go with what brain states, shows that the self is, in Derek Parfit's phrase, some kind of 'further fact'.

There is, of course, an obvious Parfitian reply here.

It is a fashionable criticism of an argument of this kind that it assumes that personal identity is indivisible. We do not make this kind of assumption with respect to inanimate things, such as cars and countries. These survive in part. If half the bits of my old car are used together with bits of another old car in the construction of a new car, my car has survived in part. And if the other bits of my old car are used in construction of another new car, then my old car has survived in part as one car and in part as another car. If we succeed in dividing humans, why should not human survival be like that? If half my brain is put into one body, and half into another body, do I not survive partly as one person and partly as another? (149)

Swinburne thinks that this option makes no sense.

However, persons such as men are very different from inanimate beings such as cars. They have hopes, fears, and memories which make it very difficult to give sense to the idea of their partial survival. Consider again the victim in the mad surgeon story. If he survives to the extent to which his brain survives, his choice of who is to suffer will make no difference; however he chooses one person who is partly he will suffer, and one person who is partly he will be rewarded. In that case he has reason both for joyous expectation and for terrified anticipation. But how can such an attitude of part joyous expectation and part terrified anticipation be justified, since no future person is going to suffer a mixed fate? *It is hard to give any sense to the notion of there being a half-way between one having certain future experiences which some person has, and one not having them, and so to the notion of a person being divisible.* [Italics added.] (149–50)

This idea forms the core of the argument I shall present in the next chapter, but it will not concern division but certain counterfactuals concerning origin. This is because Swinburne's conclusion so far, though intuitively appealing, is not conclusive, as he acknowledges.

But even if this notion of partial survival does make sense, it will in no way remove the difficulty, which remains this. Although it *may* be the case that if my two brain hemispheres are transplanted into different bodies, I survive partly as the person whose body is controlled by one and partly as the person whose body is controlled by the other, it may not be like that at all. Maybe I go just where the left hemisphere goes. As we have seen, the fate of some parts of my body, such as my arms and legs, is quite irrelevant to the fate of me. And plausibly the fate of some parts of my brain is irrelevant – can I not survive completely a minor brain operation which removes a very small tumour? But then maybe it is the same with some larger parts of the brain too. We just don't know. If the mad surgeon's victim took the attitude that it didn't matter which way he chose, we would, I suggest, regard him as taking an unjustifiably dogmatic attitude. For the fact that a resultant person has qualitatively the same memory and character is certainly no guarantee that he is me – in whole or in part. For while I continue to exist quite untouched by any change of brain or character or memory, some other person p with my character could, through a long process of hypnosis, be given 'my' apparent memories in the sense of being led to believe that he had the same past experiences as I did. But that would not make me any less than fully me; and if I remain fully me, there is no room for p to be me, even in small part. (150)

The trouble with this argument, I think, is that it treats as metaphysically possible something which some philosophers might claim is only *conceivable* or epistemically possible. The argument is that, although the 'other' side of the brain might be qualitatively like me, 'I' might have gone with 'this' side. But if the bundle theory of the mind is correct, with its associated theory of personal identity as constituted by psychological continuity, then it follows that I have divided as a subject.

Swinburne augments this argument by claiming that swopping bodies and disembodied existence both make sense and so are possible. It is also not obvious that these could not be allowed as logically possible by a bundle theorist; certainly Hume would have allowed them.

This uncovers what, as far as I can tell, is a major weakness in Swinburne's argument, namely that he does not directly tackle the bundle theory, but begs the question in the way he handles the concept of substance. He defines it as follows:

I follow normal philosophical usage in understanding by a 'substance' a component of the world which interacts causally with other components of the world and which has a history through time. Tables and chairs, stars and galaxies, cabbages and persons are substances. Substances have (monadic) **properties** – such as being square or yellow, or having a mass of 2 lbs. They also have polyadic **properties**, or relations to other substances, such as being taller than, or lying between.

This account of substance is entirely neutral on any deeper analysis of the concept – someone who thought that substances were just organised systems of properties or property instances (tropes) would accept it. Such a neutrality is indeed what Swinburne intends.

One view is that substances are simply bundles of co-instantiated properties. The alternative view is that some substances have thisness . . .

If no substances have thisness, then the history of the world will consist of co-instantiated properties having further properties, including spatiotemporal relations to earlier bundles, coming into existence and ceasing to exist, and causing the subsequent existence and properties of other bundles. (2014: 145)

There is no suggestion that this option is ruled out by Swinburne's account of substance, because

I'll operate with a conception [of substance] which does not, I think, beg the question at issue . . . (2014: 139)

But can Swinburne do what he wants with such a neutral conception and he stand by his neutrality? He says, for example:

Whenever [substances] exist, they exist totally. If the desk exists on Tuesday, all of it exists on Tuesday; it's not that some part of it exists on Tuesday, and another part exists on Wednesday. I shall count anything of the kind just described as a **(p.5)** substance, whether or not it is of a kind which features in scientific laws or is of importance in our lives. (2013: 4–5)

And in a footnote Swinburne claims that his concept of substance is essentially the Aristotelian one. What he means by this is that it covers ordinary macroscopic objects. But this anodyne conception does justice neither to Aristotle nor to what Swinburne requires. First, it differs significantly from Aristotle in at least three ways. First, and, in a sense, least important, Aristotle was not keen on artefacts, such as desks as substances because their unity is not natural. Second, Swinburne also says that substances can be made of other substances. Aristotle does not, in my opinion, believe this and for very fundamental reasons. This is a major reason why he was not an atomist. The matter of things is a potentiality, not an actuality, and is, therefore not a 'this such'; one is not allowed to have rival substances contesting the same space. This raises the third point. Swinburne is a relativist about what counts as a substance, in that you can cut the world in many different ways. Nothing could be more unAristotelian than this.

Fairly clearly there are different ways of cutting the world up into species of substance, any of which would give us a true and full description of the world. Suppose I have a car which I turn into a boat. I can think of cars as essentially cars. In that case one substance (a car) has ceased to exist and has become instead another substance (a boat). Or I can think of it as essentially a motor vehicle, in which case it has continued to exist but with different (nonessential) properties. (2014: 143–4)

Now it does not matter in this context if Swinburne's use of 'Aristotelian' is loose and unscholarly, but he must hang on to something, other than certain intuitions, that rule out psychological fission, and it is not clear where he gets this necessary unity from, except stipulation.

Is Swinburne helped by the way he develops the second stage of his argument? I do not think so, and partly because it also shows an unjustified appeal to Aristotle.

And so I come to the second stage of my argument. How are we to bring out within an integrated system of thought, this fact which the first stage of my argument has, I hope, shown conclusively – that continuing matter is not (logically) essential for the continuing existence of persons. For persons are substances, and for substances of all other kinds continuing matter *is* necessary for the continuing existence of the substance. If a substance S_2 at a time t_2 is to be the same substance as a substance S_1 at an earlier time t_1 it must (of logical necessity) be made of the same matter as S_1, or at least of matter obtained from S_1 by gradual replacement. If my desk today is to be the same desk as my desk last year it must be made largely of the same wood; a drawer or two may have been replaced. But the desk would not be the same desk if all the wood had been replaced. In the case of living organisms such as plants, we do allow for total replacement of matter – so long as it is gradual. The full-grown oak tree possesses few if any of the molecules which formed the sapling, but so long as molecules were replaced only gradually over a period while most other molecules continued to form part of the organized tree, the tree continues to exist. That continuing matter was necessary for the continued existence of a substance, was a central element in Aristotle's account of substances. But now we have seen that persons can survive (it is logically possible) without their bodily matter continuing to be part of them. In this situation we have a choice. Either we can say simply that persons are different – in their case continuing matter is not necessary for the continued existence of the substance. Or we can try to make sense of this fact by liberalizing Aristotle's account a little. We can say that the continuing existence of some of the stuff of which a substance is made is necessary for the continued existence of the substance. Normally the stuff of which substances are made is merely matter, but some substances (viz. persons) are made in part of immaterial stuff, soul-stuff. Given, as I suggested earlier, that persons are indivisible, it follows that soul-stuff comes in indivisible chunks, which we may call souls. (1986: 153–4)

So Swinburne's view is that Aristotle has shown that continuity depends on matter, and as mind does not depend on physical matter, there must be a special mental stuff that performs this role. This latter is a disturbing way of expressing substance dualism, because it seems to play into the hands of Churchland and Lewis, who argue against the knowledge argument on the grounds that it would be just as mysterious how subjective experience related to immaterial stuff as it is to explain how it relates to physical matter (see Section 3.3 above). The normal response to this is to say mental substance is not any kind of stuff, but is just consciousness, or the potentiality for it. But this may not be the main objection. If Swinburne's use of 'stuff' is not empty, it seems to me to carry the following implication. A kind of stuff is not a pure atom; there is no reason why it should not be infinitely divisible. This is true of Aristotle's physical stuffs, earth, fire, air and water. In modern jargon, 'stuff' is a kind of *gunk*. This would certainly not justify Swinburne's claim that it is simple and indivisible.

What I take from Swinburne is the intuition, found also in other places, that personal identity cannot be a matter of degree but must be all or nothing. The case he makes out for this is not, however, compelling, because it involves claims that the likely opponent will not and need not concede – though the intuitions behind Swinburne's argument are strong. In the next chapter I shall try to present an argument which is not so easy to reject.

14.3   John Foster's argument for Cartesianism

Foster's strategy is to argue that Cartesianism and the bundle theory are exhaustive options and then to refute the bundle theory. Unfortunately, I think that, rather like Swinburne, he has too generous a notion of what counts as a substance theory, and, therefore, as a Cartesian theory.

Foster responds to Hume as follows.

A natural response to Hume would be to say that, even if we cannot detect ourselves *apart from* our perceptions (our conscious experiences), we can at least detect ourselves *in* them . . . Hume seems to be supposing that introspection works like sense-perception: a mental item is presented as the object of introspective awareness in the same way as a colour-pattern is presented as the object of visual awareness. (1991: 215)

Foster responds.

Surely I am aware of [my experience], so to speak, *from the inside* – not as something presented, but as something which *I have* or as the experiential state which *I am in* . . . and this is equivalent to saying that I detect it by being aware of *myself* being visually aware. (215)

There is, Foster believes, only one way for the Humean to respond to this.

Would be by denying the traditional conception of sense-experience as involving a sensory act (or state) of awareness and a phenomenal object, and claiming that the phenomenal object is the only item involved. (216)

Foster follows the original Humean line in claiming that the bundle theorist must deny that we have any introspective awareness of anything over and above the *objects* of our consciousness – no sense of an *act* of awareness or of a *subject* of the awareness (1991: 216). But the bundle theorist is not as restricted as Hume thought. The bundle consists of the objects of awareness *and the co-consciousness relation (or relations) that hold between them,* and I think the modern bundle theorist would want to say that it is the nexus of C-relations that constitutes our sense of subject and of the awareness relation we have to particular contents. The Humean point then becomes that we mistake this nexus of relations for a kind of entity, in a way similar to that in which, Hume claims, we mistake the regular succession of similar impressions for an entity called an enduring physical object. Whether this really makes sense in the end is another matter. I think that it is dubious whether it can accommodate the subject as *agent*, but it does mean that simple introspection cannot refute a sophisticated bundle theory, in the way that Foster wants. The very strict interpretation that Foster gives to Hume seems to deny that we have any 'sense of self' at all, the version which allows for our awareness of the relatedness allows for that sense and explains how it can be an illusion.

15 An argument for the existence of mental substance

15.1 Why 'mental substance'?

First, I think I owe an explanation for talking of mental substance in the title of this book and trying to avoid the term 'substance dualism'. This is because the arguments I wish to defend are consistent with idealism as well as dualism, and so it is not *dualism* as such for which I am arguing, but for the view that the mind is an immaterial substance. Nevertheless the arguments presented in this chapter – and those presented in most, if not all, of this book – are consistent with dualism. Having clarified this point, I shall feel free to use the term 'substance dualism'.

I believe that the arguments presented so far in this book refute materialism, but one might think that one should stay as near to materialism as possible, and be a property dualist. The brain is, after all, a very complex object, and perhaps for good evolutionary reasons it has developed some strange and unique properties. One might conclude, therefore, that these properties are properties *of the brain* and, hence, *of the human animal*, not the properties of some strange immaterial substance. The conscious mind, on this account, is just the integrated (integrated by their dependence on the sophisticated organisation of the brain) bundle of the human animal's conscious mental states.

As we saw above, there are modern philosophers, including Jonathan Lowe (1996), Richard Swinburne (1986) and John Foster (1991), who do not accept that the mind is just a bundle of properties associated with a human body; they think, instead, that it is an immaterial *substance* in its own right. These are the *substance dualists*.[1]

The first question that arises is 'what is substance dualism? What is involved in categorising the mind as a substance in its own right?' This, of course, raises the whole issue of what a substance is, and this is far too

---

[1] This is not strictly accurate. Not everyone who believes that the mind is an immaterial substance is a dualist. Some, like Foster (and the present author), are idealists. But, for present purposes, it is the status of mental substance that is relevant.

large an issue to deal with *en passant*.[2] For present purposes, we can stay with the intuitive contrast between objects and their properties. Objects are relatively self-standing entities – they do not exist *by* belonging to something else, whereas properties only exist *by* being the property of something, usually an object. Objects are, of course, usually causally dependent on other objects in various ways, but they are not conceptually dependent on them, in the way that, for example, the roundness property of the ball depends on the existence of the ball. Objects, in this sense, are pretty well what is meant by 'substance'. So the mind is a substance if it is not just a collection of properties of the body or brain, and if its dependence on the body or brain is mere causal dependence; it is not conceptually dependent. There are many issues that could be raised here, but this must suffice for present purposes.[3]

15.2   Minds and counterfactuals of origin

Descartes' most famous reason for thinking that the mind was a substance in its own right occurs in the *Second Meditation* (Descartes 1641/1984). It is that we can imagine that our current conscious experience be just as it is, yet, because we are being deceived by an 'evil demon'; none of the physical things we seem to experience, including our own bodies, is genuine. We could, at this moment, be in a completely hallucinatory or virtual reality, with all the physical things we seems to experience being unreal, including our own bodies. Descartes thinks that the fact that we can conceive this to be the case shows that the mind is a distinct thing from the body and can, in principle, exist without the body. If you can imagine one thing existing without another, then the latter cannot be essential to the former and they are distinct entities. So the mind is a distinct entity from the body.

Although this argument has a certain appeal and there are still philosophers who think it has force, it is also deeply immersed in many controversies. The first of these concerns the move from something's being imaginable to its being really possible. Modality – the theory of necessity and possibility – is a very difficult and murky area, but there are philosophers who hold that, though imaginability is not a complete guarantee of possibility, it is a very good – possibly the best available – guide to it

---

[2] For anyone interested in the general issue, see the entry 'Substance' in *The Stanford Encyclopedia of Philosophy*, and Robinson (2009) in the bibliography.

[3] The argument is, of course, much more complicated than I suggest. You could argue that objects are conceptually dependent on properties both because there cannot be an object without properties and at least some of these properties may be essential to the object. For a more thorough discussion, see Robinson (2009).

(e.g. Hart 1988). There are many others, however, who think that, at least in controversial matters, it is a very weak indicator. Another problem concerns the conception of mind that seems to lie behind Descartes' argument. This conception of mind is often referred to as the 'Cartesian theatre' conception, and, according to it the life of the mind is wholly internal, a kind of bubble of consciousness confined beyond and 'further inside' than the brain. Only if you take this view of conscious life, it is argued, can you imagine consciousness to be as it is and the physical world taken away. This 'Cartesian theatre' view of the mind is disputed by direct realists, who believe that our conscious life directly encompasses the external world, especially our own bodies. If this latter is the real situation, they argue, then you cannot abstract the physical world and leave experience untouched, for external physical objects constitute – and do not merely cause – the contents of our consciousness.[4]

Because of the depth of controversy surrounding Descartes' argument, that is not the argument for substance dualism on which I wish to concentrate. The line I prefer to investigate is connected with theories of personal identity and rests on the belief that bundle dualism – the theory that the mind is not a substance but only a collection of immaterial properties or states – cannot accommodate certain essential features of personal identity – what makes a person the particular person that he or she is. I made some elementary remarks about the notion of *substance* above. The argument I am about to consider is ambitious because it is intended to prove not merely that the mind is a substance, but also that it is a *simple* substance – one of the world's atomic entities, though in a rather special sense.

We have already considered the identity conditions for ordinary physical objects. There is a long tradition, dating at least from the eighteenth-century Scottish philosopher Thomas Reid (1785/1969), for arguing that the identity of persons over time is not a matter of convention or mere conceptualist interpretation in the way that we saw that it was for physical objects in Chapter 12. There is something absolute – all or nothing – about one's being numerically the same person at 70 as at 7. Unfortunately this intuition is controversial and does not command universal, or even general, assent. Growth, ageing, and especially radical changes in personality due to accidents or diseases are claimed to make one into 'a different person'. Some would say that qualitative differences in personality must be distinguished from numerical identity as the same person; and others, that there is no absolute difference between these two,

---

[4] This is one version of the fashionable doctrine called *externalism about mental content*. See, for example, McDowell (1994).

as there is not in the identity of England through invasion and radical political change.

I think that the issue can be made sharper and clearer, however, if one moves from considering identity through time to the rather less familiar matter of identity under counterfactual circumstances, especially those concerning origin. This was the strategy we used in Chapter 12 to under- mine the claim of physical objects to be true individual substances. Instead of asking whether Theseus's ship is the same object when half its planks had been replaced, we asked whether it would have been the same ship if it had been constructed with different materials in the first place. So we were not considering changes within its life as a boat, but possible differences at its origin. Thus we are considering *counterfactuals of origin*, that is, things that might have been different at the beginning of the existence of an object. We concluded above that when this happens there is no further fact than that there is more or less overlap of constitution. As I hope to show, a similar treatment cannot be meted out in the case of persons, when it comes to these counterfactual cases.[5]

Let us try to apply the same thought experiment to a human being. Suppose that a given human individual – call him Jones – had had origins different from those which he in fact had such that whether that difference affected who he was was not intuitively obvious. We can approach this by imagining cases where it seems indefinite whether what was produced was the same body as Jones in fact possesses. What would count as such a case might be a matter of controversy, but there must be one. Perhaps it is unclear whether Jones's mother would have given birth to the same human body if the same egg from which the Jones body came had been fertilised by a different though genetically identical sperm from the same father. Some philosophers might regard it as obvious that sameness of sperm is essential to the identity of a human body. In that case, imagine that the sperm that fertilised the egg had differed in a few molecules from the way it actually was; would that be the same sperm? If one pursues the matter far enough there will be indeterminacy which will infect that of the resulting body. There must therefore be some difference such that neither natural language nor intuition tells us whether the difference alters the identity of the human body; a point, that is, where the question of whether we have the same body is not a matter of fact.[6]

---

[5] Other approaches to counterfactual identity, such as Wiggins's stipulative account and the argument that leeway is fixed (Salmon), were considered in Chapter 12, which should be consulted if the 'overlap' solution is not thought to be applicable to ordinary cases.

[6] It is important to note that this problem cannot be avoided by resorting to epistemicism in dealing with vagueness. It is central to epistemicism that the determinate fact about whether something is F depends on language use, not on some independent fact in the

These are cases of substantial overlap of constitution in which that fact is the only bedrock fact in the case; there is no further fact about whether they are 'really' the same object.

My claim is that no similar overlap of constitution can be applied to the counterfactual identity of minds. In Geoffrey Madell's words:

> But while my present body can thus have its partial counterpart in some possible world, my present consciousness cannot. Any present state of consciousness that I can imagine either is or is not mine. There is no question of degree here. (Madell 1981: 91)

Why is this so? Imagine the case where we are not sure whether it would have been Jones's body – and, hence, Jones – that would have been created by the slightly modified sperm and the same egg. Can we say, as we would for an object with no consciousness, that the story 'something the same, something different' is the whole story, that overlap of constitution is all there is to it? For the Jones body as such, this approach would do as well as for any other physical object. But suppose Jones, in reflective mood, asks himself 'if that had happened, would I have existed?' There are at least three answers he might give to himself. (i) 'I either would or would not, but I cannot tell.' (ii) 'In some ways, or to some degree, I would have, and in some ways, or to some degree, I would not. The creature who would have existed would have had a kind of overlap of psychic constitution and personal identity with me, rather in the way there would be overlap in the case of any other physical object.' (iii) 'There is no fact of the matter whether I would or would not have existed: it is just a mis-posed question. There is not even a factual answer in terms of overlap of constitution.' I shall discuss (ii) in the rest of this section, and move to answer to (iii) at the end of Section 15.3

The second answer parallels the response we would give in the case of bodies. But as an account of the subjective situation, it makes no sense. Call the creature that would have emerged from the slightly modified sperm, 'Jones*'. Is the overlap suggestion that, just as, say 85% of Jones*'s body would have been identical with Jones's original body, and about 85% of his psychic life would have been Jones's? That it would have been like Jones's – indeed that Jones* might have had a psychic life 100% like Jones's – makes perfect sense, but that he might have been to that degree, the same psyche – that Jones '85% existed' – makes no sense. Take the case in which Jones and Jones* have exactly similar lives throughout: which 85% of the 100% similar mental events do they share? Nor does

world. If the identity of the sperm is dependent on how we use 'sperm' (or 'identity'), this cannot be what determines whether I would or would not have existed.

it make sense to suggest that Jones might have participated in the whole of Jones*'s psychic life, but in a rather ghostly only-85%-there manner. Clearly, the notion of overlap of numerically identical psychic parts cannot be applied in the way that overlap of actual bodily part constitution quite unproblematically can.

There are two things to notice about this argument. The first is how the identity across counterfactuals of origin case differs from that of identity through changes across time; the second concerns the peculiarly strong sense of individuality that goes along with self-consciousness.

The first of these points concerns what one might call *empathetic distance*, which is essential to the problematic nature of identity through time but irrelevant in the counterfactual case.

Suppose that my parents had emigrated to China whilst my mother was pregnant with me, and that, shortly after my birth, both my parents had died. I was then taken in by Chinese foster parents, lived through the revolution and ended up being brought up in whatever way an alien would have been brought up in Mao's China. None of this person's post-uterine experiences would have been like mine. It seems, on the one hand, that this person would obviously have been me, and, on the other, that it is utterly unclear what kind of empathetic connection I can feel to this other 'me'. If I ask, like Jones, 'would this have been me?', I am divided between the conviction that, as the story is told, it obviously would, and a complete inability to feel myself into the position I would then have occupied. This kind of failure of empathy plays an important role in many stories that are meant to throw doubt on the absoluteness of personal identity. It is important to the attempt to throw doubt on whether I am the same person as I would become in fifty years' time, or whether brain damage would render me 'a different person' in more than a metaphorical sense. It is also obviously something that can be a matter of degree: some differences are more empathetically imaginable than others. In all these cases our intuitions are indecisive about the effect on identity. It is an important fact that problems of empathy play no role in the counterfactual argument. The person who would have existed if the sperm had been slightly different could have had as exactly similar a psychic life to mine, in as exactly similar environment as you care to imagine. This shows the difference between the cases I have discussed and the problematic cases that involve identity through time. In those cases the idea of 'similar but not quite the same' gets empirical purchase. My future self feels, in his memory, much, but not all, of what I now feel. In these cases, overlap of conscious constitution is clearly intelligible. But in the counterfactual cases, imaginative or empathetic distance plays no essential role, and the accompanying relativity of identification gets no grip.

15.3   Individuality and consciousness

The second point to notice is the light it throws on the concept of what the medievals called *haecceitas*. *Haecceitas* translates as 'thisness' and is, according to certain philosophers, the feature of an object which, additional to its ordinary properties, makes an individual thing the particular that it is. Most – though by no means all – philosophers regard this as a very suspect notion; in the case of complex physical bodies, for example, it is difficult to imagine what a *haecceitas* would consists in or how it relates to the other features of the object, and so the suggestion that there is such a thing seems to be pure mystery-mongering.[7] By contrast, in the case of minds we do have a form of *haecceitas* which, in a sense, we all understand, namely our identity as subjects. It is because we intuitively understand this that we feel we can give a clear sense to the suggestion that it would, or would not, have been ourselves to which something had happened, if it had happened; and that we feel we can understand very radical counterfactuals – e.g. that I might have been an ancient Greek or even a non-human – whereas such radical counterfactuals when applied to mere bodies – e.g. that this wooden table might have been the other table in the corner or even a pyramid – makes no intuitive sense. It is possible to argue that the suggestion that my mind might have been in another body ultimately makes no sense, but it makes a prima facie sense – it seems to have content – in a way that a similar suggestion for mere bodies does not. The very fact that the counterfactuals for subjects seem to make sense exhibits something not present in the other cases, which is available to function in the role of *haecceitas*. Only with consciousness understood in a Cartesian fashion can *haecceitas* be given an empirical interpretation.

The reflections on *haecceitas* can be developed further. If one thinks of a true particular as being something that can sustain counterfactuals and still be clearly the same individual, perhaps minds are the most genuine particulars that there are. We have seen that there is vagueness in the cases of identity for complex physical objects. This, we suggested, makes such identity a matter of convention or decision and not a true matter of fact. Reverting to our original example, the statement 'there is a ship of a certain sort and composition' gives you all the real or fundamental facts out in the world; the situation is adequately characterised by a statement which is a generalised or quantified one – 'there is *some* such and such' – and one can dispense with more exact identificatory discourse in this context.

---

[7] See the discussion of Salmon in Section 12.5.

There might, however, be the following response. It might be argued that what I say is true of composite objects but not of the units that compose them. In the case of Theseus's ship, these are the planks, and obviously the same problem about their counterfactual identity can be raised as for the ship itself, for the planks are composites, too. We can ask 'would it have been the same plank if it had been composed of such and such different atoms?' and the same problem arises. One might think that this shows that composite physical objects have a precarious hold on identity and, therefore, on existence as real individuals, but that for true atoms the same problem cannot arise. But, as we saw in Section 12.7, atoms, too, are not problem-free under counterfactuals of origin. Suppose a particular electron (pretending electrons to be basic for purposes of illustration) came into existence at a particular point in space-time. If it had instead come to be in a slightly different location, would it have been the same one? Always questions of this sort can be generated for physical objects to show that there is no real or ultimate difference between qualitative similarity and real identity as particulars in their case. Only the inwardness of subjectivity can deliver the difference. It is not simply the simplicity and unity of the self that constitutes its existence as a true individual, but its nature as conscious, from which that unity derives.

Some philosophers of physics have asserted that *haecceitas* must be attributed to certain sub-atomic particles – bosons, for example – if they are to be regarded as proper individuals.[8] But it is agreed that quantum theory itself does not require quantal entities to be individuals – indeed, it makes as much sense, if not more, if they are treated as something less than individuals. It is not possible here to enter into a debate about how best to interpret quantum theory, though it seems to me that those who wish to endow bosons with *haecceitas* do so only because they believe that this is necessary to endow them with the degree of individuality possessed by more ordinary physical objects. As I am sceptical about the status of all physical objects as full individuals, this motive gains no hold. Nevertheless, none of the arguments that I have presented for treating the self as a simple individual is in any way undermined if physical simples are also individuals.

Someone who, unlike the boson *haecceitist*, was impressed by my argument that atomicity itself is not enough alone to guarantee status as a genuine individual might be led to look again at the case of the self. We considered the option that its identity might be a matter of degree, and rejected this. But what about the suggestion that there is no firm difference between qualitative similarity and numerical identity? We have a

---

[8] For a lucid account of these issues, see French (2006).

strong feeling that there must be a difference between these two in the case of bodies, yet this seems to be mistaken. Could our sense that there must be such a distinction in our own case also be an illusion? Is that conception of the self which makes us feel so sure that someone psychically just like me but with a somewhat different origin either is me or is not something that needs 'deconstructing', after the fashion of Derrida or Nietzsche or Hume? This is option (iii) that there is no fact of the matter about whether it would have been me or not, or whether there was genuine overlap.

I do not think that the idea 'just like me but the idea of whether it would be me or not has no content' can be made acceptable. Whereas in the case of physical objects we can see, after a little thought, that though the qualitatively similar gives us all we thought we needed by talking about particulars, it will not do this in the case of minds.

Consider the following example. Suppose you discover that, in the very early stages in the womb, you were one of twins, but that the other did not develop, and that it could have easily happened the other way round; the other would have survived and you died in the first few days. The similarity between you as survivor and your twin, had he survived in your stead, both in genetic endowment and environmental circumstances and subsequent experience, could have been almost complete. Nevertheless, there is no sense that, on reflection, it makes no serious factual difference, concerning your own fate, which of the two survived. Just as it is true that, if your parents had never met, then you would not have existed; equally, if the other bundle of cells had developed instead of yours, you would not have existed. This is, in no sense, a matter of decision, convention or degree.

It is possible to answer this argument by saying that the twins' case is simply a matter of two different bodies, and I do not deny that this difference can be taken as foundational. The case is an analogy to show that there really is something at stake and is a response to the 'no fact of the matter' strategy. The 'different bodies' response is explaining the supervenience base for saying it would not be me. And saying it would not be me is not just to say it would be a different body – it is something real that goes along with its being a different body. (Perhaps the situation is not even that simple: both came from the same zygote and so sameness of body might be an open issue, given that there never developed an alternative personal claimant.)

If one accepts the conclusion reached in Chapter 12, that counterfactual identity is not basic for any physical objects, and applies this to humans, the result is clearly bizarre.

It would mean that the idea that it would be you, if counterfactual p is never any different from the proposition that there would have been someone like you if p, whatever p may be. It could be that someone coughed on the other side of the world at the moment of your conception. We certainly cannot let go the idea that there is genuine and primitive sameness under these circumstances.

It would seem that the only possible answer to the question which I supposed Jones to have asked himself above, 'if that had happened, would I have existed?' is (i), 'I either would or would not, but I cannot tell.' If there is a real fact, independent of our convention or decision, in this case, then it shows that counterfactual identity facts are real facts in the case of minds, in a way that they may not be for physical objects.

15.4   An objection: that this argument shows something about our concepts but not about reality

One response sometimes made to this argument is that it is correct as an account of our *concept* of the mind, but not correct about the actual nature of the mind. Reality is, so to speak, deconstructive of the concept that we have. So our conceptual scheme does commit us to something like the Cartesian conception of the mind, but we have other grounds for thinking that this is a mistake.

As it stands, this is more an expression of unease than a worked-out objection. I shall consider two ways of filling it out. (a) One might argue as follows. If we suppose the mind to be only a collection of mental states related by a co-consciousness relation, the phenomenology would still seem to be to us as it is in fact. The argument does not, therefore, show that the bundle theory is false, for even if the bundle theory were true, it would seem to us as if we were simple substances. It could be compared to what a 'hard determinist' might say about free will, namely we cannot help but feel we have it, but the feeling is mistaken.

There are two problems with this argument. First, it does not help Jones to answer his question. In order to avoid answer (i) – that he either would or would not be identical with Jones* – he would have to make sense of one of the other alternatives, and this objection gives him no help with that. Is the suggestion that when Jones tries to imagine overlap of psychic constitution, our concepts prevent him from doing so, but, in reality, such a thing would be possible? If so, I do not think this very plausible. It seems to me to be a real fact that this makes no sense. My objections above to the other option – that there is no fact of the matter – seem also to be untouched.

Second, the argument is question-begging. It is a moot point between the bundle theorist and the substantivalist whether there could be a co-consciousness relation that would produce an experientially united mind.

My argument supports the view that experiential unity involves a simple substance and so supports the view that there is no such thing as a self-standing co-consciousness relation. So it is not proper simply to claim that it could be the same for us if the bundle theory were true, if that condition is in fact an impossible one. The analogy with free will, though illustrative of what the objector is driving at, does little to show that he is correct. First, the coherence of the hard determinist's position is controversial. Second, the determinist can give a rationale for why we *must* feel free in terms of the conceptual impossibility of replacing one's own practice of *deciding* by one of merely *predicting* one's own behaviour. There seems to be no parallel explanation of why it seems all or nothing for counterfactual identity. This is especially mysterious given that it can seem be a matter of degree in cases that turn on empathetic distance.

(b) There is a completely different way of filling the objection out. It concerns my use of counterfactuals. Counterfactuals are a controversial matter and I make no attempt to discuss them. I blatantly assume, both here and in Chapter 12, the falsehood of Lewis' counterpart analysis, for if Jones's question whether he would exist only enquired whether there would be a counterpart which possessed states very like his own, then there would be no phenomenological problem. All counterparts are strictly different objects. However, I am quite happy, along with almost all other philosophers, simply to deny Lewis' theory.[9] But it is not from this source that the challenge comes, but from someone who takes a non-realist attitude to counterfactuals. There is an empiricist tradition which denies truth values to counterfactuals and says that they express policies or attitudes. There will be no truth about what would have happened if the relevant sperm had been slightly different.

It is not possible to get deeply engaged in a discussion of counterfactuals here. I would make two points. First, most philosophers do accept a realist account of counterfactuals – the anti-realist view is not very plausible – and the argument would go through for them. Second, the anti-realist approach has a weaker and a stronger form. The weaker version simply denies truth value to counterfactuals: there is no fact of the matter about whether it is a or b that would have happened if C had obtained. C could have obtained and, if it had, either a or b (or something else) would have occurred; there is just no truth from the perspective of the actual world about which it would have been. This does not affect my

---

[9] In fact, I think that the strongest objection to Lewis' theory – beyond its massive counter-intuitiveness – is that, because the other possible worlds are isolated causally from each other, they cannot figure in an explanation of why we think modally. The resources must be in our world, so, for example, an 'as if' explanation would fit all the facts, without the profligacy.

argument at all, which only requires that the only options about what might have happened are all or nothing, not that there is a fact about which. The stronger version says that the whole notion of *might have been otherwise* is a projection of our mode of thought – of our ability to imagine things – not something that obtains in reality. This is not to say – as it might seem – that the actual world is necessary (because there is nothing else that might have been) but only that all these modal categories are mere projections. Even if we accepted this – which I do not recommend – it would not entirely deflate the argument. It would still show something interesting about the nature of mind, namely that it made no sense to treat it in the same way as bodies within the logical space of possibility that we create by projection. The fact that we create that space does not imply that what we express within it does not reflect real differences between the objects about which we are talking.

15.5   Making sense of the substantial self ...?

The argument just presented has, I think, great intuitive appeal, but, on the other hand, it also seems to leave many puzzles. The first concerns the nature of mental or immaterial substance itself: what is its 'essence' and how should one characterise it? More often than not, the answer is given that it is consciousness. Some feel unhappy with the idea that consciousness can be treated as a special kind of 'stuff'. Even if one puts aside that issue, what are we to say about the existence of the self or mind during periods of unconsciousness, such as deep sleep or anaesthesia, if its nature is consciousness? One way of avoiding this difficulty is that taken, for example, by Galen Strawson (2009). Strawson thinks that a particular self lasts roughly only as long as a single span of attention, so a given person will be composed of many selves over time. If one is to avoid this and similar counter-intuitive ways of dealing with lapses of consciousness, how can one do it? I want to give a hint on how one might approach this problem by discussing a second apparent difficulty for the theory that the self is a simple substance.

The second problem is as follows. The argument of the previous sections attributes the conscious subject a unity and simplicity unique in nature. It is unique because I have cast doubt on the existence of any true individuals that are purely physical. But putting aside the claim that there are no true atomic physical individuals, we still have a problem about the atomic and simple nature of the self: how can something as complex as a human subject be a simple entity? People have a variety of faculties and capacities, and an almost unlimited number of memories, beliefs, desires, etc. What does it mean to say that such an entity lacks parts or composition? Attempts to answer this question are liable to drive one into what Russell somewhere described as 'soupy metaphysics' and I cannot venture too far into such territory here.[10] In substance, these problems will, I hope, give rise to another work on *The Active Self*, which will deal with thought, free will and embodiment. A 'taster' of how I hope to deal with these topics can be gained by considering the 'unity in diversity' that is an essential feature of thought.

Peter Geach (1969) has argued that the 'activity of thinking cannot be assigned a position in the physical time-series' (34). His reason for this is that, though the expression of a thought using a sentence will be spread through ordinary time, one's grasp on the content must come as a whole. If it did not, then by the time one had reached '1066' in the sentence 'the battle of Hastings took place in 1066' one's consciousness of the other components of the thought would have passed into history. What the sentence expresses as a whole is the thought of which one is conscious. Something that has an essential unity finds expression in something that is complex. The position seems thus to be the following. The expression of a thought in a sentence is spread out in the normal 'flowing' empirical time. But the thinking of the thought which, in some sense, 'lies behind' (but not necessarily temporally before) this, is not temporally structured in the same way. Something which is implicit in the thought is laid out explicitly in the sentence. One experiences a thought *in* a sentence – or sometimes in other, non-verbal, images – but as a unity that a mere string of sounds or images does not possess.

Isn't this a somewhat mysterious doctrine? It is, but it is true to the phenomenology of thought, and if one tries to avoid a conclusion along these lines one reaches even more counter-intuitive conclusions. Consider, for example, the attempt to demystify thinking by treating it as a computational process. Jerry Fodor (1975; 1979) treats consciousness as irrelevant to thought, which is a computational process carried out in the purely formal 'Language of Thought' (LOT) in the brain. This leads to certain serious limitations. For example, any term not definable within the system must be primitive and innate to it. Because very few terms in natural language are explicitly and precisely definable, this leads Fodor to claim that the LOT equivalents of almost all terms, such as 'xylophone' and 'crocodile', must be innate. Furthermore, formal systems cannot 'upgrade' themselves and so there is no natural development in the power of the system. Any purely physical 'thinking' machine must be what Daniel Dennett (e.g. 1987) calls a *syntactic engine*, which means that, like a computer, it works solely from the physical properties of the

---

[10] For a 'non-soupy' defence of simplicity rather different from mine, see Chisholm (1991).

symbols it manipulates and not through any grasp of meaning. This appears to leave out anything we do in the way of responding to the meaning of what people say or unpacking meanings or being genuinely inventive: a purely syntactic engine – one in which *understanding* has no essential role – it would seem cannot do these things.[11] As Mark Baker (2011) points out, this lacuna in the scientific explanation of thought had already been indicated by Chomsky, fifty years ago. Chomsky divided language into three elements: the lexicon, syntax and the Creative Aspect of Language Use; science, he claimed, had nothing to say about the last. This is, in part, at least, because understanding is not driven by syntax alone. This would suggest that the Creative Aspect of Language, and, hence, the development of thought, when that involves more than formal inferences but depends on our grasp of meanings and our understanding of our own projects, depends on something more than features of the neural/computational machinery. The natural candidate for this source of creativity is the self. Furthermore, for long-term tasks, such as the development of our life projects,[12] Strawson's ephemeral selves would not be adequate. When I follow out an argument, let alone develop my view of the world, I am not trying to convince my heirs, but myself. It would require very coercive reasons to make me abandon the idea that this is the project of a single self and subject and Strawson does not have such arguments.[13]

This does not tell us directly, however, how an essentially conscious entity can survive periods of unconsciousness. Geach's remarks about thought, however, do give us a lead by casting doubt on our common-sense view of time and temporal relations. Geach also says:

The difficulty felt over saying that a thought need be neither long, nor short, nor instantaneous comes about, I suggest, from a (perhaps unacknowledged) assumption of a Newtonian or Kantian view of time: time is taken to be logically prior to events, events, on the other hand, must occupy divisible stretches or else

[11] There is, of course, a massive literature on these topics. A defence of a perspective similar to mine but from a scientific point of view can be found in Penrose (1995). Several physicalist philosophers, most notably Dennett, respond to the features of thought which are difficult for them to accommodate by treating the semantic features of thought as the creation of interpretation from a third-person perspective. For the problems with this, see Robinson (2010) and Chapter 13 above.

[12] Fodor now says – and says that he always said – that his computational model only worked for the modular aspects of cognition, which does not cover such things as abduction and non-mechanical rational deliberation – the kinds of things that are supposed to go on in the 'global workspace'. This is close to the admission that his original theory (as normally understood) did not include what we would usually think of as *thought* (Fodor 2000).

[13] There are other cogent objections to ephemeral selves. Richard Swinburne (1997), for example, argues that this is a less simple theory than that of the enduring, single self.

indivisible instants of time. If we reject this view and think instead in terms of time-relations, then what I am suggesting is that thoughts have not got all the kinds of time-relations that physical events, and I think also sensory processes, have. (36)

The expression of thought is a process taking time; the thought itself is not. If you think – like, in their different ways, both Newton and Kant did – that time is an all-encompassing necessary framework of events, then the thought and its thinker must be located somewhere specific within the ubiquitous time series that also houses the expression of the thought. But if what we think of as physical time is a construct from the relations between certain kinds of events and objects, and if certain other objects and occurrences are related in very different ways from the time-constructing events, then these different ones will not be in what we think of as physical time. Insofar as the apparent complexity of the self flows from the diversity of its actions within time, we can see how it may be a genuine unity, yet express itself as a diversity. We can also see how we might approach the first problem we raised for the substance dualist, because these remarks about time give us a way of understanding how a single consciousness might have what is apparently an intermittent existence with empirical time. That time is (like space) a construct from the experiences of subjects and the subject is not itself within it.[14]

But these are only hints towards a further project.

---

[14] I discuss this at length in Robinson (2007).

16 Plotinus, Locke and Hume on the unity of individual substances

16.1 Introduction

I argued in Chapter 12 that, in a strict physical realist sense, there are no physical individual substances. The notion of such individuality is a function of our conceptualisation and interpretation of things. The only true individual is the conscious mind or self. But this is not the whole story. I believe that there is genuine illumination to be got from the treatment of this issue in classic sources of metaphysics, of which Plotinus is the key figure and Locke and Hume are instructive foils. This book has been concerned almost exclusively with contemporary writings and what appear to be contemporary issues. The task of this last chapter is to show – or, at least, suggest – that it is anchored also in perennial metaphysics. To do this, in this context and the space of one chapter, will involve moments of what appear to be dogmatism in my interpretation of the historical sources: a full scholarly justification may not be possible. But I hope that what I say is suggestive and interesting enough to excuse this methodology.

In order to proceed, it is necessary to seem to re-open the question of individuality and ask what is involved in taking parts or properties to be the parts or properties of one individual object.

Two comments must be made on this question from the outset. The first is that I am well aware that the possession of many *parts* and the possession of many *properties* are importantly different. Nevertheless it is *ex hypothesi* for present purposes that there is also something that they have in common, namely that they are both forms of complexity. To what extent it is justified to assimilate these two forms of complexity is something that we will have to assess as the argument progresses. Second, and connectedly, notice that the use of the expression 'unified entity' in this context does not signify simply *coherence, cohesion* or *bondedness*, but the more abstract property of *being one thing*. Again, only the development of the argument will show whether and to what extent this rather abstract sense of unity is a valid one.

Plotinus, Locke and Hume represent the three obvious positions on the question of what makes a complex object one thing. Taking them in reverse, Hume is a conventionalist and/or sceptic; there is nothing that constitutes their unity except our habit of deeming them to be one. His position, therefore, has something important in common with the conclusion of Chapter 12. Locke believes that, at least in the case of living things, there is a genuine organic unity. In this he, rather surprisingly, appears to follow Aristotle, at least as Aristotle is interpreted by many modern philosophers. Plotinus believes in the existence of pure individuality or unity which makes any one thing to be one. These three options – conventionalism, organicism and a belief in some kind of metaphysical principle of unity – seem to me to constitute the available options. Hume and Plotinus share a belief in the same conditional statement, but in their attitudes towards it they illustrate the dictum that one man's *modus ponens* is another man's *modus tollens*. The conditional is 'if complex objects are genuine individuals, then there must be some such feature of reality (or some such *idea*) as *individuality as such*'. Plotinus takes it as obvious that there are genuine complex individuals, and so concludes that there must be *individuality as such*. He then proceeds to investigate its nature within the framework of a Platonic philosophical logic. Hume, on the other hand, takes it as obvious that there is no such idea, and concludes that there are no complex individuals. He then proceeds to construct a psychologistic account of how we come to think as if there were. The tentative conclusion of this chapter will be to bring Hume and Plotinus together – largely to the benefit of the latter – and suggest a metaphysical or transcendental conventionalism. This is how what is argued here is reconciled with the conclusion of Chapter 12. But the discussion must begin with Locke, for his position, by contrast with conventionalism and transcendentalism, represents common sense, and so must be disposed of before it is worthwhile discussing the others.

16.2   Locke, Aristotle and the organic theory

Locke presents his account in *Essay Concerning Human Understanding*, II xxvii 5 and 6. For mere masses of matter, Locke has a mereological conception of identity, and this does not interest us here. For living things and, it seems, machines (though this may just be an analogy), there is genuine identity through change. These two sections in the *Essay* go through less and more metaphysical moments. To begin with, the unity seems to be reducible to the organisation of the parts. Then he talks as if an entity – though not a substance – emerges from this arrangement of parts, called 'a common life', and he talks of '*partaking of* the same life' (my italics), which suggests that there is something of which to partake. The ontology of structures is a difficult matter, as we saw in Section 11.5, when we discussed modern hylomorphism, and Locke is not the kind of philosopher to notice this sort of problem in formal ontology; nevertheless, he does talk as if there is some one thing that is passed on through the succession of spatially continuous organised parts, rather than there being no more than a succession of closely resembling things. It seems to be a causal or metaphysical product, not a logical construct. It is this notion of identity that Hume rejects. The mind slides across similar but strictly different objects and *feels as if* there is something that is one thing persisting through these changes.

Although the Aristotelian notion of substantial form is a paradigm of what Locke is, in general, rejecting, this 'common life', which is an organisational unity, maintaining the individuality of organic things, looks suspiciously like an Aristotelian substantial form. What is the difference, and can Locke's opposition (so to speak) to Humean conventionalism be maintained along with his rejection of Aristotelianism and can these positions be reconciled? The answer to this is that they cannot.

According to Aristotle, there is no definitive science of matter. That is, how matter behaves is, within certain constraints, a function of what it is the matter of. Even in principle, there is no definitive 'bottom-up' science. Substantial forms are real because they are an essential causal factor in how the object behaves. Although this is not necessarily inconsistent with atomism – how atoms behave in complex organisation might be emergent with respect to their properties alone or in small groups – I think that we can assume that, for our purposes, Locke accepted a bottom-up determinism based on Newton's laws of motion. There is, therefore, no causal role for complex organisation as such. There are no reasons for reifying such complexes. In Armstrong's terms, such organisational properties are concepts or predicates, not real universals. Making some allowance for anachronism, that is to say that Hume was right about the ontological status of complex bodies; their reality consists in our reification of them – though, of course, the patterned events on which this reification is projected are real in a stronger sense.

Peter van Inwagen, in *Material Beings*, adopts a Lockean view. In a sense, his position is more extreme than Locke's, because he believes that the only things are simples and things with a life; hunks of matter or artefacts do not exist. It is not possible to investigate his arguments in detail here, but I want to look at both his final account of what is there in the case of things that he does not acknowledge as beings, for it is nicely illustrative of what I am calling Humean conventionalism; and at his reason for thinking that life is sufficient to endow being although material cohesion, for example, is not. We will see that he has reasons which I, in this context, can properly ignore.

Van Inwagen's account of reality under the circumstances that we would normally describe as 'there being a wooden chair here' is as follows. He uses the expression 'chair-receptacle' as a name for those regions of space believed by chair-believers to be occupied by chairs. Van Inwagen (1990: 105) affirms:

(A) The chair-receptacle R is filled with rigidly interlocking wood particles; the regions immediately contiguous with R contain no wood particles; the wood particles at the boundary of R (that is, the wood particles within R that are not entirely surrounded by wood particles) are bonded to nearby wood particles much more strongly than they are bonded to the non-wood particles immediately outside R; the strength of the mutual bonding of the wood particles within R is large in comparison with the forces produced by casual human muscular exertions.

He denies, however:

(B) There is some *thing* that fits exactly into R.

(C) There is some *thing* that the wood particles within R compose.

This, I think, illustrates what I said above about the patterns being real (as in (A)), but the reification being rejected.

Why doesn't van Inwagen apply the same account to organisms? His reason is that if he did, it would follow that he did not exist, and this is ridiculous. Van Inwagen's position on persons can be compared to Unger's (1980), and, like Plotinus and Hume, they take contrasting *ponens* and *tollens* approaches to the same conditional. The conditional is:

If I am a person then either materialism is false or organisation in a life constitutes a being.

Both van Inwagen and Unger of (1980) are materialists, so this can be simplified to:

If I am a person then organisation in a life constitutes a being.

Van Inwagen thinks that, for *cogito* reasons, it is obvious that he is a person; Unger thought it is demonstrable on grounds of vagueness that organisation in a life does not constitute a thing, so the former thinks life is sufficient to exist and the latter denied his own existence.

I have gone into this to explain why, in this context, I feel justified in not pursuing this argument further. If one rejects the truth of materialism then one can accept the *cogito* and that one is a person, without being committed to the view that life endows being. I have already argued in Sections 11.4–11.6 that causally idle macroscopic types do not enter into a realist ontology, and nothing van Inwagen says obliges me to alter this view. There seems to me to be no more reason to think that being an organism, as such, overcomes the arguments for conceptualism, than there was for thinking that the similar arguments from Jaworski, that we considered in Section 11.5, for realism about structure proved conceptualism wrong.

Locke's position does not, therefore, constitute a further option to Hume's and Plotinus's. Given the rejection of Aristotelian causally efficacious substantial forms, 'the same life' is either a mysterious emergent entity or a reification, by us, based on a succession of similar but different things.

I would make the following remark, in case one were tempted to hold on to the original Aristotelian account. Aristotle himself was worried about how forms or essences, which are complex in definition, could be genuine unities, and one answer he comes up with is to define everything by its ultimate *differentia*, so that everything else follows logically from one single property. For well-known reasons, this cannot usually be done. So even in its own terms, the Aristotelian account does not properly solve the problem of unity.

Some of the same thoughts can be raised about Locke's explanation of personal identity by reference to partaking of 'the same consciousness' as we have raised about his use of 'the same life'. The standard interpretation is to make Locke essentially Humean, and construct personal identity from memory relations. It is not clear from the way he talks that he does not regard it as something that *emerges* from such relations, or, at least, that he does not mark the distinction between 'same consciousness' as something that emerges from memory relations and as something logically constituted by them.

16.3   Plotinus's ascent to the One

Hume's account is a default position, in the sense that it is the view one adopts if nothing can be made of anything less sceptical. It is, therefore, necessary next to discuss the Plotinian option.

Although historians of philosophy within the analytical tradition are now discussing Plotinus, there is no sign of such discussions interacting with contemporary philosophy in the way that work on Plato, Aristotle and Hellenistic philosophy does. One of the respects in which he is held to be most bizarre is in his doctrine of the One. This is still treated by the philosophical community in general as the product of mysticism grafted onto the wilder bits of Plato that only Plato specialists touch. That it might constitute an argumentative attempt to deal with a recognisable problem is hardly acknowledged at large. I want to suggest that it does constitute such an attempt.

Starting from *Ennead* VI 9, the following argument for the existence of the One can be constructed.

1. It is in virtue of unity that beings are beings.
2. Unity is not identical to something else – for example, to Form or to being in general.
3. Any feature of the world not decomposable into something else has a corresponding form.

Therefore

4. There is [what one might call] the 'form of unity'.
5. Forms are self-predicating.

Therefore

6. The 'form of unity' is perfect unity – that is, pure individuality or oneness.
7. Because forms are universals, this cannot be a form in the normal sense: *individuality* cannot be a universal.
8. Because intelligibility in the normal sense involves universality, this oneness is not intelligible.
9. Because it is in virtue of unity that all beings are beings, unity is prior to all *kinds* of things – i.e. to all forms.

Therefore

10. Unity itself – the One – transcends all forms, all intelligibility, and is presupposed by them.

The argument has a prima facie validity. The first premise is stated at the beginning of *Ennead* VI 9 1.

It is by the One that all beings are beings.

It is the equivalent of the conditional shared with Hume, with the assertion of the antecedent. Because Hume believes that there is no such a thing as unity, he denies that complex objects are, as such, beings at all.

VI 9. 2 argues for the second premise, claiming that *Being* takes complex forms and so cannot itself be unity. Plotinus's remarks on this may seem very dark but our discussion of Locke above provides good reasons of a different kind for thinking that the appeal to form or structure is not enough to secure the being and hence unity of composite objects.

3 is a general principle for all realists about universals – it applies to Armstrong as much as to Plato. The crunch comes with 5. There are two objections to my appeal to self-predication. The philosophically most important is that the doctrine seems obviously false; the fact that the argument rests on it is the kind of consideration that guarantees that

Plotinus will not be taken seriously. The second is that it is not clear that Plotinus accepts it. This for two reasons: First, as John Rist (1967: 61) points out, Plotinus denies it for some forms – for example, quantity – and accepts it for others, for example, truth. It cannot, therefore, be appealed to as a general principle. True, there is some inclination to distinguish those that it does and those that it does not in terms of whether the form concerns a property of bodies, to which it does not apply, which might mean that individuality gets by as self-predicating. This would not help us overcome the unacceptability of the doctrine. But there is an historical point which can help us philosophically. Neo-Platonists read Plato through the eyes of Aristotle – as well as Aristotle through the eyes of Plato – and, in doing so, accepted at least some aspects of his criticism of the traditional theory of forms. For example, forms are in an intellect, not a strange category of particulars in their own right. I want now to look further into this matter, for it might help us both to understand and to assist Plotinus.

16.4   From Platonism to neo-Platonism on the nature of forms, via Aristotle and Frege

The doctrine of self-predication is often taken to be the edifying part of the theory of forms, rather than a strictly philosophical part. Plato wants the form of the Beautiful to be beautiful and the form of the Good to be good, so he says that they are. But though the doctrine serves the purpose of metaphysical uplift, that is not, in my view, its origin. Without glibly invoking the notion of 'abstract object', we tend to forget that it is very difficult to say what the intrinsic nature of concepts or universals in themselves is, especially so that they are distinguished from each other. Redness, we now glibly say, is not itself red, but then what are its intrinsic properties? Plato is giving the most immediately appealing answer to this question. In the words of Ian Crombie's neat summary:

> The essential characteristic of [the classical theory of forms] seems to be the belief that there are such things as the very thing which is X ... that is, for every 'common name' there exists a 'common nature'. The beautiful, the equal, the large, fire, the bed, the shuttle; for each of these there exists a single form, and it is the form alone that the common nature fully exists. In so far as the common nature exists also in things, it does so because they 'partake' in it, or because it is 'present' to them. Furthermore the form is not only the sole pure case of the common nature, it is also *nothing but* the beautiful, or whatever it may be. (1963: 253)

A reconstruction of Plato's position could be put as follows.
Plato's position.

(1) There are kinds (call them *Forms*) as well as particulars.
(2) Because these Forms exist they must have a nature – there must be an account of what they are in themselves.
(3) The only account to hand is that they are the property they represent, pure and unadulterated. This also explains how something's participating in them gives that thing the appropriate property.

Therefore

(4) Forms are self-predicating.

Aristotle rejected this theory on the grounds that it made forms into a kind of particular.[1] His explicit solution was:

Aristotle: part one.

(1) You do not want entities that are hybrid between universals and particulars, and this is what Platonic forms are.
(2) You avoid this by having individualised forms as particulars in things, and universals as *acti mentis*.

This looks like a kind of conceptualism, but is not, as we can see if we follow the story. Frege had a similar problem with the Platonic theory to Aristotle, though he was a Platonist; he, too, thought one had to avoid treating universals as objects. His account runs as follows.

Frege's position.

(1) There are transcendent universals, – called 'concepts' – but they are incomplete entities.
(2) Only complete entities, which are objects, can be named.

Therefore

(3) When we refer to a concept or universal we are really referring to a dummy object that stands in for it for purposes of reference: 'the concept "horse" is not a concept'.

(Frege 1952: 46)

The two premises are his recognition of the same problem as Aristotle identified, but the solution is more ludicrous than Plato's own theory and leaves the ontological status of the concepts themselves utterly obscure. The answer is to be found in Aristotle's implicit position, for which all the materials are provided, but which Aristotle never articulates – which, as the ancients complained, is often the case with his more important metaphysical cruxes.

Aristotle: part two.

---

[1] Aristotle's criticism of Plato's theory of forms is found principally in his *Peri ideon*, fragments of which are preserved in Alexander of Aphrodisias's commentary on the *Metaphysics*. The text, translation and discussion of Aristotle's views are to be found in Fine (1993).

(3) You cannot have individualised forms (instances of universals) without forms (universals).

Therefore

(4) There is (are) some mind(s) which think(s) all things for which there are forms (universals). For the individual, this is the active intellect, for the cosmos as a whole, it is the prime mover.

This – that is, providing a solution to the problem of universals – is a use to which Aristotle never explicitly puts either the active intellect or the prime mover, but as (3) – which is studiously ignored by most tropists – seems blatant, this development of the theory seems obvious, as all the bits are provided. It gives one the neo-platonic *Nous* in a straightforward manner. It does not yet get us to the One because it does not tell us why unity is self-exemplifying.

16.5   Other reasons for thinking Unity is self-predicating

Plotinus begins VI. 9. 3 by asking 'what then could the One be, and what nature could it have?' His answer is that we must 'ascend to the principle within oneself'. The centre of the soul is compared to the centre of a circle (ch. 8), but this is not itself the One, which will be 'a Principle in which all these centres [of individual souls] coincide; it will be a centre by analogy with the centre of the circle we know' (ch. 8). So we ascend by way of the unity of our own self, which we might think we can grasp in a 'Cartesian' manner, as presupposed by all our diverse thinking, to a similar principle behind Intellect itself. This path for understanding the One makes eminent sense, *once one has grounds for believing that there is such a thing*: it does not provide such grounds, however. We still need a reason for thinking that the universal 'unity' or 'individuality' is self-exemplifying. What reason have we got for going beyond a *concept* of unity, which is more or less well exemplified by the various kinds of things that exist?

We already have material for an answer to this question in the argument of Chapter 15 for the simplicity and, therefore, unity of the self, which expresses itself in the diversity of its thought. If we combine this with what I deem to be the Aristotelian solution to the problem of universals, one has a philosophical reason for following Plotinus's ascent. This argument does not rest on the nature of unity itself, but on the nature of mind and the way that mind is the source of all intelligibility, both in macrocosm and microcosm. This would give the following argument. The first two steps remain as above.

(1) It is in virtue of unity that beings are beings.

(2) Unity is not identical to something else – for example, to Form
    or to being in general.
(3′) But beings also presuppose forms and
    forms are aspects of *nous*.
(4′) The existence of *nous* includes the existence
    of a thinking subject.
(5′) Thinking subjects are simples
    (unities).

Therefore

(6′) *Nous* presupposes a unity.

To this can be added (8), (9) and (10) from the original.

8. Because intelligibility in the normal
   sense involves universality, this oneness is not intelligible.
9. Because it is in virtue of unity that all beings are beings, unity is prior to all *kinds*
   of things – i.e. to all forms.

Therefore

10. Unity itself – the One – transcends all forms, all intelligibility, and is pre-
    supposed by them.

This argument definitely represents a line of thought in Plotinus – and,
indeed, seems to me to be a sound argument in its own right. It is plain
from the text, I think, however, that Plotinus looks both to intuitions
resting on the philosophy of mind and to ones resting on the feeling that
there must be an archetypal instance of unity, as represented in the
original argument. Can one do justice to both these intuitions? Perhaps
one might try to combine them as follows. Again, (1) and (2) remain
unchanged.

(1) It is in virtue of unity that beings are beings.
(2) Unity is not identical to something else – for example, to Form or to being
    in general.

Therefore

(3″) There must be some sort of principle of unity.
(4″) This cannot be a form or concept because these are universals and unity
    is not.

Therefore

(5″) One needs another paradigm
(6″) This is provided by the subject of thought, especially as it occurs in the
    unchanging Intellect to which the Aristotelian criticism of Plato leads, as *per*
    (3′) – (6′) above.

To this, (8), (9) and (10) of the original argument can be added.

It is natural to object to this argument that it is question-begging at (4″). In some obvious sense, unity/individuality is a concept, and, insofar as there are many individual objects, it has many instances, and so is a universal. Nevertheless, it is a strange concept or universal because its instances are not themselves universal in nature; they are not, that is, qualities or properties. When one confronts the red or the square of this or that object, one confronts it as a property. One does not confront individuality as a property. This is, I think, a version of the problem of transcendentals. They fall into none of the categories and are, therefore, not forms or universals proper. It is not surprising that it is a version of this problem, for the discussions in the *Sophist* from which much neo-Platonism takes off are precisely about how such concepts can be treated by a Platonist. Interesting though this may be, however, it does not follow from this, as far as I can see, that there *must* be some other exemplification of the principle of unity. It is tempting to see a Platonic argument that relies on the doctrine of recollection. Insofar as our concepts are derived not from their imperfect instances, but from some purer intellectual source (I put it this way to avoid imputing self-predication from the start) and insofar as these are normally forms, but unity cannot be a form, then some other source is required. But the claim that unity cannot be a form rests on the claim that it cannot be a universal because it *is* pure particularity, which takes us back to self-predication.

The positive situation seems to me to be, therefore, this. We have an argument for a Plotinian One which rests on a certain view about the self and a certain neo-Platonised Aristotelian view of universals, both of which theories seem to me to be true, or, at least defensible. Insofar as we want a more purely 'philosophical-logic' argument, if we are sufficiently mystified by transcendentals, we can push the argument from mind into service to help. Surprisingly enough, this situation leads us back to Hume.

16.6   Conventionalism and transcendentalism

I have been representing Plotinus as an absolutist about unity, but, in Platonic manner, this only applies to the One itself; everything else is only imperfectly one, and physical objects, barely so at all. His reason for thinking this is no different from Hume's, namely that objects are plural in their parts and their properties. The similarity does not stop there. The apparent unity of objects, for Hume, is an act of the mind. So it is for Plotinus. The Intellect, in its outwardly active form as World Soul, produces and understands objects in the light of the forms that it thinks and the unity presupposed by itself as thinker. This differs from Hume and conventionalism on two points. First, it applies not only to the human mind, but also to the intellect which is the source of everything: a feature not to be found in Hume's system. Second, in Plotinus, the imperfect unity of derived objects is a reflection of the unity in the self, in which Hume also fails to believe. But we need not worry about Hume's problems with the unity of the mind, for we do not have that problem, as the argument in our previous chapter showed. Whether we have reason to believe in a perfect unity that lies behind the Platonic world of universals will depend on whether one thinks that that world is best thought of as an Intellect and, if so, whether it would follow that a pure unity need lie behind it, in the way a simple self lies behind the human thinker. I have given at least a sketch of a reason, resting on Aristotle's criticism of Plato, and Frege's dualism of concept and object for thinking that the 'noetic' model of universals is better than an 'infinity of separate entities' account. I think that there are further reasons for preferring the noetic account, but they must wait for another work.

16.7   Overall conclusion

Although I hope that the various arguments in this book can stand alone, I also hope that an overall picture emerges which is sustained by those arguments. That picture does not merely resurrect the mind, but reinstates its role as the centre of our reality. The physical world in itself is an array of organised properties, without any true individuals being present. Individuality flows from the understanding of minds, which are true individuals. This still allows one to see the physical world as a mind-independent structure of property-placings. The move to a full idealism requires further argument.

Bibliography

Abbott, E. A. 1884. *Flatland: A Romance in Many Dimensions*. London: Seeley and Co. Republished many times, most recently by Princeton University Press, 2015.

Alter, T. 2007. 'Does Representationalism Undermine the Knowledge Argument?', in Alter and Walter: 65–76.

Alter, T. and Walter, S. 2007. *Phenomenal Concepts and Phenomenal Knowledge*. Oxford University Press.

Armstrong, D. M. 1968. *A Materialist Theory of the Mind*. London: Routledge.

Armstrong, D. M. 1978. *A Theory of Universals*. Cambridge University Press.

Armstrong, D. M. 1997. *A World of States of Affairs*. Cambridge University Press.

Armstrong, D. M. 2010. *Sketch for a Systematic Metaphysics*. Oxford University Press.

Ayer, A. J. 1968. *The Origins of Pragmatism*. London: Macmillan.

Baker, M. 2011. 'Brains and Souls; Grammar and Speaking', in Baker and Goetz: 73–93.

Baker, M. and Goetz, S. (eds). 2011. *The Soul Hypothesis*. New York: Continuum.

Balog, K. 1999. 'Conceivability, Possibility and the Mind-Body Problem', *The Philosophical Review* 108 (4): 497–528.

Balog, K. 2012a. 'Acquaintance and the Mind-Body Problem', in *New Perspectives on Type Identity: The Mental and the Physical*, Christopher Hill and Simone Gozzano (eds). Cambridge University Press: 16–43.

Balog, K. 2012b. 'In Defence of the Phenomenal Concept Strategy', *Philosophy and Phenomenological Research* 84: 1–23.

Beall, J. C. 2003. *Liars and Heaps*. Oxford: Clarendon Press.

Blackburn, S. 1990. 'Filling in Space', *Analysis* 50 (2): 62–5.

Block, N. 2007. 'Max Black's Objection to Mind-Body Identity', in Alter and Walter: 249–306.

Block, N. and Stalnaker, R. 1999. 'Conceptual Analysis, Dualism and the Explanatory Gap', *Philosophical Review* 108: 1–46.

Burge, T. 1993. 'Mind-Body Causation and Explanatory Practice', in Heil and Mele (eds): 97–120.

Carnap, R. 1934. *The Unity of Science*. London: Kegan Paul.

Carnap, R. 1955. 'The Logical Foundations of the Unity of Science', in Neurath, Carnap and Morris (eds): 42–62.

Chalmers, D. 1996. *The Conscious Mind*. Oxford University Press.

Chalmers, D. 2003. 'Consciousness and Its Place in Nature', in *The Blackwell Guide to the Philosophy of Mind*, Stephen Stich and Ted Warfield (eds). Oxford: Blackwell, 102–42.

Chalmers, D. (ed.). 2009. *Metametaphysics*. Oxford University Press.

Charles, D. 1992. 'Supervenience, Composition, and Physicalism', in Charles and Lennon (eds): 265–96.

Charles, D. and Lennon, K. (eds). 1992. *Reduction, Explanation and Realism*. Oxford: Clarendon Press.

Chisholm, R. 1991. 'On the Simplicity of the Soul', *Philosophical Perspectives* 5: 157–81.

Churchland, P. 1989a. *The Neurocomputational Perspective*. Cambridge, MA: MIT Press.

Churchland, P. 1989b. 'Reduction, Qualia and the Direct Introspection of Brain States', in Churchland 1989a: 47–66.

Churchland, P. 1989c. 'Knowing Qualia: A Reply to Jackson', in Churchland 1989a: 67–76.

Crombie, I. 1963. *An Examination of Plato's Doctrines*, vols. I and II. London: Routledge and Kegan Paul.

Cussins, A. 1992. 'The Limitations of Pluralism', in Charles and Lennon (eds): 179–223.

Davidson, D. 1970. 'Mental Events', in Foster and Swanson (eds): 79–101.

Davidson, D. 1984. 'Truth and Meaning', in his *Truth and Interpretation*. Oxford: Clarendon Press, 17–36.

Davidson, D. 1987. 'Problems in the Explanation of Action', in Pettit, Sylvan and Norman (eds): 35–49.

Davidson, D. 1993. 'Thinking Causes', in Heil and Mele (eds): 3–17.

Dennett, D. 1987a. *The Intentional Stance*. Cambridge, MA: MIT Press.

Dennett, D. 1987b. 'True Believers', in Dennett 1987a: 13–35.

Dennett, D. 1991. *Consciousness Explained*. London: Penguin Press.

Dennett, D. 2000. 'With a Little Help from My Friends', in Ross, Brook and Thompson (eds): 327–88.

Dennett, D. 2007. 'What RoboMary Knows', in Alter and Walter, 15–26.

Descartes, R. 1984. *The Philosophical Writings of Descartes*, translated by John Cottingham, Robert Stoothoff and Dugald Murdoch. Cambridge University Press.

Dretske, F. 1981. *Knowledge and the Flow of Information*. Cambridge, MA: MIT Press.

Dretske, F. 1988. *Explaining Behavior: Reasons in a World of Causes*. Cambridge, MA: MIT Press.

Dretske, F. 2000. *Perception, Knowledge and Belief*. Cambridge University Press.

Feigl, H., Scriven, M. and Maxwell, G. (eds). 1958. *Minnesota Studies in the Philosophy of Science, vol. II*. Minneapolis: University of Minnesota Press.

Fine, G. 1993. *On Ideas*. Oxford: Clarendon Press.

Fodor, J. 1974. 'Special Sciences, or the Disunity of Science as a Working Hypothesis', *Synthese* 28: 77–115.

Fodor, J. 1975. *The Language of Thought*. Cambridge, MA: Harvard University Press.

Fodor, J. 1979. *Representations: Philosophical Essays on the Foundations of Cognitive Science*. Harvester Press (UK) and MIT Press (US).

Fodor, J. 1997. 'Special Sciences: Still Autonomous After All These Years'. *Philosophical Perspectives* 11: 149–63.

Fodor, J. 2000. *The Mind Doesn't Work That Way: The Scope and Limits of Computational Psychology*. Cambridge, MA: MIT Press.

Foster, J. 1982. *The Case for Idealism*. London: Routledge and Kegan Paul.

Foster, J. 1991. *The Immaterial Self: A Defence of the Cartesian Dualist Conception of the Mind*. London: Routledge.

Foster, J. 2008. *A World for Us*. Oxford: Clarendon Press.

Foster, L. and Swanson, J. (eds). 1970. *Experience and Theory*. London: Duckworth.

Frege, G. 1952. 'Concept and Object', in *Translations from the Writings of Gottlob Frege*, P. Geach and M. Black (eds). Oxford: Basil Blackwell.

French, S. 2006. 'Identity and Individuality in Quantum Theory', in *The Stanford Encyclopedia of Philosophy*, http://plato.stanford.edu/entries/qt-idind/

Geach, P. 1969. 'What Do We Think With?', in his *God and the Soul*. Cambridge University Press: 30–41.

Goff, P. 2006. 'Experiences Don't Sum', in Strawson: 53–61.

Graham, G. and Horgan, T. 2000. 'Mary Mary, Quite Contrary', Philosophical Studies 99: 59–87.

Harman, G. 1990. 'The Intrinsic Qualities of Experience', *Philosophical Perspectives* 4: 31–52.

Hart, W. 1988. *The Engines of the Soul*. Cambridge University Press.

Heil, J. and Mele, A. (eds). 1993. *Mental Causation*. Oxford: Clarendon Press.

Hempel, C. G. 1980. 'The Logical Analysis of Psychology', in *Readings in Philosophy of Psychology*, vol. 1, N. Block (ed.). London: Methuen: 14–23. (Originally published in French in 1935.)

Hohwy, J. and Kallestrup, J. 2008. *Being Reduced: New Essays on Reduction, Explanation, and Causation*. Oxford University Press.

Hornsby, J. 2001. *Simple Mindedness: in Defense of Naïve Naturalism in the Philosophy of Mind*. Cambridge MA: Harvard University Press.

Horwich, P. 2006. *Reflections on Meaning*. Oxford University Press.

Hume, D. 1739/2000. *A Treatise on Human Nature*, D. F. Norton and N. J. Norton (eds). Oxford University Press.

Jackson, F. 1982. 'Epiphenomenal Qualia', *Philosophical Quarterly* 32: 127–36.

Jackson, F. 1986. 'What Mary Didn't Know', *Journal of Philosophy* 83 (5): 291–5.

Jackson, F. 1998/2004. 'Postscript on Qualia', in his *Mind, Methods and Conditionals*. London: Routledge, 76–9. (Reprinted in Ludlow *et al.*, 417–20.)

Jackson, F. 2004. 'Mind and Illusion', in Ludlow *et al.*: 421–42.

Jaworski, W. 2011. *Philosophy of Mind: A Comprehensive Introduction*. Oxford: Blackwell.

Kemeny, J. and Oppenheim, P. 1956. 'On Reduction'. *Philosophical Studies* 7: 6–19.

Kim, J. 1993a. 'Can Supervenience and "Non-Strict Laws" Save Anomolous Monism?', in Heil and Mele (eds): 19–26.

Kim, J. 1993b. 'The Non-Reductivist's Troubles with Mental Causation', in Heil and Mele (eds): 189–210.

Kim, J. 1998. *Mind in a Physical World*. Cambridge, MA: MIT Press.

Kim, J. 2005. *Physicalism, or Something Near Enough*. Princeton, NJ: Princeton University Press.

Kirk, R. 1994: *Raw Feels*. Oxford: Clarendon Press.

Kirk, R. 2005. *Zombies and Consciousness*. Oxford: Clarendon Press.

Kirk, R. 2013. *The Conceptual Link from the Mental to the Physical*. Oxford University Press.

Kovacs, D. 2010. 'Is There a Conservative Solution to the Many Thinkers Problem?', *Ratio* 23: 275–90.

Kripke, S. 1972. *Naming and Necessity*. Oxford: Blackwell.

Kripke, S. 1976. *Wittgenstein and Rule-Following*. Oxford: Clarendon Press.

Levin, Janet. 1983. 'Functionalism and the Argument from Conceivability', *Canadian Journal of Philosophy* 11: 85–104.

Levin, Janet. 1986. 'Could Love Be Like a Heatwave?', *Philosophical Studies*, 49: 245–61.

Levine, Janet. 2007. 'What Is a Phenomenal Concept?', in Alter and Walter (eds): 87–110.

Levine, J. 1983. 'Materialism and Qualia: The Explanatory Gap', *Pacific Philosophical Quarterly* 64: 354–61.

Lewis, D. 1983a. *Philosophical Papers*, vol. I. Oxford University Press.

Lewis, D. 1983b. 'Mad Pain and Martian Pain', *Philosophical Papers* I: 122–30.

Lewis, D. 1986. *Philosophical Papers* vol. II. Oxford University Press.

Lewis, D. 1995. 'Should a Materialist Believe in Qualia?', *Australasian Journal of Philosophy* 73: 140–4. (Reprinted in Lewis (1999): 25–31.)

Lewis, D. 1999. *Papers in Metaphysics and Epistemology*. Cambridge University Press.

Lewis, D. 2004. 'What Experience Teaches', Ludlow *et al.*: 77–103. (Reprinted from *Proceedings of the Russellian Society*, 1988. University of Sydney, 13: 29–57.)

Lewis, D. 2009, 'Ramseyan Humility', in *Conceptual Analysis and Philosophical Naturalism*, David Braddon-Mitchell and Robert Nola (eds). Cambridge, MA: MIT Press: 203–22.

Loar, B. 1997. 'Phenomenal States', in *The Nature of Consciousness*, N. Block, O Flanagan and G. Guzeldere (eds). Cambridge, MA: MIT Press: 597–616.

Lockwood, M. J. 1989. *Mind, Brain and the Quantum*. Oxford: Blackwell.

Lockwood, M. J. 1993. 'The Grain Problem', in *Objections to Physicalism*, H. Robinson (ed.). Oxford: Clarendon Press: 271–91.

Loewer, B. 2008. 'Why There Is Anything Except Physics', in *Being Reduced*. Oxford University Press: 149–62.

Loewer, B. 2009. 'Why Is There Anything Except Physics?', *Synthese* 170: 217–33.

Lowe, E. J. 1996. *Subjects of Experience*. Cambridge University Press.

Lowe, E. J. 2004. 'Non-Cartesian Dualism', in *Philosophy of Mind: A Guide and Anthology*, J. Heil (ed.). Oxford University Press: 851–65.

Ludlow, P., Nagasawa, Y. and Stoljar, D. (eds). 2004. *There's Something about Mary: Essays on Phenomenal Consciousness and Frank Jackson's Knowledge Argument*. Cambridge, MA: MIT Press.

Lycan, W. 1987. *Consciousness*. Cambridge, MA: MIT Press.

Lycan, W. 1996. *Consciousness and Experience*. Cambridge, MA: MIT Press.

Macdonald, C. and Macdonald, G. 1986. 'Mental Causation and Explanation of Action'. *Philosophical Quarterly* 36: 145–58.

Madell, G. 1981. *The Identity of the Self*. Edinburgh University Press.

Maxwell, G. 1978. 'Rigid Designators and Mind-Brain Identity', in *Perception and Cognition Issues in the Foundations of Psychology: Minnesota Studies in the Philosophy of Science*, vol. IX, C. Wade Savage (ed.). Minneapolis: University of Minnesota Press: 365–403.

McDowell, J. 1994. *Mind and World*. Cambridge, MA: Harvard University Press.

McDowell, J. 2008. 'Responses' in *John McDowell: Experience, Norm, and Nature*, J. Lingaard (ed.). Oxford: Blackwell: 200–67.

McGinn, C. 1989. 'Can We Solve the Mind-Body Problem?' *Mind* 98: 349–66.

McGinn, C. 1993. *The Problem of Consciousness*. Oxford: Blackwell.

Mc Laughlin, B. 1993. 'Davidson's Response to Epiphenomenalism', in Heil and Mele (eds): 27–40.

Molnar, G. 2003. *Powers: A Study in Metaphysics*, Oxford University Press.

Nagel, E. 1961. *The Structure of Science*. London: Routledge.

Nagel, T. 1974. 'What Is It Like to Be a Bat?', *Philosophical Review* 83: 435–50.

Nagel, T. 2012. *Mind and Cosmos: Why the Materialist Neo-Darwinian Conception of Nature Is Almost Certainly False*. Oxford University Press.

Neurath, O., Carnap, R. and Morris, C. 1955. *International Encyclopedia of Unified Science*. University of Chicago Press.

Nozick, R. 1981. *Philosophical Explanations*. Cambridge, MA: Harvard University Press.

Oppenheim, P. and Putnam, H. 1958: 'Unity of Science as a Working Hypothesis', in Feigl, Scriven and Maxwell (eds): 3–36.

Papineau, D. 2002. *Thinking about Consciousness*. Oxford University Press.

Papineau, D. 2007. 'Phenomenal and Perceptual Concepts', in Alter and Walter: 111–44.

Peacocke, C. 1979. *Holistic Explanation*. Oxford: Clarendon Press.

Pettit, P., Sylvan, R. and Norman, J. (eds). 1987: *Metaphysics and Morality*. Oxford: Blackwell.

Place, U. T. 1956. 'Is Consciousness a Brain Process?', *The British Journal of Psychology* 47: 44–50.

Plotinus, 1958. *Ennead VI, 6–9*, translated by A. H. Armstrong. Cambridge, MA: Harvard University Press.

Price, H. 2004. 'Naturalism Without Representationalism', in *Naturalism in Question*, M. De Caro and D. Macarthur (eds). Cambridge, MA: Harvard University Press: 71–88. (Reprinted in Price (2011): 184–99.)

Price, H. 2011. *Naturalism Without Mirrors*. Oxford University Press.

Priest, G. 2003. 'A Site for Sorites', in *Liars and Heaps: New Essays on Paradox*, J. Beall, (ed.). Oxford University Press: 9–23.

Prinz, J. 2012. *The Conscious Brain*. Oxford University Press.

Putnam, H. 1975a. *Mind, Language and Reality: Philosophical Papers, Volume 2*. Cambridge University Press.

Putnam, H. 1975b: 'Minds and Machines', in his 1975a: 362–85.

Putnam, H. 1981. 'Brains in a Vat', in his *Reason, Truth and History*. Cambridge University Press: 1–21.

Reid, T. 1785/1969. *Essays on the Active Powers of the Human Mind*. Cambridge, MA: MIT Press.

Rist, J. 1967. *Plotinus: The Road to Reality*. Cambridge University Press.

Robinson, H. 1982. *Matter and Sense*. Cambridge University Press.

Robinson, H. 1989. 'Structural and Functional Criteria for the Identity of Mental States: A Dilemma for Physicalism', *Hermes* 3: 128–42. (This is a journal of the *Centre National de la Recherche Scientifique*: the paper was delivered in English to a CNRS seminar in Paris, but published in French.)

Robinson, H. 1993a. 'The Anti-Materialist Strategy and the "Knowledge Argument"', in *Objections to Physicalism*, H. Robinson (ed.). Oxford: Clarendon Press: 159–83.

Robinson, H. (ed.), 1993b. *Objections to Physicalism*. Oxford: Clarendon Press.

Robinson, H. 1993c. 'Dennett and the Knowledge Argument', *Analysis* 53: 174–7.

Robinson, H. 1994. *Perception*. London: Routledge.

Robinson, H. 2001. 'Donald Davidson and Non-Reductive Physicalism: A Tale of Two Cultures', in *Physicalism and Its Discontents*, K. Gillett and B. Loewer (eds). New York: Cambridge University Press.

Robinson, H. 2003. 'Dualism', in *The Blackwell Guide to the Philosophy of Mind*, S. Stitch and T. Warfield (eds). Oxford: Blackwell: 85–101.

Robinson, H. 2007. 'The Self and Time', in *Persons, Human and Divine*, P. van Inwagen and D. Zimmermann (eds). Oxford: Clarendon Press: 55–83.

Robinson, H. 2008. 'Why Frank Should Not Have Jilted Mary', in *The Case for Qualia*, Edmond Wright (ed.). Cambridge, MA: MIT Press: 223–45.

Robinson, H. 2008–9. 'Vagueness, Realism, Language and Thought', *Proceedings of the Aristotelian Society* 109: 83–101.

Robinson, H. 2009a. 'Idealism', in *The Oxford Handbook to the Philosophy of Mind*, B. McLaughlin, A. Beckermann and S. Walter (eds). Oxford University Press: 186–205.

Robinson, H. 2009b 'Reductionism, Supervenience and Emergence', in *The Routledge Companion to Metaphysics*, P. Simons and P. LePoidevin (eds). London: Routledge: 527–36.

Robinson, H. 2010. 'Quality, Thought and Consciousness', in *The Metaphysics of Consciousness*, Royal Institute of Philosophy Supplement 67, P. Basile, J. Kiverstein and P. Phemester (eds). Cambridge University Press: 203–16.

Robinson, H. 2011. 'Benacerraf's Problem, Abstract Objects and Intellect', in *Truth, Reference and Realism*, Z. Novak and A. Simonyi (eds). Budapest: CEU Press: 235–62.

Robinson, H. 2012a. '"Are There Any *F*s?" How Should We Understand This Question?', for a special edition of the *Hungarian Philosophical Review*, dedicated to 'current issues in metaphysics': 55–68.

Robinson, H. 2012b. 'Qualia, Qualities and Our Conception of the Physical World', in *The Case for Dualism*, Benedikt Goecke (ed.). Notre Dame: Notre Dame Press: 231–63.

Robinson, H. 2013. 'The Failure of Disjunctivism to Deal with "Philosophers' Hallucinations"', in *Hallucinations*, Fiona Macpherson and Dimitris Platchias (eds). Cambridge, MA: MIT Press: 313–30.

Robinson, H. 2014a. 'Naturalism and the Unavoidability of the Cartesian Perspective', in *Contemporary Dualism*, Lavazza and Robinson (eds). London: Routledge: 154–70.

Robinson, H. 2014b. 'Modern Hylomorphism and the Reality and Causal Power of Structure: A Skeptical Investigation', *Res Philosophica* 91: 203–14.

Robinson, H. 2014c. 'Substance', in *The Stanford Encyclopedia of Philosophy*, Edward N. Zalta (ed.), http://plato.stanford.edu/archives/spr2014/entries/substance/.

Rorty, R. 1965–6. 'Mind-Body Identity, Privacy and Categories', *Review of Metaphysics* 17: 24–54.

Rorty, R. 2010. 'Naturalism and Quietism', in *Naturalism and Normativity*, M. De Caro and D. Macarthur (eds). New York: Columbia University Press: 55–68.

Ross, D., A. Brook and D. Thompson (eds). 2000. *Dennett's Philosophy: A Comprehensive Assessment*. Cambridge, MA: MIT Press.

Russell, B. 1927. The Analysis of Matter. London: Allen and Unwin.

Russell, B. 1931. *The Scientific Outlook*. London: Allen and Unwin.

Ryle, G. 1963: *The Concept of Mind*. Harmondsworth: Penguin Books.

Sainsbury, M. 1988. *Paradoxes*. Cambridge University Press.

Salmon, N. 2005. *Reference and Essence*. Amherst: Prometheus Books. (Original edition, 1981, Princeton: Princeton University Press.)

Scerri, E. R. and McIntyre, L. 1997. 'The Case for the Philosophy of Chemistry', *Synthese* 111: 213–32.

Seager, W. 2000. 'Real Patterns and Surface Metaphysics', in Ross, Brook and Thompson: 95–129.

Searle, J. 1992. *The Rediscovery of the Mind*. Cambridge, MA: The MIT Press.

Shoemaker, S. 1981. 'Some Varieties of Functionalism', *Philosophical Topics* 12: 93–119.

Shoemaker, S. 1994. 'The Mind-Body Problem', in Warner and Szubka (eds): 55–60.

Smart, J. J. C. 1959. 'Sensations and Brain Processes', *The Philosophical Review* 68: 141–56.

Smart, J. J. C. 1963. *Philosophy and Scientific Realism*. London: Routledge and Kegan Paul.

Smith, A. D. 1993. 'Non-Reductive Physicalism?', in Robinson (ed.): 225–50.

Smith, P. 1992. 'Modest Reductions and the Unity of Science', in Charles and Lennon (eds): 19–43.

Sosa, E. 1993. 'Davidson's Thinking Causes', in Heil and Mele (eds): 41–50.

Stalnaker, R. 2008. *Our Knowledge of the Internal World*. Oxford University Press.

Stoljar, D. 2006. *Ignorance and Imagination: On the Epistemic Origin of the Problem of Consciousness*. Oxford University Press.

Strawson, G. 1994. *Mental Reality*. Cambridge, MA: The MIT Press.

Strawson, G. 2006. *Consciousness and Its Place in Nature* edited by A. Freeman, keynote paper (pp. 3–31) and reply to commentaries (pp. 184–280). Thorverton: Imprint Academic.

Strawson, G. 2007. *Real Materialism and Other Essays*. Oxford University Press.

Strawson, G. 2009. *Selves: An Essay in Revisionary Metaphysics*. Oxford University Press.

Strawson, P. F. 1959. *Individuals*. London : Methuen.

Suppes, P. 1984. *Probabilistic Metaphysics*. Oxford: Blackwell.

Swinburne, R. 1986/97. *The Evolution of the Soul*. Oxford University Press.

Swinburne, R. 2007. 'From Mental/Physical Identity to Substance Dualism', in *Persons: Human and Divine*, P. van Inwagen and D. W. Zimmermann (eds). Oxford University Press: 142–65.

Swinburne, R. 2013. *Mind, Brain and Free Will*. Oxford University Press.

Swinburne, R. 2014. 'What Makes Me Me ? A Defense of Substance Dualism', in *Contemporary Dualism: A Defense*, A. Lavazza and H. Robinson (eds). New York and London: Routledge: 139–53.

Tye, M. 1992. 'Visual Qualia and Visual Content', in *The Contents of Experience*, T. Crane (ed.). Cambridge University Press.

Tye, M. 1995. *Ten Problems of Consciousness*. Cambridge, MA: MIT Press.

Unger, P. 1980. *Ignorance*. Oxford University Press.

Van Inwagen, P. 1990. *Material Beings*. Ithaca and London: Cornell University Press.

Walker, R. 1993. 'Transcendental Arguments Against Physicalism', in Robinson (ed.): 61–80.

Warner, R. and Szuba, T. (eds). 1994. *The Mind-Body Problem*. Oxford: Blackwell.

Wiggins, D. 1974. 'Essentialism, Continuity, and Identity', *Synthese* 28 (3/4): 321–59.

Wiggins, D. 2001. *Sameness and Substance Renewed*. Cambridge University Press.

Williamson, T. 1992. 'Vagueness and Ignorance', *Aristotelian Society*, suppl. 66: 145–62.

Williamson, T. 1994. *Vagueness*. London: Routledge.

Index

abilities hypothesis (AH), 36–43
Alexander of Aphrodisias, 255
Alter, Torin, 10, 64, 71
anomolous monism, 100, 102, 103
argument from illusion, 67
Aristotle, 105, 161, 183, 195, 229, 230, 249, 250, 252, 254, 255, 256, 259
Armstrong, David, 4–8, 9, 11, 42, 50, 92, 95, 97, 107, 120, 122, 175, 182, 183, 192, 250, 253
Ayer, A. J., 126

Baker, Mark, 246
Balog, Katalin, 74, 75, 76, 77, 85, 90
behaviourism, 7, 20, 22, 29, 34, 35, 43, 48, 49, 77, 78, 80, 96
Blackburn, Simon, 120
Block, Ned, 65, 85, 87, 88, 90, 112, 154, 263
Broad, C. D., 12, 160

Carnap, Rudolf, 95, 96, 149, 150, 152, 219, 260
causal efficacy, 182
Chalmers, David, 14, 15, 29, 52, 77, 90, 91, 118, 122, 133, 153, 180
Charles, David, 95, 96
Chisholm, Roderick, 245
Chomsky, Noam, 7, 246
Churchland, Paul, 17, 45, 89, 110, 230
competance of logic, 166
conceptualism, 178, 179, 191
Crombie, I. M., 254
Cross, Sir Rupert, 143

Davidson, Donald, 4, 8, 93–101, 102, 103, 104, 109, 110, 111, 152, 156, 165, 186
Dawkins, Richard, 185
Dennett, Daniel, 7, 14, 18, 20, 22–34, 35, 36, 92, 95, 104, 110, 115, 158, 159, 192, 210–19, 245, 246
Mary and blue banana (MBB), 22

RoboMary (RM), 22
Swamp Mary (SM), 22
Dretske, Fred., 64, 66, 68, 70
dualism, 14, 15, 16, 21, 45, 59, 75, 76, 82, 97, 100, 104, 107, 116, 128, 133, 152, 156, 159, 160, 178, 179, 181, 210, 212, 223, 225, 226, 230, 233, 235, 259
Dummett, Michael, 163

emergence, 74, 112, 113, 124, 126, 127, 129, 130, 131, 147, 148, 155, 156, 158, 215
epiphenomenalism, 15, 45, 52, 53, 54, 56, 58, 59, 88, 98, 99, 100, 103, 156
epistemicism, 163, 236
Essentialism, 195
exclusion principle, 184, 186, 211
explanatory gap (EG), 14, 15, 16, 29, 74, 75, 76, 81, 85, 87, 112, 127, 128, 155

Feyerabend, Paul, 4
Fine, Gail, 255
Fodor, Jerry, 70, 103, 104, 151, 152, 153, 156, 158, 159, 186, 187, 189, 245, 246
Foster, John, xiv, 119, 120, 231, 232, 233
Frege, Gottlob, 164, 175, 254, 255, 259
functionalism, 7, 8, 9, 20, 29, 30, 34, 36, 48, 49, 51, 52, 53, 59, 77, 78, 94, 96, 100, 125, 153

Geach, Peter, 245, 246
Godel, Kurt, 114
Goff, Philip, 129, 130

haecceitas, 197, 198, 199, 200, 201, 202, 204, 206, 207, 208, 239, 240
hallucinations, 63, 67, 68, 70, 72
harmonisation requirement, 166
Hart, W. D., 235
Hempel, C. G., 149
Hornsby, Jennifer, 192

Made in the USA
Monee, IL
05 September 2021